ROBIN SMITH

Robin Smith was born in apartheid South Africa, but qualified to play for England on account of his British parents. Smith made his Test debut against the West Indies in 1988 and looked instantly at home on the big stage. He played 62 Tests, scoring over 4,000 runs at an average of 43.67, and is remembered as one of England's greatest ever players of fast bowling. He also made the then highest score by an England batsman in a one-day international, hitting a spectacular 167 not out against Australia in 1993, a record that stood for 23 years.

In retirement, he has settled in Perth, Western Australia, but he remains a club hero at his career-long county, Hampshire.

ROBIN SMITH WITH
ROB SMYTH AND
KARIN LWIN

The Judge

More Than Just a Game

VINTAGE

1 3 5 7 9 10 8 6 4 2

Vintage
20 Vauxhall Bridge Road,
London SW1V 2SA

Vintage is part of the Penguin Random House group of companies
whose addresses can be found at global.penguinrandomhouse.com

Penguin
Random House
UK

First published in paperback by Vintage in 2020
First published in hardback by Yellow Jersey Press in 2019

penguin.co.uk/vintage

A CIP catalogue record for this book is available from the
British Library

ISBN 9781529112863

Printed and bound in Great Britain by Clays Ltd, Elcograf S.p.A.

Penguin Random House is committed to a sustainable future
for our business, our readers and our planet. This book is
made from Forest Stewardship Council® certified paper.

With love to Harrison and Margaux for ever

Contents

Foreword
by Shane Warne

ROBIN SMITH IS THE nicest bloke I have ever met in cricket. The Judge, as he's known to all of us, is one of life's true good guys. I first met him in 1990, when I was playing for the Australian Cricket Academy against England in Adelaide. He approached me with Allan Lamb, who said, 'Hey, china, we hear you're the man to tell us where to go out round here.' I said, 'Well, I might know a few good spots ...'

We had a great night out and have been mates ever since. With Judgie, you know you've got a friend for life. He's always got your back, and he is so loyal. We were born on the same day – 13 September – so we have a lot of similar traits. But I reckon I'm a bit tougher than Judge. He's a big softie at heart, and sometimes he's too nice for his own good. When I played with him, he worried too much about what other people thought. He never really stayed in the present, and always had something on his mind.

It was a really tough time to be an England batsman in the late 1980s and early 1990s, because people were being dropped all the time, yet Judgie had an outstanding record. He was one of the most talented and skilful players in the world, and the courage he showed against the West Indies fast bowlers was amazing. The fact he was only on the winning side in 14 of his 62 Tests is a bit of a joke and hard to fathom, though it shows what a mess the team was at the time.

Let's get one thing straight: it's an absolute fallacy that he couldn't play spin. People said he had an issue against me. But I was knocking over most of their batsmen for fun on that 1993 Ashes tour, including Mike Atherton, Alec Stewart and Graham Gooch, so I'm not really sure why Judgie was singled out. It was very unfair.

Judgie has told me he didn't like facing me, though. When I joined Hampshire in 2000, I was bowling in the nets on one of my first days when Judgie wandered in. I knocked him over a couple of times straight away and he said, 'That's it! Bugger off! You're not allowed to bowl in my net any more!'

Judgie trained bloody hard. Each morning I'd get to the ground and he'd already be there with his dad feeding the bowling machine. He was always the last to leave at night and the first to arrive the next morning. What's that new saying, 'fear of missing out'? Judgie definitely had FOMO! If anyone was going for a beer or dinner at the end of a day's play, Judgie would say, 'Ah, no, look, boys, I'm going to bed, I want to get an early nigh— I'm coming! Where are we going?!''

He was always the life of the party. He had a very good sense of humour and was a really calming voice in the dressing room. He was the main reason I joined Hampshire. I was really keen to experience county cricket and had pretty much agreed to join Lancashire when Judgie gave me a big spiel about Hampshire. He said, 'Listen, we're a fairly small club, we've got a lot of talent, but we like the good life a bit too much. With your experience and winning mentality, I think we can really go somewhere.' That challenge resonated with me, and I also knew playing with Judgie would be a lot of fun.

My first game was away at Essex in the Benson & Hedges Cup. I drove down with Judge the night before, and on the way he said, 'Just reach round the back, there's a couple of cold ones in the Esky.'

I looked behind me and there were six extra-tall cans of Carling. I thought, 'Jesus, no wonder England are bloody shit, they're all drinking before the game, not after!'

When we arrived, there was a cake for Peter Hartley's fortieth birthday, or Jack, as we all called him. After everyone had sung happy birthday, I leaned over to Judge and said, 'He's the team manager, is he?'

'He's our opening bowler.'

'What?! Come on, mate, you've got to be kidding.'

'Mate, he bowls at eighty to eighty-five miles per hour.'

'Horseshit! You can't be serious.'

The next day I stood at slip as Jack took the new ball, and he bowled bloody beautiful outswingers at good pace. He became my car buddy – whenever we were driving to away games, Jack and I went together because we were both smokers.

In the end I spent eight years of my life with Hampshire. I bought a house there and got to know the area. It was great fun. I was captain in the last few years, and in that time we won more first-class games than any other county. We just missed out on the Championship in 2005 but we won the C&G Trophy and helped turn the club around. I thought we had a very entertaining style of play, which the members enjoyed, and I was absolutely blown away when they named one of the stands at the Ageas Bowl after me. I'm very honoured and proud of that. And if it wasn't for Judgie, I wouldn't have gone to Hampshire in the first place. Who knows, without Judgie there might not even have been an Ageas Bowl.

I still touch base with him all the time. Unfortunately, it's not as though he's just down the road – he's five hours away on a plane! But I see him when I'm in Perth or he's in Melbourne, and we talk all the time. You know what it's like. You text to say, 'Hey mate, fancy a quick chat?' You get going and two hours later you're still talking. Even if it's been six months since I last met him, we always pick up where we left off and start chatting like we'd seen each other yesterday. Like I said, with Judgie you know you've got a friend for life.

He has had his problems since retirement but it's great to see that he's turned his life around. I'm really proud of him. He's switched on, he's working so hard – and he's still the nicest bloke you could ever meet.

Shane Warne
February 2019

Foreword
by Mark Nicholas

WHEN WE FIRST SAW the Judge, it was his physical strength that made the most overwhelming impression. He was a delightful young guy and already able to bat better than most of the rest of us – but he was just 17 years old, and so strong! During a damp pre-season fielding practice, he slid to stop a ball near the whitewashed iron railings that guarded the boundaries of the old Hampshire ground at Northlands Road – these were the cold spring days before the advertising boards took up their summer residence – and crashed into the railings. The damage was all theirs: the Judge simply dusted himself down, straightened out the iron work and apologised, like he was a guilty party. Typical Judgie – always trying to keep other people happy.

Robin Arnold Smith, the best of men. For the first 40 years of his life, it was a mainly happy story of free-spirited youth signed off by a mountain of runs made with courage, power and style. Alongside him, variously, were devoted parents; a driven and engaging brother who could bat a bit himself; marriage; kids; a few business interests to keep the wolf from winter's door and a pint or two on Easy Street. That was then.

The July day in 2003, the one on which Hampshire dropped the bomb that was the decision to move forward without him, was the day that Easy Street disappeared from view. A new life, the one beyond the arms that wrap themselves around professional cricketers from the moment bat and ball become their closest friends, was to be an almighty challenge. It is a familiar theme, first of loss and then of direction, amid the crushing of identity and confidence. Robin's story has ended safely and with promise for a bright future; others have not been so lucky. In the pages that follow, he explains the years of darkness with both a hitherto unseen perception and with tenderness, as if he knew more about the depth of man than he let on. Perhaps his recent studies in psychology have expanded a previously one-dimensional mind and encouraged it to investigate the soul.

In some ways this makes for a sad book – at times while reading it, I shed a tear – for the stripping-back of so gregarious and popular a personality is cruel enough; that it was self-inflicted seems somehow worse. In short, the Judge had it all and let it go. After which he became a victim and, as with most victims, the inability to see a way forward led to insularity, depression and, ultimately, a fall from grace. Some passages in the story make for painful reading. Thankfully, entwined into the soul-searching are wonderful recollections of battles won and lost against many of the finest cricketers to have played the game, along with the lighter entertainment that comes with them.

It has long been my view that Robin is the greatest Hampshire cricketer, as distinct from the greatest cricketer to have played for Hampshire. The list is star-spangled – in batting order think Richards, Greenidge, Gower, Smith, Pietersen, Clarke, Pothas (wkt), Akram, Marshall, Warne, Roberts. Only one of these is English-born, but who should we push aside for Phil Mead, Derek Shackleton, Peter Sainsbury, Leo Harrison or James Vince? The point is that the Judge plays in any Hampshire team and, for me, always will.

For all the hundreds made – the certainty of that forward defence, the bravery against fast bowling, the thrilling square cuts, the immense driving and pulling and the irresistible modesty in his acknowledgement of the appreciation – there is one innings, played far from the madding crowd, that will live with me for ever. In the quarter-final of the 1988 Benson and Hedges Cup, against a very strong Worcestershire side who made just 169 on a difficult, uneven pitch, the Judge got us over the line with 87 unbeaten runs of the highest imaginable quality. In front of just a few loyal folk as the match bled into its third rain-ruined day, he transcended both the conditions and the talents of every other player in the match. I defy him to claim a better innings for the county. (Richie Benaud used to talk with unbridled enthusiasm of the 148 not out for England against West Indies at Lord's. I wish I had seen it.)

Paul Terry scored a hundred in the semi-final against Essex that year and Hampshire made it to a Lord's final for the first time – at last! Stephen Jeffries bowled out Derbyshire cheaply and, after the loss of a couple of quick wickets, Judge arrived at the crease to thrash their much-vaunted attack all around the old ground. Miraculously caught on the boundary for 38 by the Derbyshire substitute, he left the field to a standing ovation. On commentary Benaud said, 'The game needed an innings like that.' A week later, Robin was chosen for England and made his Test match debut against West Indies. Outside of Mum and Dad, whose devotion to Robin knew no bounds, the greatest joy in that selection came from the Hampshire dressing room.

Robin has been the most popular cricketer I have known, with kindness shown to friend and foe in equal measure. Worldwide affection for him remains strong to this day: men such as Viv Richards and Allan Border, Ian Bishop and Merv Hughes pass messages of warmth and encouragement through those of us who see him more often.

I imagine that if he was able to do it all again, he might be rather less concerned about other people and a little more attentive to himself. He was always trying to please others, to the point of distraction from his own needs. He listened to the few of us in whose counsel he trusted, but too often he failed to hear. This applied to his delightful sense of bonhomie, for there was a charm and attraction in his personality that led to plenty of late nights with mates from all corners of the cricketing kaleidoscope but, latterly, to the reputation of him becoming a party animal. Yes, he burned the candle at both ends a little too often but not to the cost of his high standards and commitment to practice and preparation. It also applied to his batting, which retreated from its originality and sense of adventure into something no less admirable but somewhat less exciting. By this, I mean that he allowed himself to join the pack and in so doing no longer had the point of difference in his play that set him apart from the likely lads in waiting.

He was back in Hampshire last summer for the first time in 11 years. The light had not dimmed. He was the star attraction at a dinner for all the living captains of the club and at every turn there was joy and glory in his presence. He is greatly missed. The eyes still sparkle, the smile has lost none of its warmth and the wig is rather charmingly grey; that once oh-so-strong body holds on with admirable resilience through the ebb and flow of life's journey and, best of all, his mind is alive with possibility. Late in the afternoon before the dinner, we wandered together to the middle of the Ageas Bowl, a moment for quiet reflection on what has been and what is to come. George Dobell, writing a Test match preview piece for *Cricinfo,* added a most generous footnote to the piece he was about to file. It said:

> There was one nice moment at the end of training on Thursday. Once all the players had left the field, Mark Nicholas and Robin Smith - both hugely popular and significant figures in Hampshire cricket - emerged from one of the function rooms overlooking the ground and took some pictures of one another playing imaginary shots on the Test pitch. Smith has had some tough times in recent years so to see him in fine fettle and, even without a bat, unleashing that famous square-cut was heartening and reviving. How England could do with a batsman of his class now.

I am not embarrassed to say I love this man. Once Hampshire cricket's talisman, he has to me, at the very least, become Perth's greatest attraction. Fun, funny and formidable, Robin was both colleague and compadre, and is now simply the dearest of friends. I once read that he was 'too nice' to have had the international career he might have done. Nonsense, he's a great bloke, and there is no shame or sense of regret in that. This is the man with whom I would choose to go to the trenches but dare not lose in the battle for the pain would be too great. I hope that when you have finished the pages to come, you are able to see why.

Mark Nicholas
April 2019

Prologue

I'M LYING ON A plastic sunlounger by the pool outside a Perth apartment block. It's a still winter's night and there's nobody else in sight. Behind me, towards the Swan River, I hear laughter and chatter; the sound of youth, the sound of the future. I pick up the plastic water bottle to my left and take an absent-minded swig. The warmth of the vodka calms me instantly.

I am Robin Smith, and in a former life I played cricket for England. Back then I was the Judge, the macho man who went toe-to-toe with the meanest fast bowlers on the planet. At one stage, I was officially the second-best batsman in the world. That was then and this is now. This is May 2013 and this is my life. The words of my ex-wife Kath on the phone earlier today – 'You are a fucking loser!' – ring sound my head. She's right. I've lost my marriage, my home, my children, not to mention my identity, money, dignity, direction, purpose and hope. There isn't much left.

Chris, my brother, has sacked me from my job at his embroidery company. He says I'm beyond redemption, an embarrassment to the family. He tells me to stay away from him, tells my friends to stay away from me. I have been staying on a sofa bed at my parents' apartment but Dad chucked me out this morning when he smelt alcohol on my breath. Both he and Chris have told me to go to the Salvation Army. I'm not ready for that. I'll never be ready for that. Instead I'm here, catching my breath by the pool outside Mom and Dad's apartment block – a 49-year-old man hiding from his father in plain sight because he has nowhere else to go.

Dad is struggling as Mom is in hospital with a fractured hip. The sight of my wonderful mother in such a state is what has driven me back to drink. Mom has broken bones, I have a broken mind and nobody can cope.

Ten years ago, I was starting my testimonial year at my beloved Hampshire Cricket Club. Twenty years ago, I was scoring a record 167 not out for England against Australia in a one-day international, when I received a standing ovation from the entire ground and praise from the prime minister. During my career, I was described as both the nicest bloke in world cricket and the most popular. Where are your friends tonight, Judgie?

Not here, thankfully. I don't want anyone to see me like this, least of all the people who remember me so fondly.

I think back to the days when I took on the West Indies' fast bowlers with unwavering courage, and compare that to what I have become.

I was the world's strongest man.

I am the world's softest bastard.

I hear the click of the gate that leads to the swimming pool and look to my right to see Karin, a petite, elegantly dressed lady who lives in one of the apartments upstairs. We have spoken quite a bit around the pool in the past few months. She rarely talks about herself, and she never flirts, despite my worst efforts, but she is friendly and listens to what I say without judgement. I've forgotten what that's like.

Karin knows nothing about my former life. She calls me Robin, not Judgie like everyone else. To her, I'm just a greying middle-aged man who's down on his luck. I haven't told her about how bad things are but she has a pair of eyes. I'm the skinniest I've ever been, I can't remember the last time I shaved, my surfing shorts have holes where they shouldn't and my body language is screaming for help. I know I look frail, jittery and dishevelled. I don't care.

We make small talk and I respond as enthusiastically as I can. I'm not quite drunk, not quite sober, not quite anything. I tell her Mom is in hospital, though not that Dad and Chris have disowned me. As she talks, I drain the last of my water bottle and calculate how I can top it up without her noticing. There's a bottle of Finlandia vodka in the vegetation to my right, and a $4 bottle of white wine in one of the hedges behind me in case of emergency. I wander away as if to go home for a minute and discreetly fill my bottle before heading back.

When I return, Karin is very quiet. She isn't hostile, but the mood has changed and I can't figure out what she's thinking.

'I have to go up and cook for my children before it gets too late,' she says. 'What are you up to tonight, Robin?'

I have become an autopilot liar and I can feel a response forming. 'Ah, not much, Karin, I'll sit here for a bit and go back to see Dad.'

Bugger this. I'm so tired.

She waits a few seconds and then asks again. 'Robin, what are you going to do tonight?'

What am I going to do tonight? What do people do when they don't want to live and they don't want to die?

I feel my chest tighten. 'I'm going to grab a couple of bottles of vodka, Karin. I'm going to drink them by the river and sleep there.'

She asks why and I explain that Dad has chucked me out, that I'm so ashamed and sorry for the hurt I've caused everyone.

'Well, you aren't going to sleep by the river,' she says. 'Tip your drink out, I know it's not water and I saw you top it up just now. You'll come and sleep on my sofa. I'll get you up early tomorrow, you can have a coffee and a shower and then jump on your bike and go to see your mum. You can have a fresh start, because you can't take the same day into tomorrow.'

I'm uncomfortable with the imposition, especially as I know she and her three young children live in a two-bedroom apartment, so I tell her I'll be fine.

'No, it's no problem,' she says. 'Robin, you can't sleep by the river. I'll go up in a minute and tell the children you've been locked out and that your dad is staying at the hospital with your mum. It will be okay.'

Karin disappears and returns 15 minutes later to collect me. Up in her flat, she tells me to relax, have a long hot shower and a cup of tea. I drink half my tea and thank her before climbing into the sofa bed. I fall into a deep sleep almost instantly.

When Karin wakes me at 6 a.m., I have another shower and then shiver my way through a cup of coffee.

'Robin,' she says matter-of-factly, 'I know you'll have the urge to drink today, but if you care enough about anyone in this world, think of them and ask if it's really worth touching another drop.'

I cycle the 15 kilometres to see Mom and spend the day with her. The piercing sadness of seeing her in a hospital bed is compounded by alcohol withdrawal and overwhelming anxiety. I feel like I've had twenty cups of coffee. My heart is a drum-and-bass track, I'm caked in sweat and sometimes I have to close my eyes for a few seconds to stop my head exploding. I'm tempted to get into one of the empty beds myself and beg for help.

When Mom drifts off to sleep, I walk outside to call Chris and tell him how she is doing. His wife Julie answers and says in an apologetic tone that he doesn't want to talk to me. I am shaking so much that I can barely hold the phone, and I feel my teeth chattering as I try to give her an update about Mom.

I know one swig of vodka, one swig of anything, will stop the cold turkey. I don't want a drink but I sure as hell need one. The bottle shop is only half a mile away and the temptation is relentless.

Ask if it's really worth touching another drop, Robin.

After spending a few hours at the hospital by Mom's bed, I call Dad to tell him she is doing well and in good spirits.

'Yes, I know, Robin. The hospital called me earlier and I'm coming to visit in a minute. Have you been to the homeless shelter?'

'No. I haven't, Dad. Please, can I come home?'

'Robin, make sure you go there, and don't come back here this evening. I've had enough. We've all had enough.'

I do go back, but only to the pool. I know it'll almost certainly be deserted as nobody goes there in the winter, certainly not Dad. I'm still suffering a vicious hangover – from last night, from the last ten years. I stand by the fence that backs onto the river, as I look across the Swan River towards the city lights, gripping the fence tight. I hear the gate click and turn around, hoping it's Karin.

It is. She feels like the only human contact I can face right now. She asks how Mom is, how I am, and we start chatting. I tell her how hard the day has been, how much I craved a drink but thought about what she said and managed to control myself. I tell her that I'm trying – really, really trying – and that I don't want to be like this.

Karin knows I'm in a state but she doesn't pry so she doesn't know why. I haven't really talked to anyone about how my life went so wrong, which is part of the problem. I tell her a couple of things and am struck by her empathy and lack of judgement. Unlike everyone else, she seems to listen rather than waiting for her turn to bollock me. I feel an instant, simple relief from sharing things that have been eating up my insides, and so I keep talking. For the next three and a half hours, on a calm winter's night by a deserted pool in Perth, I pour my heart out and cry it out too. I tell Karin everything – the full story of how I went from the Judge, superstar cricketer, to Robin Smith, homeless drunk.

Chapter 1

Winnie the Pooh

I GREW UP IN apartheid South Africa, but I didn't know it at the time. I didn't even hear the word 'apartheid' until I was in my late teens. South Africa was so sheltered from the outside world, and I was so content in my childhood bubble, that I had no sense of what the bigger picture looked like. I barely knew there was a bigger picture, or a world outside South Africa.

I was born at the Addington Hospital in Durban on Friday 13 September 1963. My brother was born in the same place five years earlier, and Mom had the same midwife each time. When I arrived, and the midwife delivered a little new-born parcel to Mom, she said, 'You've already got Christopher, now here's Robin.' As you probably know, Christopher Robin was a character in the Winnie the Pooh stories. Mom liked the name so much that she and Dad kept it – although these days Christopher and Robin are known to pretty much everyone by their nicknames of Kippy[1] and Judgie.

We had a really nice standard of living when I was growing up. Mom was South Africa's leading ballerina and Dad had a very successful

---

[1] When he was very young, Chris pronounced his name as Kiptopher, so he became known as Kippy.

business as a leather merchant, which he bought from his father. Among other things, his company provided all the leather gear for *Zulu Dawn*, the 1970s film that starred Burt Lancaster, Peter O'Toole and Bob Hoskins. I've always been so grateful for how comfortable we were, and my childhood was without doubt the happiest time of my life. It really stayed with me how lucky I was, and when I became a professional cricketer I tried to concentrate all my charity work on helping children get a decent upbringing.

We lived in La Lucia, an upmarket suburb just outside Durban, in a house called Mucklenook. When we moved there we didn't have any direct neighbours as ours was one of the first houses to be built. When I looked out towards the sea, all I could see was sugar cane – we were absolutely surrounded by it. Eventually, the suburb became more populated but at first the nearest house to us was about a kilometre away, owned by the diamond baron Harry Oppenheimer, who was one of the wealthiest men in the world. I may once or twice have stretched the truth and told people I was neighbours with Harry Oppenheimer!

The Durban weather was almost always beautiful. It was very humid but we had these lovely afternoon storms that would roll in and cool the place down. The winters weren't too cold, though it could be brisk in the morning, especially when Dad was dragging me out of bed at 5 a.m. for rugby or cricket practice.

It was an exclusively white area, and in those days we had black people working at our home. It's impossible to imagine that kind of racial segregation and suppression happening in today's society, but that's how it was in South Africa at the time. I didn't come across black people at school and I had no idea that was unusual. I had nothing to which I could compare my life. When you're a kid, the day-to-day reality of life defines what is normal.

We were a liberal family and the people who worked at our house were treated well. They felt like part of the family to me, and our maid Florence was my second mother. She changed my nappies, bathed me and cooked my meals. In fact, I saw more of Florence than Mom, who spent a lot of time teaching ballet and Spanish dancing at Natal University, and I absolutely adored them both. Florence used to call me her 'little Nunu', a South African word for a small creature. She doted on me.

We also had two 'garden boys' – that was the phrase of the time, not one I or anybody else would use now – called David and Simelane. David, in particular, was one of my best friends; he was a real charmer and a bit of a rogue. At the end of each day, he would grab a *juba* (an African beer), sit on the verge and chat to all the other maids as they walked past.

Maybe I'm being naïve, but it seemed to me that they were very happy. They had en-suite accommodation with TVs, they shared our food and cooking facilities, they were well paid and they stayed with the family for at least twenty-five years. Apartheid was utterly deplorable, and I know some unimaginably appalling things happened across South Africa, but I wasn't aware of any of that at the time.

When you're that age you don't read newspapers or think too much, you just play sport, and I was in a cocoon of cricket, rugby and athletics. There was full censorship in the media anyway, covering television, newspapers and radio. The first Kippy knew about apartheid was in 1973, when he was 15 and Dad sent him to England to Alf Gover's famous coaching school in London.[2] Kippy went with Mom's brother, Vernon Jr, and one day they were walking through Wandsworth when Kippy noticed some white guys collecting rubbish. When he asked about it, our uncle began to explain the political situation in South Africa.

Florence always cooked dinner for us when we got home from school. Kippy, being the older brother, would take butter from the silver tray and flick it at my face with a knife. If I started crying he'd say, 'Harden up, you bloody baby. You're a soft cock.' I was a bit portly as well and one day he said, 'You're a fat little shit, you shouldn't be eating anyway.'

'Don't say that.'

'Well you are, you're a fat little shit.'

---

[2] Gover, a fast bowler who played for Surrey and England, was the most famous cricket coach in the world for many years – visitors to his school included Sir Viv Richards, Sir Andy Roberts, Brian Lara and Sunil Gavaskar.

Florence came through and saw me crying. 'Christopher, do not treat your brother like that!'

There are four years and eleven months between us, which is quite a big gap for two brothers, and as you'd expect he bullied me a bit. Kippy is hard, really hard, and being his younger brother toughened me up – through playing sport or just messing around and fighting. By the time I was 15, I was bigger and stronger than he was, and the bullying mysteriously stopped!

My earliest childhood memory is hanging out with my wonderful grandfather, Dr Vernon Shearer, who was the mayor of Durban. We used to be treated to ice creams in the mayor's car and would play hide and seek at his beautiful home. He was a liberal member of parliament and therefore in a huge minority, especially as he was always very public in his anti-apartheid views. My grandfather was a people person, a very empathetic man who was a member of parliament for 25 years, while also working as a dentist, before he became mayor.

Kippy remembers being picked up from school in the black mayoral limousine, with flags on the front of the car and the licence plate NDC1, though my memories aren't quite as vivid. I was young and didn't realise quite how big a deal he was. I knew he was fairly special, as he drove round in the best car in Durban, but to me he was just my grandfather.

He was Mom's father and mixed in some impressive circles. When Queen Elizabeth had a twenty-first birthday party in Cape Town, Mom, as a daughter of a parliamentarian, was one of the guests. He also encouraged Mom to study ballet in Paris and London, where she was tutored by Russian royalty and shared a classroom with the likes of Dame Margot Fonteyn.

If I inherited any sporting genes, they probably came from my grandfather. He qualified as a dentist from Edinburgh University but he was also a triple Blue in swimming, cricket and rugby – I think it was the first triple Blue ever awarded there. He played a few games of cricket at the Grange, the ground where Scotland famously beat England in a one-day international in 2018.

That's not all I seem to have inherited from him. I'm emotionally soft and I worry a lot about others, which apparently my grandfather did too. He was a very compassionate, optimistic man. I've always seen the best in people, sometimes to my cost, and I think much of that comes from Mom's side of the family. She says I was quiet and a little introverted as a child, and could be sensitive and emotional. Apparently, I used to leave notes on her pillow saying, 'I love you so much it's unbelievable'!

Mom and Dad were both born in the UK in 1931 – Joy Shearer in Edinburgh and John Smith in Walsall. By coincidence, their families moved to Durban in 1932, thinking there would be better prospects during the Great Depression, and they ended up meeting at kindergarten. They've known each other for 85 years.

They started dating when they were in their early twenties, though my grandfather was initially against Mom going out with Dad. He thought his beautiful daughter, the best ballerina in the country, might marry a barrister or someone like that, not a leather merchant.

Dad got Mom's number from a mutual friend and asked her on a date.

'Hi, this is John Smith.'

That's a great chat-up line, isn't it, using the most common name in the world?! Mom said thank you, but no. Dad persevered and tried to impress her with his flash MG sports car. Eventually she agreed to a date, they fell in love and were married a few years later in 1955.

When Kippy was born in 1958, Dad encouraged Mom to continue her studies and, after discussing it with my grandfather, bought her a plane ticket to Spain. She studied there for three months and when she came back she started teaching at Natal University. We also converted our garage, which could fit ten cars,[3] into a big dance studio. That's another of my early memories, coming home from school every day to see Mom teaching 120 gorgeous young ballerinas. She even had a couple of rugby players as students – two huge lock forwards for Natal, our provincial side, who wanted to improve in the lineout. Ballerinas can jump very well and there was no lifting in the lineout in those days. I'm glad to say I didn't see them in their leotards.

---

[3] Not that we had ten cars, by the way, only a couple!

Mom and Dad had very different parenting styles, which gave me a nice balance between being loved and disciplined. Mom was soft and gentle and Dad was the authoritarian. I love him every bit as much as Mom but he could be very tough. In those days, I got the cane on many, many occasions. I would go to his study, pull down my pants and wait for the smack. I didn't ask any questions – that's just the way it was.

When I was six or seven, I told the next-door neighbour's mother to 'fuck off'. I'd heard my brother say 'fuck', and I didn't really know what it meant, so I thought I'd find out by telling her to 'fuck off'. It got back to Dad, who called me into his study. I tried to plead with him.

'Dad, I didn't know what it meant.'

'You'll soon know after this, my boy!'

I got the hiding of my life.

Mind you, I'm not sure Dad's message got through. I should apologise in advance for some of the language in this book. Swearing is just part of the way I talk, and it's certainly a big part of the vocabulary of sport at any level.

When Kippy went to Alf Gover's coaching clinic in London, he returned with a couple of porno mags. We'd never seen anything like *Mayfair* or *Penthouse* because they were banned in South Africa. If you had topless women in a magazine, their nipples would be covered – and that was the most explicit pornography you could get.

One day I found these magazines in his room and decided to bring them to school to impress the boys. We had those old school desks that you could open up and I had the centre spread on display with a couple of my mates gawping and giggling. The teacher soon noticed.

'Smith!'

'Yes, ma'am?'

'You seem to have something very interesting in your desk.'

'No, not really, ma'am.'

'May I come and take a look?'

'Yes, ma'am.'

I went pale. She walked around, opened the desk and saw the full glory of the *Penthouse* centre spread. Without saying a word, she went back to her desk to write a note, put it in the middle of the magazine and said, 'Would you like to take that down to the headmaster?'

The honest response – 'Not particularly, ma'am' – wouldn't have been appropriate, so I trudged nervously down the corridor. When I got to the headmaster's office, he said, 'Robin, I've had a call from your teacher. I believe you have something to show me.'

'Yes, sir.'

'You know this is banned from South Africa, never mind this school. I'll have to give you six of the best.'

'Yes, sir, I understand.'

I got six of the *best*.

He took the mag and wrote a letter to my parents saying that I'd been caned. When it arrived a couple of days later, Dad summoned me to his study. You can imagine how I felt. My arse was already yellow and blue, and now Dad was brandishing his cane!

'You know what happens, my boy. In you come.'

I took six more on the same bruises. I honestly reckon the pain of being caned was as bad as being hit in the face by a cricket ball. It stung viciously and occasionally I was reduced to tears. But even though it hurt, I was never scared of being caned. Even as a child I had no real fear of physical harm. I would swim in water that was well out of my depth or surf in areas with no shark nets, and when I was a bit older I got a buzz from steadily upping the speed on the bowling machine – or in my car – to see if I could still cope. Mind you, I have always been absolutely petrified of snakes. In South Africa all snakes are highly venomous – particularly the green or black mamba, which used to live in the sugar cane fields around our house. If I saw one of those I'd be on top of the cupboard. I've never understood people who have snakes as pets. What the hell do you get back from a snake?! Devious little buggers. At least a budgie will sit on your finger and look at you for a bit.

I had to sleep on my side for a few days after that double caning, and sitting down at school wasn't much fun either. And then I had to face the hardest thing of all: telling Kippy his special magazines had been confiscated.

I knew if I got the cane, it was justified. Always. In those days if you did something wrong – if you swore, misbehaved, showed disrespect – you got caned. Those were the rules and we accepted the consequences of not doing the right thing. In South Africa, the first thing you were taught was that respect for your elders and seniors was non-negotiable.

In so many ways, it was a very different world.

Chapter 2

The all-rounder

IN ALL WALKS OF life, people ask the same question. Nature or nurture? Are we the way we are because of genetics or environment? With my sporting career, and I'm sorry this is a boring answer, I really do think it was about fifty-fifty. I was lucky enough to pick up most sports pretty quickly but I also, thanks to Dad, had the privilege of excellent and intensive coaching.

My first memory of playing sport is at the local soccer club when I was seven or eight. It's strange that this is the first thing I recall because I wasn't particularly good at soccer and I never really enjoyed it. I used to have a bit of dandruff and I would stand there scratching my head while the game was going on. I got a real bollocking from the old man after one game.[1] 'You just stood there scratching your head! Why don't you bloody get involved in the game?'

Dad loved sport, particularly rugby and cricket. He was a very good rugby player at school. He never got beyond the 2nd XI at cricket – but he's asked me to mention that he once took a hat-trick bowling his phantom legspinners. His sister, Jackie Mercer, was South

---

[1] I should stress that 'old man' is a respectful term in South Africa, as it is in England!

Africa's ladies golf captain for twenty-five years. There were never any half-measures with Dad; if you were going to do something, you did it properly. The great golfer Gary Player had a coastal home in La Lucia and Dad loved his famous quote: 'The harder I practise, the luckier I get.' If it was good enough for Gary Player, Dad thought, it was good enough for his sons. And bloody hell did we work hard.

When I was growing up, the seasons weren't summer, autumn, winter and spring. They were cricket (October to March), rugby (April to mid-August) and athletics (the rest of August and September). Dad set up a special training routine for all three. He would get me out of bed at 5 a.m. every morning in the middle of winter for rugby practice, usually when I was half asleep. We'd fill the car with a tackling bag, heavy landing mats and rugby balls and head down to the local school. It didn't matter if it was pissing down; in fact, Dad preferred it if it was. He was all for training in tough conditions – whether it was rain, poor light, or running five miles in the burning lunchtime heat. He reasoned that if you trained in extreme conditions then playing matches in milder weather would be much easier.

It was only a six-minute drive to school, but I was often so tired that I'd fall asleep in the car. When we got to the school, we'd warm up and then run up and down the sideline while he gave me instructions:

'Robin, do a dummy!'

'Robin, do a sidestep!'

'Robin, sprint for the twenty-five!'

I thought, 'Bloody hell, this bloke's nuts!' I'd practise everything, from hitting the tackling bag to goal-kicking. It was usually dark and all I could see was the silhouette of the rugby posts, with the sun yet to rise up over the Indian Ocean. Dad would bring a bright electric lantern, about two feet high, and perch on the case while I practised kicking from various distances and angles.

The lantern was right under the posts, so I had to aim for that. He usually couldn't see the ball coming because it was dark but he could hear the bounce, so if it landed off target he'd say, 'Not good enough, my boy! Make sure you follow through straight.'

Every now and then I would absolutely nail a kick that would sail between the posts. Then I'd hear a massive clatter and the light would go out. I'd think, 'Shit! I'm in trouble here.' After a couple of seconds of silence, he'd turn the light back on, cup his mouth with his hands and shout, 'Great kick, my boy!'

At that age I loved rugby as much as cricket, if not more so. I played inside centre and dominated my team at Clifton Preparatory School. When I was about ten I started to get a lot bigger, both in height and strength, and Dad has got some footage of me doing the 400m where everyone else comes up to my shoulder. One school even refused to play rugby against Clifton if I was in the team.

At the age of 16 I was one of the reserves for the South Africa Schools team, playing alongside blokes a lot older than me. That was also my last year at Northlands Boys High School, when I scored 208 points for the rugby team. The next highest was my best mate John Laurie with 11. I dislocated my shoulder during the season but I didn't miss any games – in those days it was just a sore shoulder, so you had to grit your teeth and get on with it. We used to play on what is now called the Smith Oval. There's also a Pollock Oval, because Shaun Pollock went to the school as well. I didn't know him then – he's ten years younger than me – but our paths would cross in Test cricket many years later.

There was a grandstand on one side of the field where everyone sat, and on the other side there were just the two coaches, the linesman and Dad patrolling the sideline. I never knew how he was always able to get on that side, as it was supposed to be for officials only. He always wore his white safari suit and white socks, even in the middle of winter.

Whenever we had possession you could hear him, with his hands cupping his mouth, shouting, 'Pass the ball to Robin!' How embarrassing. I thought rugby was a team game, Dad!

I swear that most of the people came to watch him rather than the game. If I was taking a kick he'd be behind the posts, right in line with where I was aiming, giving an extravagant signal for me to follow through straight.

I think I was always his favourite son. Kippy would agree with me on that, though there's no doubt Dad's proudest moment was when Kippy first played for England. It's a tremendous credit to him that he brought up two sons to play international cricket, even though he barely picked up a bat himself. I suppose, like many parents, he lived his sporting dreams through his children.

My cricket really got going at Clifton when I was about nine, thanks to our wonderful cricket master, Neil Fox. He hadn't played at a high standard and was only really an English and handwriting teacher, so he was limited in the finer aspects of batting technique, but he ignited my love for the game. He was also the cricket master when the great Barry Richards was at the school, so he could tell his grandchildren he taught Barry Richards and Robin Smith how to play the game – even if he probably taught me more about handwriting than cricket!

He taught me a couple of other important things – to take my cap off as a mark of respect when I asked for my guard, and again if I reached a half-century. You never, ever spoke to a senior with your cap on.

While I was at Clifton I broke a couple of records that belonged to Barry Richards, who at the time was widely recognised as the best opening batsman in the world. He only played four Test matches, because South Africa were banned from international sport due to the apartheid regime, though he averaged 73 in those games – and they were all against Australia. He also scored tens of thousands of runs for Natal, Hampshire and South Australia. He was my first cricket hero, so to break his records was surreal.

The fact I showed early promise made Dad doubly determined to ensure I had the best facilities. He bought the house next door, knocked it down and built a cricket pitch. We also had one of the first bowling machines in South Africa. Dad imported a Jugs pitching machine from America, the kind they used in baseball. The facilities were unbelievable, really – we had a full pitch, which was made of concrete with an Ozite[2] overlay, and if you cranked the bowling machine up the ball really flew off the pitch. It meant I was exposed to serious pace and bounce when I was barely a teenager, and it helped me to pick up the short ball quickly. That type of bowling became my bread and butter.

---

[2] Ozite was the Astroturf of its day, though not quite as advanced.

Dad also found out that Grayson Heath lived nearby and approached him to see if he would be interested in coaching me. He was the captain of Natal, our provincial team, who were South African champions at the time. Grayson's a really intelligent, wise man who also did a degree in psychology – he's been a huge influence on my life, never mind my cricket. Dad could afford to pay him to coach me for an hour each day before I went to school, so he came down at 5 a.m. every morning.

Grayson also gave me a mantra for batting: A+H=C. I thought it was a mathematical formula until he explained it. 'Robin, A is arrogance and H is humility. Put those together and you will achieve C, the wonderful balance of confidence.'

Grayson taught me to have the arrogance to try to score off every ball and the humility to know this wouldn't always be possible – and that the bowler was entitled to bowl a good ball which might get me out. It's fair to say that, for most of my career, the humility came more naturally than the arrogance.

He also made me appreciate the importance of technique, another thing which stayed with me throughout my career. I've always loved seeing a player with great technique. Mark Ramprakash, Ian Bell, Martin Crowe, John Crawley – I know that might surprise some people – and Rahul Dravid were some of my favourites.

The most important lesson Grayson taught me was the one about the hot potato. Let me explain. Grayson said to imagine I had a hot potato under my left armpit when I batted, so if I didn't keep my elbow nice and high I would get scalded – and, more importantly, my bat would come down across the line of the ball. Remembering the hot potato helped me to play straight throughout my career. I'm not sure if there are too many hot potatoes in T20 these days!

That was one of many eternal truths of technique that Grayson taught me. Another was that my eyes were my camera and my computer, so unless I was cutting a wide ball I should always try to get my eyes parallel to the ground and right behind the line of the ball – not behind the line of my pad. You want your pad to be just inside the line of the ball so that you are not playing around it. If your eyes and bat are aligned correctly, you will automatically get into the right position. But it's such a hard thing to do, because your head is so heavy that it's natural to fall over towards the off side. Once your head goes, your body will follow and you'll have to play across the line.

These days I do some coaching and I've had to say to a couple of parents, 'Look, I don't want to coach T20 players. I want to instil a solid technique, which will give your son or daughter a great foundation. Then when they're 15 or 16 they can become more creative with their shots.' It's a lot harder to turn a great T20 player into a Test match player than the other way round. You can't build the Penthouse Suite first.

Steve Smith has made life more difficult for batting coaches. It's not easy explaining to 12-year-olds that he has a fundamentally poor technique which only works because he has freakish hand–eye coordination.

All that practice against the bowling machine was brilliant for developing my technique and grooving certain shots. If you spent 500 hours practising the cover drive over a long period of time, you had a much better chance of nailing it when Sir Curtly Ambrose bowled his yearly half volley. I'd like to think I'm the best player in history on a bowling machine!

I became very programmed, so that if the ball was in a certain area I would play the appropriate shot without having to think. This was generally, but not always, a good thing. Though practice is vital for a batsman, it's not quite the same as golf, where you are hitting a stationary ball. There are more variables in cricket – length, line, movement off the pitch or in the air, uneven bounce – and the technology of that time couldn't really replicate them. And nobody has yet invented a bowling machine with a setting that allows you to simulate batting in the middle when you've got no confidence.

It wasn't great for learning how to play slow bowling, either. The technology was not that far advanced so, though it was superb for practising against pace or swing, it couldn't really deliver an off-break or a legspinner. Nor could it replicate the subtle variations in pace and flight that are such a big part of high-class spin bowling. It took ages to change the speed, so you couldn't do it from ball to ball, and

I didn't bother practising against 50mph bowling because it wasn't spinning anyway.

I probably did between 15–20 hours a week on the bowling machine in addition to playing for my school or in club cricket. People often said how talented I was – and maybe that was true, certainly when I was younger – but I also worked a lot harder than anyone else. Even when I was playing my final season for Hampshire at the age of 39, I was first to the ground in the morning with Dad loading the bowling machine. I always giggled inside when people said how lucky I was to be so naturally talented. I sometimes felt like saying, 'Yeah, and if you'd practised three or four hours a day maybe you'd be more talented.'

I've always had an innate belief that hard work is rewarded on and off the field. You work hard and then you get to play hard. That all goes back my childhood, because with Dad, everything was based around effort and achievement. Kippy and I didn't get pocket money – he'd be livid with Mom if she gave us any – but if we scored a fifty or a hundred, we would be rewarded with a few rand notes. It was like having a sponsor from an early age, and we always seemed to end up with more pocket money than our mates.

Sometimes I had to work seriously hard for a reward, though. I can remember a period when I was eight or nine and Dad would regularly take me on a three-mile run with him. If I didn't do the run I wouldn't be allowed on the beach later on. I must have had some sort of undiagnosed asthma because there were times when I found it very difficult to breathe. In Dad's mind, I was either not breathing properly or I wasn't fit enough. He would pick up a strong branch from the side of the road, and if I was breathing heavily or not running quickly enough he'd whack me on the bum. Sometimes I was in tears because I couldn't breathe, and he'd stand there and inhale really extravagantly. 'This is how you do it, my boy. Breathe through your nose and exhale through your mouth. You're just not fit enough.'

I know what you're thinking. But these were very different times, and he did give me a lot of love. An hour later we'd be sitting on the beach and he'd be building sandcastles with me or gently cutting up my fishing bait and putting it on the hook.

We had a gorgeous beach cottage in a little village about 100 kilometres south of Durban, which we would visit in school holidays or at weekends when we weren't playing sport. It was so close to the Indian Ocean that, at high tide, the water would come over the sand and into our garden. Kippy and I still had to practise an hour every afternoon – Dad had a cricket net put up at the cottage as well – but if we did that we were allowed to go fishing.

Every year there was a three-week period in July, during the school holidays, which was known as the 'sardine run'. We used to collect hundreds of sardines, pack and freeze them and then sell them to the local tackle shop to get our pocket money. There were hundreds and hundreds of them, right in front of our beach cottage. Sardines on toast, anyone?

There were other rewards, too. When I was 12, Dad bought me a motorised go-kart, which went at around 60km/h. It was like a little F1 racer, and I'd go whizzing up and down the road with my little dog Candy in my lap. In fact, I first broke the speed limit at the age of 12. One day the police pulled me over for going 60km/h when the speed limit was 50km/h. There was a newly laid tarmac road near our cottage, so they were just making sure all the residents were aware of the speed limit. I've been an adrenalin junkie for as long as I can remember. I've got my fix in various ways, from driving high-speed cars (and go-karts) to facing the fastest bowlers in the world. Even at the age of 12 I was living life at 100 miles an hour. Well, okay, at 60 kilometres an hour.

My size meant I was good at athletics, so Dad had a long-jump pit and shot-put area put up in the garden. We were so lucky to have a huge garden, about an acre in total, with a lovely swimming pool and all these sporting facilities. We also had a high-jump area with a huge landing mat. All this was done just for me – by that stage Kippy was 17 and had other priorities in life. It just happened that by the time I became a teenager Dad was able to take a bit more time off work and devote it to me. When Kippy was the same age, Dad was still building the business.

Kippy still used the cricket pitch and bowling machine but he certainly wasn't being dragged out of bed in the small hours. He stood up for himself more than me and occasionally told Dad where to go. In those days it was compulsory to do two years' military service. Kippy chose the police force because they had barracks in Durban, which meant he could still play cricket, and if Dad tried to discipline him he was able to say, 'I'm not getting at up five in the morning, I'm a bloody policeman.'

If I wasn't getting up at 5 a.m. for cricket or rugby practice, then I was off to school to practise the 100m, 200m and 400m. Dad paid my brother's best friend to come and train with me. If I was doing the 400m, Dad would be my pacemaker for the first 100m before dropping out and leaving me to do the second 100m on my own. Then Peter would start at the 200m mark. We had a few close races, but at the end I was absolutely exhausted.

I also had an athletics coach who trained me for three or four hours a day during school holidays, covering every single discipline. Dad had a book in which he scribbled down all my personal bests and records. Before my first sports day at Northlands, he said he would give me a certain amount of money if I broke a school record, and for each subsequent record he would double it. He budgeted for me to break four or five records, and his plan was that he would look after the money until I was old enough to buy my first car.

I was excited and knew I had a chance of breaking some records. I didn't feel pressure – I was too young for that – but I was slightly uneasy about the expectation. Having said that, I knew Dad just wanted me to do my best. He was a humble man and that was enough for him.

The first event was the 100m, a tight race against a really good sprinter who represented Natal, but I won it and also broke the school record. Because I was taking part in so many events, there was no gap in between each discipline. It was like an assault course: I remember running from the 110m hurdles track to the shot-put area. Then it was back to the athletics track, then over for the long jump, then back again for the 400m. When I broke the long-jump record it was my fifth of the day, and Dad beckoned me towards him before the next event. I looked forward to hearing how proud he was of my achievements.

'Robin! All bets are off!'

That day, at the under-14s, I broke the record in every event I entered: 100m, 200m, 300m, 110m hurdles, shot put, discus, javelin, triple jump, long jump and the high jump. The school had been going for 80 years and most of the records had stood for at least two decades.

The 400m record had stood for 70 years, and I put about 30 per cent on the previous best in the shot put. I was really good in that because of the power in my shoulders and at one stage I had an unlikely double when I held the South African under-17 records for that and the 110m hurdles.

The fastest 100m I ever managed was 11 seconds – I really wanted to get down to 10.9 but I never did. They kept records for each age group so a year later there was the same expectation. I broke the under-15 records in the same ten events, although the 300m had become the 400m, and the year after that I got eight out of ten at the under-16s. I'd bulked up a bit by then so I missed out on the 100m and the high jump. Actually, the high-jump record was broken by my best friend John Laurie. That wasn't the only thing he stole from me. He was a charming, good-looking bugger who was forever nicking my girlfriends.

I don't know if I was a celebrity at school but I suppose you're a bit of a ledge if you break that many records in one day. It got a bit embarrassing when they had the annual prize-giving in front of the students and parents at the end of the day, because I was going up every couple of minutes. I guess it was no surprise who got the *victor ludorum* trophy.[3]

I could go on, but I don't want to sound like, well, a broken record. I was a fairly shy young bloke so I felt uncomfortable with the attention, and I still don't really like talking about records and achievements. It's going back 40 years, but I still feel arrogant and big-headed telling people I've done this or that.

At that age, even though it was clear I was talented, it was too early to think about being a professional sportsman. I just focused on the three seasons, whether it was cricket, rugby or athletics. It was an

---

[3] The trophy was awarded to the most successful competitor at the end of each sports day. *Victor ludorum* is Latin for 'the winner of the games'.

idyllic life – I played sport all the time and had some great friends. I had a core group of mates but I got on well with everyone and I always had a liking for the underdog. When I was around 10 years old, I stood up for a bullied schoolmate called Philip Patel. I was much taller and stronger than everyone else so nobody really took me on. When school ended that day, he jumped in Mom's car with me and we headed for home. She thought it was nice for me to bring a friend back to the house for a couple of hours. I hadn't told her that he had decided to come and live with us and I had said that would be absolutely fine. I got him to ring his mum and tell her. His parting words to her were, 'Don't worry about me, Mum, I'm very happy here.'

A few minutes later his mum's car came screeching up to our house, at which point she let go a deluge of abuse to all of us – especially Mom, who she accused of kidnapping her son. She dragged Philip back home and my poor mother, who still had no idea what had happened, said, 'Well, that was very rude, Robin. His mother seemed a little stressed.'

My most memorable moment at Northlands was during my last game for the rugby side. We were unbeaten going into the last match of the season – and we were playing Beachwood, our big rivals from down the road.[4] There were two or three thousand spectators in the grandstand. I can still picture that day – it was pissing down with rain, and our school colours of brown and white soon became all brown as we dived around in the mud.

We were a couple of points behind with time running out. Even at that age, I was very competitive and couldn't stand the thought of losing. We were on our own ten-yard line and Dad, as usual, was barking, 'Pass the ball to Robin!'

When the ball was eventually passed to me, I fizzed off one of their players and sidestepped another. I had my head down and started to bolt diagonally towards the corner flag, knowing I only had to beat the full-back to score the winning try. Dad, as usual, was patrolling the touchline with the coaches and the linesman, and after I beat the full-back I noticed out of the corner of my eye that Dad was hurtling

---

[4] The schools have since merged to form Northwood.

down the touchline as well. He was fit and strong in those days because of our training every morning, so he matched me almost stride for stride from the halfway line. When I slid in the corner to score the winning try, he dived at exactly the same time. Because it was so wet, we both skidded about five yards and he ended up right next to me. When he got up, his safari suit had turned green and brown.

Dad, bless him, was totally oblivious. He was so cocooned and focused on me doing well that he had no idea about the impact of his celebration. Children usually get embarrassed by their parents and at the time I was mortified. But as I grew older I looked back on that moment with so much pride and fondness, because I knew how much it meant to him. This was the same ground where we trained every morning for years, often in the same pouring rain. The harder we practised, the luckier we got.

Chapter 3

The Judge's wig

You won't find the details in *Wisden*, but believe me, Test cricket was played in South Africa in the 1970s and 1980s. It just went by a different name. The Currie Cup, our domestic competition, produced cricket of the highest standard. South Africa was isolated from international sport because of the apartheid regime, so these games – and the rebel tours that came later – were the equivalent to Test cricket for players and supporters. The matches were played with the same intensity and quality as Tests, if not more so, and the games between the three big sides – Natal, Western Province and Transvaal – were absolutely ferocious.

I'm certainly not alone in believing that, had South Africa played Test cricket in that period, they would have challenged the great West Indian side. They would have had an awesome XI: Barry Richards, Jimmy Cook, Peter Kirsten, Graeme Pollock, Ken McEwan, Clive Rice, Mike Procter, 'Tich' Smith, Denys Hobson, Garth Le Roux and Vincent van der Bijl. Look at that team! As Mike Procter and Clive Rice were such great all-rounders, it's effectively a 13-man team – seven brilliant strokemakers, four proper fast bowlers, a leggie and a specialist keeper.

When I was 11 or 12, Mom used to drop me off at Durban's Test ground, Kingsmead, with a picnic: Fizz Pops, Jelly Tots and an ice cooler full of drinks and Eskimo ice creams. I'd sit behind the picket fences watching the guys play through my binoculars. I can still hear the chorus of beer cans being thumped on the advertising boards whenever a fast bowler was charging in.

Allan Lamb became another hero of mine whenever he came to play with Western Province. Kingsmead was always a difficult pitch to bat on, because Natal had such a strong pace attack that the groundsman was told to prepare seamer-friendly wickets. I loved Lamby's confident attitude, and how he always tried to dominate those bowlers no matter what the pitch was doing. He was always bantering with the opposition, never flinched when he was hit, and always seemed to have a smile on his face. I sometimes wondered what he was talking about with his batting partner between overs as half the time they seemed to be laughing their heads off.

I vividly remember running after him at lunchtime one day.

'Mr Lamb, may I have your autograph please?'

'Okay, mate, how are things going, china?[1] All good, eh? Are you enjoying the cricket?'

'Yes, Mr Lamb.'

'Great, you might see some shots after lunch.'

If you'd told me then that he would become one of my best friends, and one of the biggest influences on my career, I'd have thought you'd caught too much sun.

I got to meet a lot of my heroes around that time. From the age of eight until 12, I went to a coaching clinic called the Kingsmead Mynahs, which was run during the school holidays by all the Natal cricketers – Barry Richards, Mike Procter, Vincent van der Bijl, Bob Woolmer and others. Around the same time, Barry was approached to do a book about batting technique. The publisher wanted to include

---

[1] A slang expression for 'mate' that was very popular in South Africa when I was growing up. It originated in East London so don't ask me how it found its way to Durban!

some pictures of him showing a youngster how to play certain shots, so that the kids who bought it could relate more easily to the text.

He wrote to all the parents of the kids he coached at Kingsmead Mynahs to see if they might be interested – but you had to be at least ten years old. Mom saw the letter and knew I'd love to do it. The trouble was that I was only nine, so she decided to keep quiet about that.

We were told to report to the ground of Barry's club side, DHS Old Boys.[2] On the way there, Mom made one thing clear: 'Don't get your hopes up, Robin, there will be hundreds of boys there and only one can get picked.' When we got there, it was completely deserted, and I was just starting to think we'd gone to the wrong place when Barry came out to say hello. It turned out he'd picked me ahead of all the other kids. It's easy to forget, as time passes, just what an unbelievable honour that was for my nine-year-old self.

I looked at the book recently and the pictures stand the test of the time, even if the haircuts haven't! It shows how technically correct Barry was. I know techniques evolve, and I'm in awe of some of the shots the guys play in T20 cricket, but I hope they don't throw the MCC Coaching Manual out the window. Those basics are so important.

I grew up as a very correct batsman. I played straight – remember the hot potato – and all my strokes were orthodox. You might be surprised to read that I hit only 11 sixes in my Test career, though I cut loose more often in one-day cricket and for Hampshire. Dad drilled into me Sir Donald Bradman's mantra that if you hit the ball in the air you risked being caught. When I was batting at school, he would park himself by the sightscreen with his umbrella, his deckchair and his Esky, and if I ever hit the ball in the air he would stand up and make an exaggerated motion for me to keep the ball down. So I did – not because I was worried about getting out, but so that the old man wouldn't continue to embarrass me!

Barry and Mike Procter lived near our house in Durban and used to come to practise in our back garden. They could have gone to the

---

[2] Durban High School Old Boys.

club but we were nearby and there were advantages at our place – David and I would feed the bowling machine to them for as long as they wanted, and Florence would feed them as much lunch as they wanted.

It was another surreal privilege, having two all-time great cricketers in my back garden. I was used to being in their company by then, but I was still totally in awe of them and their ability. I used to look at the speed dial, because I had it up high to practise avoiding or cutting short balls. When Barry came over he turned it up even higher and then started driving off the back foot through extra cover. You can cut quicker bowling but it's unheard of to play back-foot drives. And this was when he was in his late thirties. Honestly, you would not believe how good he was.

Even a genius like Barry knew you could only develop your technique through a great deal of practice. There are no shortcuts: never have been, never will be. One of the shots I practised the most, usually with my coach Grayson Heath, was the square cut. I didn't enjoy working on some shots – if you miss a hook, for example, you know you'll probably get hit on the head – but the square cut was always fun. The ball was wide of off stump, so if I missed it, it would just crash into the net behind me.

In our garden, we had a tree that was about seven yards away, directly square of where I was batting. Dad put a little white circle on the bottom of the tree as a target, so that I was hitting the ball downwards rather than at catchable height. Whenever the ball was in the slot I'd get back and smash it towards the tree. The Durban air was quite thick and it was very quiet in the morning, so it made a hell of a racket. By then we had next-door neighbours, and when they heard the sound every morning they thought we were chopping wood at 5 a.m.

They rarely complained but we thought the right thing to do was to put all our gear in the car and head down to my school so that our neighbours could get a decent sleep. This presented a different problem. I used to hit so many square cuts to the same part of the net that eventually the mesh start to break. Every now and then Dad would get a call from the school telling him it might be time to repair the nets.

Believe it or not, the square cut wasn't my favourite shot – nothing compared to hitting an on-drive off the front foot back past the bowler – but it's the one I'm associated with. I was pretty flattered when, a couple of years ago, somebody sent me a link to a YouTube coaching video in which Sir Alastair Cook was demonstrating the cut shot. At the end he said, 'I hope that helps, and I hope you're hitting them like Robin Smith after this.' Thanks for pumping my tyres up, Cookie! If I was a good square-cutter, it's because of years and years of practice from the age of nine. There's no magic secret, although I suppose a well-positioned tree in the back garden doesn't hurt.

In my opinion, there are seven elements that make up the square cut.[3]

1. **Picking up the line of the ball very quickly**. If you're shaping to play a drive off the back foot, and you pick the line early enough, you're in a really good position to move into the cut.
2. **Body shape**. You have to stay sideways on. If you open up your body it becomes difficult to hit the ball square or behind square with any real power. If you're sideways on, you can turn your left shoulder towards the wicketkeeper and get your back foot parallel to the crease, with your right foot pointing towards square cover and your left towards extra cover. You keep the bottom half of your body completely still and twist the top half. And stay upright. If you are leaning backwards that means you are cutting too close to your body.
3. **Wait for the ball.** It sounds silly to say you have to wait for the ball, given you have less than half a second's reaction time, but it's true. Your reflexes are so fast, and your eyes light up when you see a ball that is short and wide. It's so important to have the confidence to wait for the ball that extra split-second, until the ball is level with your eyes and your back knee. Watch the ball onto the bat and then off the bat.

---

[3] All these tips apply if you're a right-handed batsman. If you're left-handed, reverse them where appropriate.

4. **Don't get too far across your stumps**. If you do that, you will cramp yourself. You need room to free your arms through the shot. The longer you wait for the ball, the more you can bring your right shoulder through and explode into the shot, accelerating through the ball like a tennis player.

5. **Lock your wrists**, only rolling them at the end of your follow-through. If you do that, the angle of your bat will mean you naturally keep the ball down. If you lock your wrists you will gather more momentum into the shot, and if you don't you increase the chance of a top edge.

6. **Aim to hit the ball just to the right of square cover**. That way, if you are fractionally late on the shot, it will still go square or just backward of square. But if you aim to hit it behind square and are late, you will hit it too fine. The shot should ways end up going the left of gully.

7. **Don't try to hit the ball too hard**. It's vital to get the perfect balance between strength and timing, and the way to do it is to retain your composure and control of the shot.

You know if you've nailed it because you'll hear that lovely rifle crack at the point of impact. When you really get hold of a square cut, and you hear the primal roar of the crowd as it flashes to the boundary, there's a lovely feeling of power and dominance over the bowler.

The strength in my shoulder must have helped me play the square cut. I never really bothered with weights but I did press-ups from a young age, usually 200 a day, which made my shoulders and forearms quite strong. All that shot-put training had an impact, too, as it allowed me to get that explosion through the shoulder. I always tried to tailor my fitness work with batting in mind. I did wrist exercises – that was one time I did use weights – and also practised using only my top hand. Every day, at the start of practice, I would face 50 or 60 balls with just one hand to build up the strength in my left forearm. I don't know if I was gym-fit but I was definitely cricket-fit and naturally fit.

The fact I was bigger and stronger than my peers helped me progress quickly as a batsman and I made my club cricket debut, playing against grown men, at the age of 12. At 14 I was the youngest player ever to be picked for Natal Schools under-18s and the second youngest ever to appear at Nuffield Week. It's a bit of an institution in South African cricket, a week-long tournament where schoolboy talent is unearthed. At the end of the seven days, the best XI is picked to play for South African Schools against the host provincial team.

I made it into the South African Schools XI in 1979, on my second visit to Nuffield Week, and again in 1980. That was the year I broke another of Barry Richards' records, this time for the most runs ever scored in a school season in South Africa. I was starting to get a decent reputation.

I also had a new nickname. When I was 16, I played in an A-grade club game in Durban, with each team having a handful of Natal players. One of theirs was Mark Hedley, who had played a bit of provincial cricket – mainly as a batsman, but he also fancied himself as a tearaway fast bowler. I had my hair down over my ears and my collar, which was the fashion in 1980. At least I think it was. I was batting without a helmet or cap, and because it was a hot, humid day, my hair had gone a bit crinkly. Kippy and I were developing a nice partnership when Mark shouted to the captain, 'Oi, skipper, gimme the ball, I'll knock that Judge's wig off his bloody head!'

He came on and bowled a short ball that I pulled for four. 'Little prick! I'll knock that fucking wig off your head!' Later in the over he dropped another one short and I clattered it for six. Eventually he was taken out of the attack and I got a hundred. I went into the bar afterwards and he called to me from about ten yards away, 'Oi, Judge!' I didn't turn around but he kept saying it and eventually came over.

'You've got a bloody wig like a judge,' he said. 'Is that your real hair? Mate, really well played, let me buy you a beer.' He was a fun, jovial bloke, very well respected, so the name stuck. It didn't matter what length my hair was – after that, I was always the Judge.

I was 17 when I was first drafted into the Natal squad as 12th man. The senior players who had been involved in my development wanted me around the dressing room to learn and understand the game. They'd been my coaches and were still my heroes, so I referred to them respectfully as Mr Procter, Mr van der Bijl, Mr Richards and so on. I couldn't exactly say, 'Hey, Barry! What d'you wanna drink?'

I was so nervous when I first walked into that dressing room. I said, 'Good morning, Mr Procter.'

Silence.

'Who's your bloody Mr Procter? You make me sound old! Call me Prock or Procky.'

After that day's play, he told me to go to the dressing-room attendant and get a couple of crates of Castle lager and a load of miniature bottles of Cane, a spirit drink that we always had in South Africa. I put those down, had a shower and started to get ready to go home. He said, 'Judge! What are you doing?'

'Mom's waiting in the car park to take me home.'

'No, no, I don't think you understand.'

He took me down to the car park to see Mom, and said to her, 'Joy, don't worry about Robin, at the end of the day's play we always enjoy a beer and a chat about the game. He's been a great twelfth man today, he's looking after the boys well, so I'll keep an eye on him and give him a lift home.'

Those end-of-play beers were my entry to a fantasy world. Only a few years earlier I'd been watching these blokes from the pickets, pestering them for autographs, and now I was having a beer with them while they dissected the game. If we played Transvaal, Graeme Pollock would come into the dressing room and Clive Rice might be sitting two yards away from me. Sometimes it was an overseas player like Sylvester Clarke or Alvin Kallicharran. I'd sit there listening to these blokes chatting about cricket and think, 'This is unbelievable.'

I remember one match against Western Province in Cape Town. We were having a few drinks in our hotel bar after getting back from the ground. It was my job to collect 50 rand from everybody and make sure their glasses were full at all times. At last orders, 10.20 p.m., Procky said, 'Go and collect another twenty-five rand from everyone and order fifty Cane and Cokes.' This was between about ten players. Barry didn't drink much and neither did the late Paddy Clift, a lovely Zimbabwean who played for Leicestershire. The rest of the team used to put away a lot, but they never really seemed to be affected by the alcohol. They'd drink their Cane and Cokes, go back to their rooms, fall asleep at 11.30 p.m., wake up at 8 a.m. and be raring to go for another day's cricket. Amazing! That was the culture I was introduced to, and I learned so much from listening to them talk about this fantastic game.

The South Africa in which I grew up had a very clear definition of masculinity. Young men were taught to believe in God; to be respectful; to be strong, hard-working breadwinners. In sport, they played hard on the field and even harder off it. Women's roles were defined in equally old-fashioned terms. They nurtured the children and their husbands, and kept themselves looking feminine and attractive.

Nobody really questioned those values and gender roles because they were so entrenched. But I think that, at a young age, I understood on some level that I did not fit my country's masculine ideals. My brother noticed it too, repeatedly telling me to toughen up and that I was a 'soft cock'. He was right – I was soft and sensitive, unacceptably so in such a tough environment

But that's who I am. I'm not too embarrassed to say that books, music and films can make me very emotional. I'll sit at home watching a film like *The Notebook* and I'll feel a few tears rolling down my cheek. People might say, 'What are you doing?' but I get invested in these films. Understanding the human experience and human condition moves me profoundly. I care about people, even when they're fictional!

Mom and Flo were both proud of that side of my personality and encouraged it. Through their actions, they taught me that masculinity should be defined not by brute strength but by moral strength. It's no good being mentally and physically tough if you don't have empathy and humility. This might sound a bit odd if you only remember me facing up to the West Indies pace bowlers, but there have always been two sides to my personality. In my day-to-day life I thrive on harmony and peace. I jump out of my seat if there's a sudden loud noise (this makes me a constant target for pranks at work), and I hate confrontation, especially raised voices. When people start screaming abuse, especially if it's at me, I can't handle it.

To me, being a man – being a human being – is about fighting for what you believe is right and for those you love. That's why I always tried to stick up for people who were being bullied, like Philip Patel at school. I always identified with the outsiders because I felt like one myself. I didn't fit the mould either, but I had a facade of athletic power and sporting ability. That was my protection, and that was the masculinity I could showcase to satisfy expectations of me. I also loved the rush of adrenalin that came with more traditional masculine pursuits. There was such a contradiction between the two sides of my personality that I wasn't really sure about my identity.

It may seem like I was always destined to have a professional career in one sport or another, but it didn't feel like that at the time. I had no entitlement or expectation, and just being 12th man for Natal was a magical experience. I was happy to go with the flow, and enjoy rugby, cricket or athletics depending on the season. The vague plan was for me to become a sales rep at Dad's company, with a view to eventually taking over from him when he retired. That way I could potentially play both rugby and cricket for Natal, which was possible in those days. Provincial sport was the extent of my ambition. South Africa was isolated so I had no thoughts of international honours.

Things started to change, though I didn't know it at the time, when Kippy went over to England to spend a season with Glamorgan's 2nd XI in 1979. During that time he made a terrific hundred against Hampshire 2nds. He should have been given out caught behind early in his innings, but he didn't walk and received loads of abuse. Our lives might have been very different had he been given out. Instead, Hampshire were so impressed that they offered him a contract for the following season.

Each county was allowed to play a maximum of two overseas players – Hampshire usually had Sir Gordon Greenidge and Malcolm Marshall, but they were due to miss most of the 1980 county season because the West Indies were touring England. It meant Kippy would go straight into the first team and open the batting. The last two overseas players to do that for Hampshire had been Barry Richards and Sir Gordon. He had big boots to fill!

Kippy was a very different player to me – a watchful, patient batsman with incredible mental strength who made the absolute most of his ability. He once said he had 'zero talent'. That's total nonsense, but it's definitely true that he was limited when it came to reflexes and timing. Kippy won't mind me saying that; in fact, he'd be annoyed if I didn't. It's his badge of honour that he had such a brilliant career despite his limitations, and he enjoys playing down how much natural ability he had. He is really proud, and rightly so, of how mentally tough he was.

He had a really good debut season at Hampshire in 1980 and was their top scorer in the County Championship. The club were thrilled they had discovered such a fine player. 'If you think I'm good,' he told them, 'you should see my brother.'

He arranged for me to have a trial at the start of the following summer in 1981. It was too good an opportunity to miss – especially as, if it came off, I would be able to play cricket all year round for Hampshire and Natal. It meant I wouldn't be able to complete my studies at school. I still had a year to go but instead I finished in November 1980, just after Dad went sliding down the touchline in his safari suit. I've always been a bit insecure about my intelligence, and maybe that goes back to the fact I didn't finish high school.

I decided to get a job for a few months and then see how things went at Hampshire. Paddy Clift, the Natal bowler, arranged a really good contract for me to do some coaching with Barclays Bank at various schools around Durban. Dad had other ideas. He asked me how much I would earn and said he'd pay me the same if I practised five hours a day for five months before going to England. Talk about a dream job!

He wanted me to be properly prepared for my trial at Hampshire and gave me every opportunity to realise my dream. He even bought me Sir Gordon Greenidge's book to read thoroughly before I went to England and said it was an important part of my preparation to learn about one of the greats.

It wasn't long after that I made my first-class debut, on New Year's Day 1981. It was for Natal B against Transvaal B in the SAB Bowl, which was effectively the second tier of the Currie Cup. I was 17 years old and I got 16 and 15 in my two innings, out each time to the future England Test bowler Neal Radford. That's not the main reason I remember the match, though. There was a downpour during the game and I forgot to close the roof of my beloved Ford Escort XR3I, the car I bought with my savings from sports day all those years ago. It was absolutely soaked, and I had to clear about three inches of water out of it.

At least I could still drive it. Kippy couldn't do much with his beloved Fiat 19 open-top sports car after I persuaded him to swap cars on the way home one night. I let him lead the way and then turned off so that I could go on a little excursion. In my teenage wisdom I decided to give the car a thorough test run. I was having the time of my life, slowly cranking the speed up, when I came towards an S-bend. I took it too quickly and the car took off like something out of *The Dukes of Hazzard*. It flipped in mid-air, landed on the passenger side and kept rolling over. It went through a fire hydrant, backed into the wall of a house and landed two yards from their pool.

I was pretty lucky to survive. I was miraculously lucky to walk away without a single broken bone. The scary thing is that, under normal circumstances, my best mate John Laurie would have been in the passenger seat and he would have been killed instantly. I'd been to see him earlier that day – he was in hospital having knee surgery.

Kippy was working for the police force at the time. The officers who attended the scene knew me through him and made sure nothing more was said. But Kippy didn't have third-party insurance, and the car was a write-off, so I spent the next few years paying him back!

I didn't realise the enormity of the incident at the time. I was just a teenager who loved getting an adrenalin rush any way I could. I was starting to discover the opposite sex, and playing in South Africa domestic cricket gave me great exposure to extreme pace bowling. There were so many brilliant quicks around at the time – and unlike the bowling machine, most of them looked and spoke like they wanted to kill you.

Although there were a handful of excellent spinners like Denys Hobson and Omar Henry, they often struggled to a get look-in as the seamers ran riot on green pitches. The upshot was that, in my formative years, I hardly faced any spin. At the time, I had no idea how significant that would be. Besides, I had other things to think about. For the first time in my life, I was about to leave South Africa.

Chapter 4
South Africa to Southampton

IN MARCH 1981, AT the age of 17, I went on an aeroplane for the first time. Mom and Dad dropped me at Durban airport, where I said my goodbyes before embarking on an adventure to England and a mysterious place called Hampshire. I knew I'd miss my parents but we weren't too emotional as it didn't feel like I was cutting ties with South Africa. I was only going for a three-week trial – and even if it went well and I stayed the whole summer, I'd still be back to play for Natal during the English winter. I was slightly apprehensive as I'd never been abroad and I'd barely been outside Durban, but the fact Kippy was in England made such a difference.

All I had with me was one light suitcase. I didn't even take any cricket equipment. I'd been sponsored by Gray-Nicolls for a couple of years in South Africa, so they said they would send some new equipment to Hampshire from their factory in Robertsbridge.

It was a long plane journey and after a while the main lights were turned off. A few minutes later I switched on the overhead light to read, and all I saw was a huge plume of fag smoke right in front of my face. It was so thick that I could hardly see the book so I gave up.

When I arrived at London Heathrow I marched innocently to the immigration desk and handed over my passport, only to be told I had the wrong visa if I wanted to play cricket for Hampshire. Kippy was there to pick me up and he persuaded them I'd only be there for three weeks. The immigration officer said, 'Ah, okay, son, enjoy your holiday. Maybe one day you'll be a professional cricketer and play for Hampshire.' Then – I'll never forget this – he barked, 'Next please!' and waved me on my way. He was so condescending. What a knob. I wish I could have bumped into him when I was returning from one of my England tours!

We jumped in Kippy's car and drove down to Southampton. That journey was the first time I'd ever seen snow – and this was in the middle of March. I was naïve about everything. From the time I landed in England I had my eyes wide open and a big smile on my face as I discovered everything about life and cricket. I was never homesick, not even at the start, and it worked out perfectly because for the next four years I spent every English winter back in the comforts of our family home in South Africa. Life was one long summer – not just for me, but for Mom and Dad as well. They bought a place in Hampshire so that they could spend the English summer with me and Chris, and head back to Durban for the South African summer.

The food in England was less of a shock than I expected. I loved Indian food in Durban and had no idea I would be able to get it in England, never mind that it would be of such high quality. I also took a liking to Sunday roasts at one of the village pubs and quickly developed a taste for Ploughman's lunches with Cheddar cheese. But I did miss Florence's wonderful home-cooking. A microwave chicken korma from Sainsbury's didn't quite compare.

The first day of my Hampshire trial was also the start of pre-season training. The captain Nick Pocock welcomed everyone and said we'd start with a little run around the ground. Then a guy called Mike Bailey came up and said, 'Mate, the coach has heard a lot about you, he wants to see you have a bat. Go and get your pads on.' While everyone else was running round the ground, I went down to the dressing room and proudly put on my pristine Gray-Nicolls gear. As I walked out onto the field the players were all running past. They all stopped and stared at me. The coach, Peter Sainsbury, walked over and looked me up and down. I assumed he liked my kit.

'What the hell do you think you're doing?'

'I've been told to put my pads on, sir, to have a net.'

'Well, you can bloody well get back in the dressing room, take your pads off and come back out here and start running with the rest of us. And, by the way, you won't be seeing those pads or that bat for the next week!'

Everyone pissed themselves laughing. It had all been set up by Kippy, and I soon learned that Mike Bailey was the dressing-room joker.

I eventually got to have a bat, and I must have done okay because at the end of the three-week trial they offered me a four-year contract. My first weekly pay cheque was for £17, which in those days was enough for 14 pints and a couple of burgers!

When I signed my Hampshire contract, Dad arranged to have my Ford XR3I shipped over. He and Mom had planned to come over later in the summer to watch Kippy bat, and he liked a cigarette or 20 while he was sitting by the boundary in his deckchair. Cigarettes were much cheaper in South Africa, so he decided to fill my car with enough to keep him going for the summer. And I mean fill it: he put them everywhere except the exhaust pipe. Dad was old school, so he assumed nobody would bother checking at customs. They checked all right, and made him pay import duty on every last cigarette.

Dad has always been a loveable eccentric. Another thing he did was keep scrapbooks of my career, one for every season. I always thought he was a bit of a muppet but they have been so helpful while writing this book – not just to check facts but also to remind myself what I was thinking or what people were saying at different points of my career. It's been a lot of fun reading the articles. Well, most of them.

The Hampshire contract took me up to 1985, at which point I'd have the option of playing as a non-overseas player. Kippy and I were eligible for British citizenship because Mom and Dad were born in the UK, and he had already decided to go down that path. In those days, you had to purchase a property in the UK and spend 200 days a year in the country for four consecutive years, which we both did. It was my dream to play cricket all year round. But it meant a change of plan at home, as I wouldn't be able to take over Dad's business. Dad was really fond of John Laurie, my best friend, so he invited him to join the business, and eventually John and my cousin, Malcolm, took over from Dad. They still own the business to this day.

My naivety made me an easy target for the usual dressing-room tricks. Halfway through my first summer I travelled with a young batsman called Mark Nicholas, who would become one of my greatest mentors, and Kippy for a 2nd XI game against Glamorgan at Swansea. Mark was driving, my brother was in the front passenger seat and I was in the back. As we drove towards the Severn Bridge into Wales, Kippy turned round to me.

'Throw me your passport, Judge.'

'What passport?'

They pulled over to the side of the road and Kippy said, 'Judgie, you need a passport, we're going to Wales.' He pointed to the toll booths in the distance. 'Look up ahead, that's passport control. How the hell will we get you through there?'

Their faces were deadpan and I thought I'd messed up massively. Mark chimed in, sounding really worried. 'It's too late for us to go back. We'll have to try to smuggle you through somehow. But if we get caught we're in serious shit, we could go to prison for this. Nice one, Judgie.'

We pulled over and moved all our coffins[1] and cases into the back seat so that I could hide in the boot. I was terrified as we drove slowly through 'passport control'. As the minutes passed, and the car didn't stop, I started to realise I'd been stitched up. An hour or so later we pulled into Swansea and they opened the boot, laughing their heads off!

During those first four years I played 2nd XI cricket and covered occasionally for the overseas players – mainly Malcolm Marshall, Sir Gordon Greenidge and Kippy, who qualified as a non-overseas player in 1983. I got a lot of runs in the 2nd XI, and I remember smashing a double-hundred in a low-scoring game against Gloucestershire in my first summer. Mind you, I then got nought in the second innings, so it wasn't all plain sailing. I also played club cricket for Ickenham in 1981 and had a good season.

---

[1] Coffins are big rectangular cases in which cricketers put all their gear.

The 2nd XI played most of their home matches at Northlands Road, the main county ground. It was a lovely place, a typical old ground with loads of character and beautiful architecture, particularly the Edwardian pavilion with its burnt-orange roof. The capacity was around 3,000, but we usually had around 300–400 diehard supporters for first-team games. I liked that, as you get a better atmosphere with 300 fans at a small ground than with, say, 900 at a bigger stadium.

The difference with the 2nd XI games, apart from the even smaller crowds, is that they were usually played on a strip near the edge of the square, which meant a very short boundary on one side of the ground. There was a block of flats on one side and over the years I broke a few windows with my pull shots. One day an old lady marched over, refusing to give the ball back until she found out who'd done it. She demanded I pay her there and then. I didn't know what to do – I didn't generally bring my chequebook out to bat with me – but I apologised profusely and told her to talk to the club secretary to see whether it was insured.

It even made the broadsheets. This story from *The Times*, which I found in one of Dad's scrapbooks, is a beauty.

> A woman marched onto a cricket pitch yesterday demanding an apology from opening batsman Robin Smith, who had just hit the ball through the window of her flat overlooking the ground.
>
> Mrs Iris Clarke, aged 62, refused to give back the ball and a quarrel erupted in front of spectators at the match between Hampshire Second XI and a Southern League side on Hampshire's county ground in Southampton.
>
> Mrs Clarke said: 'They told me I was holding up their game. I said that if they could break my windows I could spoil their silly cricket. That seemed to stump them for a moment. They were all so smug about it. I didn't think it was funny at all.'
>
> A Hampshire Cricket Club spokesman said: 'We will not pay for damage of this kind as the flats have an insurance policy.'
>
> Mrs Clarke vowed: 'They are not getting their ball back.'

That wasn't the only time I got in trouble for big hitting. I lost a fair few balls during practice, which irritated the coach Peter Sainsbury. The guys used to encourage me to run down the wicket and smack the ball towards the housing estate because they knew how the coach would react.

'Sod this, I've had enough! We've lost enough balls, we can't afford to lose any more. We've lost thirty quid's worth today! Pack up, end of practice.'

And he'd storm off. The guys cheered, 'Great performance, Judge!'

Peter was harsh and tough but very fair. In fact, everyone at Hampshire was so welcoming and affectionate, from the secretary Jimmy James to the captain Nick Pocock. There were plenty of senior pros in the dressing room like David Turner and Trevor Jesty, who also made me feel really comfortable. It helped that Kippy was there and such a popular bloke, and the more I played in the 2nd XI the more confidence I gained.

At first it was a bit strange to be sharing a lunch room with Sir Gordon Greenidge and Malcolm Marshall, because of the racial segregation I was used to in South Africa. I was so unworldly that, when they talked really fast to each other in their Bajan accent, I thought they were speaking a different language. I even asked Kippy what they were speaking. 'English, you bloody idiot!' I got on with them straight away and they became two of my best friends, along with other Hampshire players like Mark Nicholas and Paul Terry.

Sometimes people forget what an amazing batsman Sir Gordon was. I'm not sure he realised how good he was, either. He was like a butcher, and watching him bludgeon the ball definitely had an influence on me – it was terribly exciting being at the other end when he played those savage pulls and cut shots.

When I was batting with Sir Gordon in my early years, I was convinced he received more bad balls than I did. I was intrigued when, later in my career, if I went back to Hampshire after playing with England, the younger blokes said the same to me. You can imagine the team talks. 'Don't bowl short and wide to Smith, don't bowl short and wide and by the way don't ball short and wide.' You're focusing on the negative when you should be accentuating the positive: 'Pitch it up, we'll bring one more on the leg side. Smith can play across his pad and get out LBW, so that's the area to bowl.' It's the same message delivered in a more psychologically effective way.

Sir Gordon was a fascinating character. He wasn't always the most popular – he could be very dry, very serious – but he's a lovely bloke and he was always fantastic with me. He was very professional, incredibly neat, with his numbered gloves and his kit always immaculately folded and positioned. As I said, he could be very serious and sometimes he made us laugh without realising. One year, Rod Bransgrove, who later became Hampshire chairman, chartered a magnificent 120-foot yacht in the Caribbean and invited my family to join his family for a two-week cruise. Sir Gordon, Malcolm and Desmond Haynes were invited on board for dinner one evening. We were having a great time, being very well watered with some magnificent Chablis, and Rod – who never played county cricket, never mind at Test level – said, 'Around this table we've scored about 14,000 Test runs and taken nearly 400 Test wickets.' We all started laughing, and then about ten seconds later Sir Gordon said, 'But Rod, you haven't played Test cricket?' We all groaned. 'Oh, *Gordon!*'

At Hampshire, we felt Sir Gordon lived in the shadow of Sir Viv Richards. One story summed this up for me. In 1985 we were playing Warwickshire, and a week earlier Viv had smashed a triple-century against them for Somerset. Sir Gordon was approaching 200 and taking Norman Gifford, the wily left-arm spinner, to the cleaners. Giff was just about the most effective sledger in county cricket. After each over, he would come down the wicket to talk to the wicket-keeper Geoff Humpage. I was at the other end and everything they said was designed to be just in earshot.

'Bloody hell, good shots these,' said Humpage. 'I reckon he's hitting it further than Viv was last week.'

'Come on, mate. He's hitting it beautifully but Viv was smacking it further.'

Suddenly, Gordon's head snapped round. 'Did you hear that, Judge?'

'Hear what?' I said.

'What they said about Viv?'

I'd heard but pretended I hadn't. In Norman's next over, Sir Gordon launched another huge straight six. Humpage walked past him and said, 'He's getting close, Giff ...' You can guess what happened next. Sir Gordon came down the pitch again, tried to hit the ball out of Birmingham and was caught at long-on. It was sledging at its best.

I don't know why Sir Gordon felt like that about Viv because he was a sensational player. I've never seen anyone hit the ball harder. Never. He was so destructive – and he opened the batting, so he was doing it against the new ball. There are a lot of attacking openers these days but Sir Gordon was a trailblazer.

The only thing he lacked was Viv's aura. Viv was, and will always be, my hero. I loved the confidence and the arrogance that oozed from the man. The two people I have met with the greatest presence are Mother Teresa and Nelson Mandela, but when it comes to cricket, Viv was out on his own. He has such an aura that you don't need to see him to know when he's entered a room.

I tried to emulate his presence by getting in character when I walked onto the stage. When I crossed the boundary rope I was no longer Robin Smith, I was the Judge. I never had an aura like Viv – nobody did – but I know that when I was batting in a dominant fashion, bowlers could be intimidated. I could tell by their body language.

It was all an act, really. I may have looked and performed as though I was bulletproof, but I was hiding a heart and mind of glass. For all the fun, laughs and clowning around off the pitch and the toughness and strength I exhibited at the crease, I was as caring and fragile as they come.

The persona of the Judge was reinforced by the media and perpetuated by the supporters. It became something I felt I had to live up to at all times – not just when I was in the middle. Privately, I felt like I was caught between two types of masculinity. The Judge was a tough, arrogant competitor who thrived on conflict; Robin Smith was a gentle, emotional character who dreaded it.

Overseas players like Sir Gordon, Malcolm and Viv had such an influence on my career, both as teammates and opponents. The value of playing with and against the best in the world is enormous – you absorb so much from being around them on and off the field, often without even realising it, and it also makes it so much easier if you then play against them in Test cricket. If you've spent time with them they become less intimidating, and you're less likely to put them on a pedestal. It wasn't a deliberate tactic but I noticed the effect as time went on. I always felt there should be at least two if not three overseas players in our county teams. That still allowed eight England-qualified players per team. If you were the ninth, tenth and 11th best in your county, you probably weren't going to play for England anyway, although you might have had a chance in 1989!

I always used to go to the ground early to practise on the bowling machine with Dad, and one morning I saw the great West Indies captain Clive Lloyd running around the ground on his own. None of the other Lancashire players had arrived at the ground. At that stage he was pushing 40. I walked up to him and said, 'Good morning, Mr Lloyd. I see you've been training hard this morning.'

'At my age,' he said, 'you need to do that.'

It really rammed home Dad's message that you have to work bloody hard whatever you do. Those lone runs around the ground were one of the many reasons Clive Lloyd scored so many runs in the middle. So much of greatness is down to simple hard work.

I certainly believed in working hard. And now that I was away from South Africa, it was time to play hard as well.

Chapter 5
Off the leash

ENGLAND WASN'T JUST A different country, it was a different world. I arrived as a 17-year-old who'd had a very regimented upbringing, a sheltered and almost entirely sport-focused life, and suddenly there were no restrictions on anything. Dad wasn't getting me up at 5 a.m. for practice; I could make my own decisions about everything. Any teenager would have enjoyed that freedom, and I certainly did. Over the next few months, I discovered my inner scallywag!

I lived with Kippy, who had bought a nice house in a quiet area just outside Southampton called Fair Oak. We were all single and there were usually three or four Hampshire players staying there. Paul Terry, Jon Hardy and Richard Scott were all tenants at different times.

Paul became one of my best mates in the Hampshire team. I shared with him when we played away from home – he'll tell you my snoring kept him up but there's no proof as far as I'm concerned – and I'm the godfather to his daughter Siobhan.[1] I was also his best man when he married Bernadette. Paul was an extremely good opening batsman who played a couple of Tests for England against

---

[1] The circle of life goes on – Siobhan has just had her first child, Edward. They also live in Perth, so maybe he's a future Australian Test player!

West Indies in 1984. It was really sad – in his second Test he had his arm broken by Winston Davis and, though he batted in a sling to help Allan Lamb reach a century, that was the last time he played Test cricket. We didn't really wear armguards or chestguards in my day, but I'm surprised more players don't do so these days. Why wouldn't you? There's no need to be macho. Who knows how different Paul's career might have been had he worn one.

We didn't think we'd be having too many dinner parties at Kippy's house, so we built a brick bar in the dining room and bought some barrels of draft beer. We often had teammates round to sit and chat about cricket all evening. As you'd expect of a load of carefree blokes in their late-teens and twenties, we had a very active social life. We might go to one of the country pubs to meet Malcolm Marshall and Mark Nicholas, and sometimes we went to watch Paul play squash. He was brilliant, as good as anyone in Hampshire, so he was playing at a serious standard. We also got to know a number of the South-ampton football players, including Peter Shilton, who we always saw in the nightclubs, and Kevin Keegan.

I've always adored the social side of cricket. I built friendships that will last for ever, and many of the happiest memories of my life involve sitting round a table with teammates and opponents, roaring with laughter or discussing the game. I often didn't say much, I just loved listening to all these great players and characters. Even now, I'd rather be sitting around a table chatting about anything and nothing than sitting in front of the TV.

Mind you, sometimes I got mixed messages. There was a game at Northlands Road against Essex at the start of the 1984 season, when Graham Gooch was in great form. He was 100-odd not out at lunch, so I thought I'd sit next to him and try to find out what the secret was. It turned out it was about 1500 calories! He had a huge lunch, and I sat there thinking, 'How can you have a meal like that and still smack us everywhere?' After lunch he marmalised our bowlers and went on to get 220.

In England, I realised I had a constitution that allowed me to burn the candle at both ends. There wasn't a moment of revelation – it just steadily became normal for me to be the last out of the bar and the first into the nets the following morning. I socialised a lot throughout my career, but it never compromised my work ethic. If anything, it increased it – that extra work was my way of earning my reward at the close of play, or paying my penance for any excesses the previous night. Every day at Hampshire, without fail, Kippy and I would stay on after training and do an hour each on the bowling machine. And when I was on tour with England, I ran from the ground back to the hotel every day, usually around six kilometres, sometimes with weights in each hand. The bus would pass me and the team would all shout, 'Wa-hey, Judgie!' as they went past. By doing that, I felt I'd earned my beers when I got back to the hotel.

I'd had a taste of alcohol before I left South Africa, but only really in the Natal dressing room. In England I discovered pubs, bars and clubs. At Hampshire, our two favourite haunts were Simon's Wine Bar and the Concorde nightclub. They were typical 1980s places, with wooden beams and brick bars, the sort of place where Del Boy might fall through the bar. They seemed so sophisticated compared to what I had experienced. The atmosphere was warm and relaxed, and we started to get to know all the people who worked there.

I looked a lot older than I was, so I was able to get into the Concorde Club at 17, even though it was over-21s only. Then, in my second year at Hampshire, I played for the local club Trojans and scored a few runs. There was a feature in the local paper, including a picture with the caption '18-year-old prodigy Robin Smith'. The manager of the club, a wonderful lady called Jan White who we are still in touch with, read it and told Kippy and me that I couldn't go in any more. It was a bit of a problem – especially as I used to tell the women in Simon's Wine Bar that I was 22, so if one of them suggested we move on to the Concorde Club I had to make some lame excuse why I couldn't go!

It was at Simon's Wine Bar that I developed my liking for lager. It was an instant cure for my shyness and social anxiety, and it went hand in hand with my other great discovery – the opposite sex. I know it's a cliché, but honestly, I went from a boy to a man in the space of a few weeks. Having lived at home all my life, suddenly I was playing in a team of professional cricketers and living a bachelor lifestyle.

There's no point denying that I've always had a pretty high sex drive. It wasn't a big part of my life until I got to England as South Africa was such a puritanical place. There was no sex education in school, pornography was banned – as I knew to my cost – and any sexual references on TV or in films were usually censored. On top of that, Mom was reasonably religious, so I wasn't even allowed to *think* about having a girlfriend until I was 16. Dad felt having a girlfriend would be a distraction from sport, and told me there would be 'plenty of time for the opposite sex'. How right he was!

I had my first girlfriend in the year before I left South Africa, a really sweet girl called Morag, although my parents had no idea about our level of intimacy so we had to duck and dive. But like most 17-year-old boys I didn't really have a clue about women. When I got to England I found them as intriguing as I did intimidating. They all seemed so confident, knowledgeable and uninhibited. Alcohol took the edge off my nerves, loosened my tongue and gave me a hit of confidence that allowed me to talk to women. I also, like most young blokes, enjoyed the competitive element of trying to pull.

The fact we were Hampshire cricketers gave us a minor celebrity, and I was taken aback at how I often didn't have to move a muscle before temptation would strike. It probably helped that I looked closer to 27 than 17. I vividly recall one night when we went for a few beers at Simon's Wine Bar and I was transfixed by a tall woman with streaked blonde hair, who looked like she had come straight from a shampoo advert.

I decided to park myself next to her at the bar, though I had no idea what I was actually going to say to her. And then *she* spoke to *me*.

'Would you like a beer?'

'P–p–p–p–pardon?'

She smiled, said nothing and ordered our drinks. The mutual attraction was obvious, and as the night went on it was clear we would be going somewhere. We couldn't go back to hers, as she lived with her parents, and my place wasn't an option because Kippy had been known to 'cut my turf' and play the sophisticated older brother when I brought somebody home.

I had a mischievous realisation that we were only five minutes from Northlands Road, and I knew where the key for the first-team dressing room was kept. We walked to the ground and I led her towards the pavilion. I walked into the dressing room, turned on the heater – ever the perfect gentleman – and we made use of the physio's table, the same place where Sir Gordon Greenidge was stretched out every morning getting his massage. The fact I was trespassing, and would be in serious trouble if anyone knew, made it even more exciting. Welcome to England, Judge!

A few days later, Sir Gordon called me over for a chat while he was on the same table getting a massage. It's fair to say that, at that particular moment in time, I didn't make much eye contact with him.

It's not that I want to brag, quite the opposite in some cases. But sex has been a huge part of my life and it's impossible to tell my story without some promiscuous detours. I was acting on instinct at the time, but I've thought about my motivations a lot in the last few years, especially while writing this book. I used to think I was living up to expectations of masculinity, not just with women but also fast cars, socialising and much else besides. But I suspect now that, though I didn't consciously recognise it at the time, I understood on some level that I had an adrenalin addiction that needed satisfying. I loved risk, too, which also gets the adrenalin flowing. Make the car go a bit faster, crank the bowling machine up a bit higher, have illicit sex. That side of my character co-existed with the more emotional, sensitive side. It's a delicate balance, and possibly a fairly unusual one, I don't know.

At the end of that first season at Hampshire, Kippy and I went on holiday before returning to South Africa. We planned to hop around the Greek islands and went to Athens for the first night, and then next morning caught a ferry to Hydra, a beautiful volcanic island.

Not long after we landed we found ourselves in a nightclub, where we were chatted up by a couple of girls. It seemed the evening was going brilliantly – until we saw the bill. Without our knowledge, they had been ordering Bollinger on our tab. It was our budget for the whole bloody holiday. Being two naïve idiots from South Africa, we hadn't realised we'd walked into an escorts club.

We sat for a few minutes trying to work out what to do. I told Kippy to go back to the hotel, and if the bouncers stopped him he should say he needed to make an urgent call to England and that I was going to settle up when I'd finished my drink. When Kippy left, I picked up my drink and floated around as if I was waiting for him to return. I walked casually towards the door – and then I bloody bolted! It wasn't long since I'd broken all those sprinting records at school, and Kippy wouldn't know how to fight anyway. I saw the bouncers running after me but they were never going to catch me. I got back to the hotel in one piece, much to Kippy's relief. After all that worry, we'd kept our budget intact and enjoyed a free night out.

We always went back to South Africa during the English winters and were often joined by some of the Hampshire boys, including Mark Nicholas and Paul Terry. They regularly visited our place and enjoyed the hospitality of Mom, Dad and especially Florence, who took great pride in preparing delicious meals for everyone. The boys had a cricket pitch, swimming pool and jacuzzi they could use anytime they fancied. Dad kept the fridge packed with ice-cold beers and told them to help themselves.

Florence was upset when I returned home from my first summer in England. Before I left I was a typical teenager, leaving my clothes strewn everywhere and my room in a mess, but now I was much tidier and there was less for Florence to do. She went to Mom in tears asking whether she was still good enough to look after me. Bless her, she was such a wonderful woman and had a beautiful, sensitive personality.

In the early 1990s, after apartheid had ended, Malcolm Marshall came to play for Natal and often went round to our house. Florence loved him and spoilt him rotten – until, one day, Dad put on a video of Macko bowling to me in a Test match. She wasn't much of a cricket fan, so she didn't know about the competitive edge that we all loved. And when she saw Macko zipping a couple of bouncers past my head, her maternal instincts boiled over. She was furious and vowed never to talk to Macko again or make him his tuna salad because 'he tried to hurt my Nunu'. It took Mom and Dad a fair while to convince her that it was all part of the game, and that Macko wasn't trying to kill me. She still gave him a stern talking-to the next time she saw him. 'You must never, ever bowl like that to my Nunu again!'

There were other people in South Africa who really did want to hurt me. I'd turned 18 in September 1981, which meant I could go out in Durban with my mates from school. One night I was in Coco de Mer, our favourite nightclub, with John Laurie and my other Northlands School buddies. We were having a real party, a *jol* as we called it, with those magic lights spinning around the club and disco music blaring out.

We used to make fun of what we called the 'okes from Johannesburg', a stream of good-looking, muscular blokes who'd come down to Durban wrapped in expensive suits and with wallets full of rand. These okes would drive down and snatch up all our gorgeous ladies, leaving us standing alone at the bar. On this particular night I was feeling sharp and mischievous, so I sidled up to one of the blokes before squeezing between him and a girl he was talking to at the bar.

'Hi,' I said to her. 'Do you fancy a dance?'

The bloke tapped me on the shoulder. 'What did you say?'

'I asked the lady for a dance. You don't own the women in Durban, you know.'

I hadn't quite anticipated his response.

'Check the ring. That's my fucking fiancée, *domkop*.'

Domkop, as you can probably guess, is not a term of endearment. I knew what was coming but decided to stand my ground. I told him his peacock behaviour was a sorry representation of *real men*.

He barked, '*Jou Bliksem*' – 'you bastard' – and motioned for me to step outside. I walked after him, knowing exactly what was coming. He gave me a solid right-hander, ripped a heavy gold chain off my neck and walked back inside. I didn't hit him back – I've never been a fighter, and it was only one punch anyway. More to the point, I deserved it for being a prick, so I had no problem with it at all. In those days, you didn't really get beaten up, it was just a single punch and that was that. It was almost like when I used to get caned – you do something wrong, you get punished.

In the morning, my dad saw my black eye and asked me what happened.

'I tried to chat up this bloke's girlfriend in the club.'

'Is that so? That's okay, my boy. At least it wasn't because you'd been hit by a bouncer.'

On reflection, any courage I showed during my cricket career was demonstrated in this early behaviour, because I knew full well what I was in for and it didn't stop me accepting a well-deserved smack in the face.

I still had a fair bit of growing up to do both on and off the field. For a sensitive teenager, South African domestic cricket was an intimidating and tough school. I made my debut for the Natal first XI in a one-day semi-final against Transvaal at the start of 1982. It was a huge step up, both in the standard of cricket and the intensity, from playing for Hampshire 2nd XI. Their attack was known as the 'Mean Machine', and on that day the legendary all-rounder Clive Rice was bowling like the wind. The first ball I faced from him was a bouncer. I swayed back, felt the breeze as it whistled past my face and saw the keeper Ray Jennings take it miles above his head. As he did so, my helmet – which had side-pieces but no chinstrap – flew over short leg and I had to go and collect it a few yards away.

Clive came down the wicket and looked at me as I was bending down to pick up my helmet. Jennings, a nasty piece of work on the field who sledged like you wouldn't believe, said, 'Mate, the next one will hit you right between the fucking eyes and you'll be straight off to Addington Hospital.'

Bloody hell! I was born there but I didn't particularly want to go back there.

Jimmy Cook was at third slip, and he walked past me and said, 'Robin, don't worry about that, that's the quickest bouncer I've seen him bowl in years.' That was a really nice touch as he could tell I was a bit shocked. There were no speedguns during my career but I reckon that was the quickest ball I ever faced. I don't think I ever received a 100mph ball but on that day, where I was in my career, that ball from Clive felt like the fastest.

The Currie Cup matches were played on lively pitches, where a par score was often around 200–250, and nobody took a backward step. I didn't set the world alight in my early years but it was such a good grounding because it made me fight for every run, which helped me cash in on flatter pitches as my career developed.

I made my Currie Cup debut, also against Transvaal, a week after my introduction to Clive Rice. I only got 6 and 10, but in the next game, at home to Eastern Province, I made a very good 91 in a match where nobody else on either side reached 50. I felt great as I headed off for my first away game, against Western Province in Cape Town. This was my big chance to play against legends like Peter Kirsten, Allan Lamb, Denys Hobson, Garth Le Roux and Stephen Jefferies.

I walked out to bat at No. 5 on the first day full of nerves. I wasn't scared of failure so much as not impressing some of my biggest heroes. The left-arm spinner Omar Henry was bowling and Lamby was at bat-pad on the off side. I had broken Barry Richards' South African school record, so they all knew a bit about me. As soon as I took my guard, Lamby started yapping.

'Aaaah, hello! We've got the new fucking Barry Richards here! We'll see how good he is now!'

I suffered much worse sledging later in my career but nothing ever unsettled me like that. When you're 17 and your hero lays into you with such aggression and contempt, it affects you. I could barely concentrate and I prodded around for a few balls before being caught at bat-pad.

Smith c Lamb b Henry 2

Lamby's farewell was even more cutting than his greeting. 'Piss off, you little prick! Go and have a fucking shower and have a think, you're playing the big boys' game now, eh?'

When I got back to the dressing room I sat down next to Mike Procter, took my pads off and felt a few tears rolling down my cheek. He looked at me and said, 'What's up, Judge?' I said nothing.

'Don't worry about getting out. You're young and you'll learn from the experience. Don't worry about it.'

I still said nothing and then he twigged.

'They've been sledging you, haven't they?'

More silence.

'They have, haven't they? I'll bloody sort this out! Don't you worry, we'll settle this later.'

Nothing more was said. At the close of play, he picked up a six-pack of Castle lager and said, 'Judgie, come with me', and marched towards their dressing room. Le Roux, Lamby and Peter Kirsten were sitting together. He went up and said, 'Garth, move up; Lamby, move over; Judge, sit down there in the middle.' They were all in awe of Procky so none of them said a word. He opened a beer and gave it to me.

'Right, Lamby, what the fuck have you been saying to my young champion?'

Lamby replied in that clipped South African accent of his.

'Eh, Procky, man, what's up? What did I say, eh?'

'He hasn't told me what went on, but you must have been sledging him.'

'Procky, hey, look I might have sledged the young oke but he's got to learn the form. It's a tough school here. You can't let the young oke go out there and think he's playing schoolboy cricket. You know it's a tough game, Prock. He might be a nice young oke, I don't know, but when he comes here and plays with the big boys he'll get sledged.'

Lamby turned to me. 'Look, let's shake on it. I just wanted to try and unsettle you.' From that moment on I realised that it wasn't personal. It was just part of the game, an attempt to unsettle or intimidate the batsman so that he made a mistake. I'm glad I was exposed to it very early on by my hero and I'm grateful to Procky for nipping it in the bud.

I still don't really understand why players get so emotionally triggered and aggravated by things that are said on the field. Then again, I get emotionally triggered watching a film like *The Notebook*! I wasn't sledged much during my career, but when I was, I really didn't care. I lost concentration and played bad shots – too many, at times – but I was never suckered or sledged out. I learned in a very good school.

In 1982, it was back to Hampshire 2nd XI. I also played club cricket for Trojans, where I broke the Southampton League record for most runs in a season (and ruined my chances of getting into the Concorde Club for the next few years). At that stage I didn't think I was good enough to play first-class cricket day in, day out, so it was great to play in the leagues and learn about batting on the different surfaces you get in England. That was very important, because the slow, seaming wickets were totally different to the quick, bouncy pitches in South Africa. I learned to use the crease a lot more, and if there was any sideways movement I would try to play more off the front foot, but without moving too early and lunging at the ball. I don't like the word 'lunging', as there's a massive difference between that and *trying* to get forward.

If I was going to make a mistake I would rather be caught forward than back. If you misread the length it's easier to manoeuvre or avoid a short ball on the front foot than it is to play a full ball off the back foot. There were other advantages – you give the ball less time to swing or seam, and if you get a good stride forward you might be outside the line if you're hit on the pad. The one thing I never wanted to do, wherever I was playing, was to be caught on the crease. That was the cardinal sin.[2]

That said, you have to adapt to all conditions. When I faced Patrick Patterson on a flyer at Old Trafford in 1986, or when I batted on the WACA trampoline in Perth, I certainly wasn't pushing forward every ball.

I'd already been exposed to first-class cricket in South Africa, so I was always going to do well in league and 2nd XI cricket. I suppose I was in limbo for a bit, and I know Mark Nicholas and Kippy think that may have stunted my development. I understand their point, though I'm not sure it was that big a factor. I was still only 21 when I qualified to play as a non-overseas player for Hampshire, so it's not like when Graeme Hick had to wait seven years to qualify for England. And even in that time, I was able to play very intense first-class cricket for Natal during the English winter.

The thing I remember most about the 1982 season is probably a trip to France with Jon Hardy. We went off in my little Ford Escort XR3I for a week during the season. We told our coach Peter Sainsbury

---

[2] Getting caught on the crease is cricket's equivalent of being in no-man's-land. You're a sitting duck because you're being tentative, not committing yourself, and you have no momentum going into your shot.

that Jon's club, Lymington, were going on a tour of the Isle of Wight, and because there was no 2nd XI cricket he was happy for us to go. We got the ferry from Portsmouth to Le Havre and then drove along the coast for miles and miles. Eventually we were close to the Italian border when I thought I should give Kippy a ring and tell him we'd arrived safely.

'Hi, Kippy, how's it going?'

'Mate, where the hell are you?'

'We're near the Italian border, about fifteen kilometres away. What's up?'

'For fuck's sake, Judgie! There's been a flu epidemic, the coach has been trying to get hold of you all day. He got them to put a message out on the ferry to the Isle of Wight and everything. He needs you and Jon to make your debuts for the 1st XI tomorrow.'

I thought about Peter Sainsbury's temper, and how it exploded on my first day when all I did was put my cricket whites on. What would he do if he knew we'd buggered off to France on the sly when Hampshire were short of players?

'Judgie,' said Kippy.

'Yes, Kippy?'

'I'm only joking, mate, enjoy your trip!'

A couple of nights later, when it was quite late and extremely hot, Jon and I drove up to a deserted pebble beach, made ourselves a barbecue and had a crate of those small bottles of Kronenbourg. We fell asleep in the car with the sun roof and windows open. Jon grew up in Kenya so he had a sarong on. I grew up in South Africa so I wasn't as fussy. When we woke up the next morning the car was surrounded by sunbathers – it turned out it was the most popular beach in the south of France, and I was there fast asleep with the sun roof and windows open, wearing nothing. We had to sheepishly drive across the pebbles, past the sunbathers and back to the road. I had so much fun on that trip. Mind you, we had a bit of explaining to do to our coach when we came back with great tans. Our stories about the Isle of Wight heatwave weren't the most convincing.

I made my County Championship debut in 1983, at the age of 19, when Malcolm and Sir Gordon were taking part in the World Cup in

England. It went well and I got three hundreds in as many weeks. The first came against Lancashire at Bournemouth, yet I almost missed the game. On the first morning, I woke up slightly late and had to race down to the ground. By then I'd graduated from a Ford Escort to a Porsche 924 Turbo which, typical me, could do up to 180mph, so I was whizzing down to Bournemouth when I was pulled over for speeding. Things weren't quite so strict in those days and luckily for me the policeman knew his cricket and had read that I was making my debut. He said, 'Mate, I should give you a fine, but I'll let you off. I hope you'll be as lucky when you bat as you are right now.'

I was. That was the day I scored my maiden first-class century. Kippy had already got a hundred, and I was on 94 at the start of the last over of the day. I'd played nicely but I knew Nick Pocock would ideally want to declare overnight. Jack Simmons, an experienced, accurate offspinner, was bowling, and there was a really short leg-side boundary so he packed the off side and speared everything outside the off stump. I was getting more and more frustrated until there was only one ball left of the day's play. He sent down a juicy full toss on leg stump that I belted over the short boundary for six. As I sheepishly raised my bat, it dawned on me what had happened. Jack fancied putting his feet up in the morning, but he knew Nick wouldn't declare if a young bloke was six short of his maiden hundred, so he gave me a freebie. I shook his hand and said, 'Thanks, Jack.' He said, 'Mate, I thought you played really well and deserved your hundred – and I really didn't want to come out again tomorrow morning!'

Even though I scored those three hundreds, I had to wait another 14 months to play again in the County Championship. I was straight out of the team when Malcolm and Gordon returned, and I was fine with that. They were two of the greats and had to play, but I was thrilled I'd made the most of my chance. It enhanced my reputation and made people a bit more aware of me – especially when Gordon was quoted as saying I was the 'best young white batsman in the world'. I couldn't believe it really as I was 19 and had played barely a handful of first-team games. It was only a couple of years since

Dad bought me Sir Gordon's autobiography to read before I went to Hampshire and now he was saying *this* about me. I was so proud but also a bit confused by that sort of praise. Who's this bloke he's talking about?

Later in the 1983 season, the Smith family had even bigger reason to celebrate – Kippy was called up by England to make his debut in the Lord's Test against New Zealand. I was still staying at his house and had a late one the night before his debut. Paul Terry came in at about 10.55 a.m. to wake me up because England had won the toss and were batting, which meant Kippy would be opening with Chris Tavaré. I rubbed my eyes and flicked the TV on just in time to see Kippy get a golden duck, LBW to Sir Richard Hadlee. I rolled over and went back to sleep, and when I woke up a couple of hours later I was sure it had been a dream. I asked Paul and he confirmed that, no, it really did happen.

It was clear after the second day's play that England would be batting again on the Saturday, so I decided to get up to Lord's to support my brother. By the time I got there play had already started, but on the way to the ground I saw someone with a radio so I asked them if England had lost any wickets. 'No,' came the answer, much to my relief. I walked through the Grace Gates, heard a big roar and thought, 'Oh, shit, he's out.' The roar was for Kippy – but thankfully it was because he'd finally got himself off a pair, having taken nearly half an hour to get off the mark in the second innings!

He ended up batting a long time to make a very important 43, which helped England win a low-scoring game. Typical Kippy, over-coming adversity through sheer mental strength. I was so proud of him. His success also switched a lightbulb on in my head. If my brother could play for England and get runs at Test level, maybe I could too.

Chapter 6
Mind games

IF YOU HAVE AN older brother, you spend most of your childhood looking up to him, so it's a strange feeling when you realise you're better than him at something. Kippy and I used to shoot thousands of balls at each other on the bowling machine, whether in Hampshire or South Africa. He would feed it to me on a decent pace, around 85–90mph and I'd always be fine with that. When it was my turn to feed him, I always had to put the pace down by 5–8mph so that he could feel equally comfortable. There's nothing wrong with that, except he was playing for England and I was in Hampshire's 2nd XI.

Those sessions on the bowling machine in 1983 were the first time I seriously started to think about playing international cricket. If Kippy could do it, then maybe I could as well. The fact another South African, Allan Lamb, had also qualified to play for England a year before Kippy made the idea even more appealing.

There was some talk in the press, after those three hundreds in 1983, about the fact I would be eligible to play for England from 1985. I loved living in England but at that stage I still regarded myself as South African. All I wanted to do was play as much cricket as possible, all year round. But a seed had certainly been planted.

Kippy's success also pricked my interest in the power of the mind. While I didn't agree with Kippy when he said he had 'zero talent', everyone would agree that I was much better when it came to things like reactions and hand–eye coordination. In fact, he probably had less conventional talent than almost all of the batsmen who played for Hampshire in the 1980s and 1990s. Lamby used to call him 'lead boots', and Vic Marks wrote in Kippy's benefit brochure that he was an inspiration to donkeys and cart horses!

If Kippy had those limitations in his reflexes but was still scoring so many runs, he had to have something the rest of us didn't have. It really got me thinking about, well, thinking. Psychology is a subject that has fascinated me ever since, and in 1993 I released a book called *Quest For Number One*, which was all about the mental side of playing sport at the highest level.

People often say 90 per cent of cricket is played in the mind. If that's the case, Kippy was world-class. He played eight Tests and four ODIs for England between 1983 and 1986, although it's no coincidence that the first time he was dropped was before the West Indies toured in 1984. He'd had a good winter, batting for a long time against New Zealand and Pakistan, but he had a weakness against extreme pace.

He was usually okay against the West Indian fast bowlers in county cricket, because each team only had one of them – and he was the best in the world at playing them from the non-striker's end! I remember once discreetly farming the strike so that he wouldn't have to face Tony Merrick on a green pitch at Edgbaston; we used to do that for each other if one of us was having trouble with a certain bowler.

I sometimes joke about Kippy's ability against pace bowling but trust me, he could play. I'll always remember a double hundred against Allan Donald on an Edgbaston greentop in 1987. He played like God in that innings.

He always said that facing four pace bowlers at the same time in Test cricket would have been too much for him, though. He didn't play a hook shot until his last season of country cricket – we were all so surprised that we ran out onto the balcony to applaud, and Kippy raised his arms as if he had scored a triple hundred. Jonathan Trott called Mitchell Johnson his 'executioner' in the 2013–14 Ashes, so goodness knows how you'd describe four fast bowlers with no limit on bouncers.

Kippy did okay at Test level, averaging 30, but his Hampshire record was outstanding. I'm going to pump Kippy's tyres up a bit here because a lot of people don't remember what a brilliant player he was. He averaged 46 in county cricket and 43 in one-day matches, which is a better record for Hampshire than Sir Gordon Greenidge, one of the finest openers of all time. They opened the innings together so they were always batting in the same conditions and against the same bowlers, and Sir Gordon averaged 45 in county cricket and 38 in one-day matches. Fascinating. I don't like comparing batsmen across different eras, because cricket changes so much – don't tell me, for example, that people averaging 50 today are as good as or better than Sir Viv Richards – but Kippy's record stacks up incredibly well against his contemporaries. From 1975–95, only two regular English openers had a better average than Kippy in county cricket: Geoff Boycott and Graham Gooch. He also shares the record for the most Man of the Match awards in the Gillette Cup/NatWest Trophy with Graham Gooch and Clive Lloyd. They all received the awards nine times – but Goochie and Clive played about 40 per cent more innings.

We're both really proud of each other's achievements, and chuffed that the little old Smiths achieved so much in the game. Between us we scored over 50,000 runs for Hampshire, and there aren't too many brothers who've done that for one club. I asked Richard Isaacs, whose dad Vic was the Hampshire scorer in my day, and he could only find one: the Tyldesleys, Ernest and Johnny, who played for Lancashire in the early 1900s. And don't think Kippy lived off my success. He scored about 40 per cent of our combined total – and he would have scored many thousands more had he not retired at the age of 32. I reckon Kippy's mental strength added at least 15 runs to his average. Sports psychology is a big thing now, but in the 1980s it was almost taboo, certainly in cricket, so Kippy was decades ahead of his time. He has always preached the importance of finding a way to control your brain. He says that positive thoughts, if dealt with correctly, can become an incredibly strong force – but the same is true of negative ones. Kippy found he could artificially stimulate confidence and has been doing so in all walks of life ever since.

There are many other examples in cricket. Look at Sir Alastair Cook's record, particularly in the subcontinent, or the Waugh brothers. Steve was nowhere near as talented as Mark in terms of timing and reflexes, yet he averaged 10 runs more in Test cricket. It's a really important message, I think, that with the right mental approach and work ethic you can achieve far more than those with more natural talent.

Kippy wasn't always so mentally tough. In 1979, he batted against Mike Procter in a club game in Durban and struggled. Afterwards, one of Procky's teammates, Mike Matthews, who was a successful businessman and a good club player, told Kippy he'd been playing the bowler rather than the ball. They got chatting about the power of the mind and he gave Kippy some books to read. One was *Believe and Achieve* by W. Clement Stone and the other was *The Power of Positive Thinking* by Dr Norman Vincent Peale, a book that has been his bible ever since.[1]

To this day, Kippy still reads it to top up his well of internal strength and belief. His view is that you can't just read these books when you are struggling; you need to be constantly studying and training your brain so that you become mentally resilient and strong. He will tell you that it takes years, even decades, to develop total control of the mind, but that unwavering, deep-rooted confidence can come from continually studying the subject. You need absolute, undiluted focus and dedication to achieving your goals. I suppose he has a different take on the 10,000-hour rule. If, say, 60 per cent of the game is in the mind, then we should spend at least 6,000 hours working on that.

Kippy's cricket career surpassed all expectations and was only the start of his overachievement. In 1984, he set up a company to market and sell Hampshire CCC's corporate hospitality and sponsorships and made a big success of that while he was also scoring thousands of runs for the 1st XI.

Throughout his life, not just in cricket, he has been proof that anyone can be successful. Kippy had no qualifications for any of

---

[1] *The Power of Positive Thinking* has sold around 5 million copies and is still in print almost 80 years after it was written.

his jobs, and limited ability, yet he succeeded in all of them. He has persistence, strength of mind, absolute focus and the clarity to know exactly what he is trying to achieve. He has also had unbelievable support from his lovely wife Julie.

I wish I'd been able to harness the power of the mind as much as Kippy. There are times when I thought too much about the game and listened to too many people, particularly during the period when everybody had an opinion on my ability against spin bowling. Maybe I should have spent more time reading Kippy's books. When I got to England he started to underline passages and give them to me. You can imagine what I, as a teenager who was just discovering the power of something other than positive thinking, made of that.

Paul Terry and I would sometimes browse Kippy's books in the dressing room while he was out in the middle scoring another hundred. We felt they were a bit religious and not for us. I preferred to sit and chat about the game with teammates and opponents – how we dealt with nerves, how we dealt with expectations, different match situations, variables in the game and adjusting to different batting and bowling conditions.

I learned early in my career that you can't have a one-size-fits-all approach to cricket. Different things work for different people. Some like to break batting down into small targets within an innings or a season, which Kippy did to great effect. Others like to have a slogan on the inside of their coffin or on their bat handle, like Jos Buttler.[2] Some like to chat about the game in the bar; some prefer to be on their own. Whatever's good for you.

One thing Kippy introduced me to, which I have sworn by ever since, is visualisation. It was my secret weapon and I later passed it on to Matthew Hayden when he was at Hampshire. When I eventually started my innings, I almost felt like I had a ten-run start because I'd already done so much work. Before each day's play I would go into the middle and imagine my innings. It was a detailed process – taking

---

[2] He has 'Fuck it' written at the top of his bat handle, which he says helps him put cricket in perspective.

guard, surveying the field and the crowd, trying to absorb the atmosphere and working out how each bowler would try to get me out, getting used to the light and the sightscreen. I visualised the bowling action of my opponents, where the fielders were, what the crowd were doing. Then I'd get my feet moving and practise my shots: rasping square cuts, bread-and-butter clips off the pads, leaving the ball outside off stump, ducking a bouncer or playing an airtight forward defensive shot. Then I'd go down the other end and do the same thing. Once, I thought of raising my bat and thought, 'Piss off, Judge. You need to get to fifty first!'

There's one other nice thing about visualisation – you never, ever play a shit shot.

Kippy has been such a big influence on my whole life. At times, brotherly love has been mixed with seriously tough love. He's brutally honest – and I mean brutally. When I mess up, he comes down bloody hard. Sometimes I think he's being unreasonable, but he only does it for my benefit. Blood's thicker than water and he has always looked after me.

We're pretty different in many ways. He's focused, driven, ambitious and gets a buzz out of creating successful companies and making money from them. I've always been happier to chill out and go with the flow. I just wish I could have found a happy balance.

He was always shrewd when it came to money. In the mid-1980s he bet £100 at odds of 50–1 that I would play 50 Tests for England. A decade later, he won £5,000. And he didn't even buy me a drink, the tight arse. That 1985 season was the first I was able to play for Hampshire as a qualified player. I hadn't appeared much in 1984, even though Malcolm and Gordon were touring England with the West Indies. We had only one overseas player that season, due to some slightly complex regulations that are far too boring to explain, and the club signed a fast bowler called Elvis Reifer from Barbados. He struggled with form and injury and I got a chance towards the end of the season. I had a good few days in August when I scored 132 and 97 against the touring Sri Lankans followed by 104 in a Sunday League match away to Glamorgan. In that Sri Lanka game I was out trying to hit the boundary that would have given me the fastest century of the English season – 83 minutes. The prize was £3,000, which would have bought me a lot of beer and burgers.

Overall, I'd had a solid start to my Hampshire career, and I knew that when I returned in 1985 I had every chance of becoming a regular in the first team as I would no longer be classified as an overseas player.

First I had to renounce my South African citizenship. I thought long and hard about it, but England was starting to feel like home – I had put down roots and I absolutely loved playing for Hampshire. If it started as a marriage of convenience, by 1985 I was definitely falling in love with England. It was a process, though, and I didn't just say, 'Yep, where do I sign?' I tried as I best as I could to understand and embrace the culture.

I can understand people being cynical about that, but national identity is a complex thing. I was born in South Africa, I played for England and I now live in Australia, so what nationality am I? As far as I'm concerned I'm still a Pom,[3] and I'm proud to be one. I was thrilled when apartheid ended and South Africa returned to international sport, but there was no sadness that I couldn't play for them. The thought barely registered. I loved England and I never thought I would have to leave the country. Even now I always want England to win, whatever the sport. The anthem used to bring a lump to my throat, and I even have 'Land of Hope and Glory' as my ringtone on my mobile, which isn't necessarily the wisest move when you live in Australia.

There was another reason why Hampshire was starting to feel like home – I was settling down with a local girl. Katherine James used to come to Northlands Road quite a lot for corporate lunches as part of her work. I didn't know this at the time but she asked Julie – my brother's new girlfriend, who was working at the club – whether I was single. One night in the bar after the day's play she came up to say hello with her brother. We hadn't really been introduced properly, and when I saw him in the toilet a few minutes later I said, 'Mate, your

---

[3] I still don't understand why the English are called Poms, by the way. Shouldn't it be the other way round?

girlfriend seems lovely.' He said, 'Oh no, that's my sister, do you want a proper introduction?'

We got on really well and soon started going out. Kath was attractive, funny and I enjoyed being around her. Morag was my first girlfriend when I was a teenager back in South Africa, but Kath was my first serious long-term relationship.

With Kippy meeting Julie and Paul Terry meeting Bernadette, who was living with Julie, things started to change in the bachelor pad. First Julie moved in to Kippy's, then PT moved in the other direction to live with Bernadette, and Kath flitted between her flat and Kippy's for a year or so before we got our own place.

My first year as a non-overseas player went well, with only my brother scoring more County Championship runs for Hampshire. I played one innings at Basingstoke against Derbyshire which really enhanced my reputation. We were chasing 380 in the fourth innings on a turning pitch, and I smacked 140 not out at quicker than a run a ball. At that stage it was the highest score of my career and included four sixes off the spinners Geoff Miller and Dallas Moir. We needed 39 off the last four overs and got there with an over to spare when I hit Miller for consecutive sixes out of the ground.

I also won the first Man of the Match award of my career when we beat Somerset at Taunton in the quarter-final of the NatWest Trophy. They were the glamour side of English cricket, with Viv, Beefy and Joel Garner, and we smashed them by 149 runs. I scored 110 and kept cutting Joel for four, even though he had three men on the boundary to stop the shot – one just in front of square, one at fine third man and one in between. It was one of those days when I just nailed everything. I'm told Joel finished with the worst one-day figures of his entire Somerset career.

There was a fine example of Beefy's aura during that game. We had Somerset in trouble, 43–5 chasing 300, when Beefy announced to the umpires that we were going off because the sun was reflecting off a rooftop and getting in his eyes! Thankfully we returned the next day to finish the job.

I received my county cap later in the summer. I was having so much fun, on and off the field, especially as I was now a regular in the

1st XI. But looking back through Dad's scrapbooks, there's an interview from *The Times* during the summer of 1985 that suggests that, though these were essentially innocent, carefree days, even then there was a bit of self-doubt. 'Chris is much stronger than me mentally,' I said in the interview. 'He knows he can succeed and has the confidence to do so. I haven't yet learned that. I am not all that great upstairs and I don't really believe in myself. You need more than talent to be a good cricketer.'

We had a real chance in the Championship that year. That win over Derbyshire put us top of the table but we came second behind Middlesex. That was the closest I came to winning the Championship in my career, though we picked up a few one-day trophies. The Hampshire boys loved a day out at Lord's.

The summer of 1985 was the first full season we were captained by Mark Nicholas. He's another great man who's been a huge influence in my life, and I can't speak highly enough of him. I didn't play under many top-class captains and he was certainly the best, though Goochie comes a good second. Mark has always been incredibly knowledgeable about the game; he was a very astute captain when it came to field placings and working out a batsman's weaknesses. He was also excellent at managing some very strong characters in the Hampshire dressing room. He was just a great all-round captain, such a pleasure to play under, which is one of the reasons I really enjoyed going back to Hampshire when I was an England player.

Mark might have played for England himself had he been more selfish and focused a little more on his own game rather than putting others before himself. He captained England A on a few tours, but that was as close as he got. In those days we played three-day cricket and he gave his wicket away on many occasions when we were trying to set a target or chase down runs in the fourth innings. His record was good but he was better than it would suggest.

There was one other incident of note during that 1985 season. Mom and Dad were over in England, watching Kippy and me bat at Taunton, when a call came over the tannoy for Joy or John Smith to urgently report to the secretary's office. There had been a call from their next-door neighbours in Durban to say our house was burning down. Florence had forgotten to switch the iron off before she went out, and eventually it caused a huge fire.

Half the house was smoke damaged, though it was still structurally okay. The other half was burned to the ground: the kitchen, laundry room, dining room, first lounge, the blue room (a second lounge), the communal bar, Kippy's bedroom, Kippy's en-suite bathroom, Kippy's lounge and Kippy's bar were all gone.

And Dad wasn't insured. He was old school and didn't believe in insurance, so he lost the lot. Flo was mortified, God bless her, but Mom and Dad knew it was an accident and didn't blame her at all. Thankfully, we were wealthy enough that Dad could have the same house rebuilt on the same plot.

I didn't get to see the new old house for a while, because I didn't go back to Durban in the winter of 1985–86. Barry Richards suggested I spend a few winters in Perth – he'd played club cricket out there for many years and felt I would develop by playing on quick, bouncy wickets against more aggressive opponents.

I played for Nedlands in the first two years and then South Perth in my final season. I really tried to make the most of every innings over there. The way the matches are structured – over two days each weekend – means you might only get a bat once every two or three weeks. I loved everything about it, from the fast pitches to the nights out at the Windsor Hotel bar. In fact, I made my debut having had about two hours' sleep after an eventful Friday night, and peeled off 147 in my first innings for the club. The wickets were great and because we were slightly closer to the river, we had a lovely sea breeze blowing through in the early afternoon. If you were inland at somewhere like Midland/Guildford, where Alec Stewart played around the same time, the breeze arrived three hours later so you had to bat in searing heat.

I had a job in a bakery during the week, which allowed me to watch a lot of Test cricket on TV. I started work at 4 a.m. and was usually home at 9.30 a.m.,[4] so I could kick back and watch Australia for a few hours before I went to the nets in the afternoon.

---

[4] Perth is a few hours behind the rest of Australia, so the Test matches in Adelaide, Melbourne, Sydney and Brisbane usually started around 9 a.m. Perth time.

It was around then that I found a new hero in Allan Border. Australia weren't great at that stage – they won only one Test series in a five-year period from 1984–89 – but Border's standards never, ever dropped. I loved his resilience and mental toughness, especially when he was playing against the West Indies. He put such a high price on his wicket. There were other players who were more exciting to watch, but if you looked deeper you saw a level of concentration and toughness that was extraordinary from such a little bloke. I also heard later from Lamby what a great guy he was.

That bakery job was quite interesting. Every morning I'd nick a dozen loaves, some doughnuts and croissants and give them to home-less people. The bakery was producing thousands of loaves so nobody noticed if a dozen went missing. I got to know some of them and after a while they started to gather in the same place in east Perth at 5 a.m. every morning, and I'd get told off if I was late. I thought I was doing them a favour! They were all lovely people who had fallen on hard times.

My boss was a strict old Italian guy called Di Campo. After a few months he asked me to clean the van every day, which wasn't in the job description. I didn't mind doing that, but then he asked me to sweep the entire bakery. Bugger that! I said no, he ordered me to do it, so I told him where I'd like to shove his broom and walked out. Credit to Mr Di Campo, I still got paid.

Barry also felt I would mature as an individual if I lived on my own in Perth. As it turned out, Kath suggested it would be nice if she could join me. There were one or two times it became a bit claustro-phobic, and had we been at home we might even have split up, but she gave me outstanding support – she spent three hours loading up the bowling machine for me every day. I was still practising much more than anybody else. The first year I got the most runs in the Perth Premier Club League, the second year I did the same and in my third season, 1987–88, I broke the record for most runs in a season, which had stood since 1943–44. This record still stands.

Barry later became chief executive at Natal and called to ask if I'd return to play for them as an overseas player. I said, 'Barry, it was your idea that I come to Perth and as much as I am grateful for the offer, I'm very happy here!'

Unlike in Perth, the innings came thick and fast in county cricket. Hampshire won the 40-over John Player League in 1986 and I did pretty well, averaging 70 in that competition. But in first-class cricket, there was sometimes criticism – particularly from Kippy – that I got too many good-looking thirties and forties and wasn't greedy enough. I found that I thrived on pressure and seemed to be better when the stakes were higher or the going tougher.

I was still learning about the power of the mind. In 1987, Hampshire went on a pre-season tour to Barbados, which was arranged by Malcolm and Gordon. One night they set up a dinner with Dr Rudi Webster, a psychologist who worked with the West Indies. He'd written a brilliant book called *Winning Ways* in 1984, all about the mental side of sport, which I've read a few times over the years. That night, Kippy, Mark, Paul Terry and I sat round a table at a nice restaurant on the west coast of Barbados, picking his brain and hanging on his every word. I remember that evening so vividly.

Another night out on that trip was memorable for different reasons. The team was doing some hard pre-season training in a rum shack, where I got chatting to an attractive tourist. We were getting on well and decided to go down to the Bamboo Beach Bar in my Mini Moke, and then we went skinny-dipping for a bit. When we returned, all my clothes had gone! It turned out Kevan James and a couple of the other Hampshire players had followed me and nicked my clothes, so I had to drive her home naked and then try to get back myself. I ran through the hotel foyer wearing nothing except a very nervous frown, and with my hands hiding my modesty. To make it worse, by that stage all the Hampshire players and their wives were in the bloody hotel bar laughing their heads off.

A few weeks later, at the start of May, we travelled to Oxford to play the Combined Universities in the Benson & Hedges Cup. We won comfortably against a side with three future England players – Mike Atherton, Nasser Hussain and John Stephenson – and then zipped across to Leicestershire for our first match of our Sunday League title defence the following day.

A few of us decided to go for a couple of drinks in the hotel bar. That was the plan, until we saw it was full of Welsh club rugby players, who were also staying at the hotel. They were hammered and making a racket, so we went to a nightclub because we thought it would be quieter! Malcolm, Gordon and I walked up to Caspers along with Cardigan Connor, our Anguilla-born fast bowler, and after a while we saw three of the rugby players come in. They knew who we were and asked for autographs, which was fine, but then they plonked themselves down and started slurring away like we were long-lost friends. They were being really rowdy and far too chummy, when all we wanted was a quiet chat, so after a while we moved to another part of the club. They followed us and were getting steadily more aggressive, at which point Gordon and Cardigan decided they'd had enough and went back to the hotel. Malcolm wanted to stay so I kept him company for a bit. It got more and more uncomfortable until I said, 'Macko, let's go.' The hotel was about a kilometre away, and as we walked back we could hear them staggering behind us. I didn't think much of it because they were staying in the same hotel.

When we got back to the lobby, it was deserted apart from the night porter. One of the rugby players walked in behind us and said, 'Malcolm, you're an unsociable black c★★t.' Malcolm ignored him and pushed the lift button, but I snapped, 'Mate, what the fuck? You can't say that.'

I'd barely finished my sentence when he said, 'And you're an unsociable c★★t as well!' As he did so he took a big roundhouse swing at me. My reflexes were quite quick so I ducked under it as if I was avoiding a bouncer. In that split second, as I was ducking, I instinctively realised I had to do something. I'm not a fighter but there were three huge rugby players looking for trouble, so the wisest thing was probably to get my retaliation in first. As I came back up I landed a beautiful right cross. I've always had good strength in my shoulder from my shot-put days, and this bloke just took off. There was blood everywhere and he was a right state. By this time the lift had arrived, so Malcolm and I pegged it while the other two players checked on their mate. Trouble was, they must have seen on the display that we had gone to the third floor. We ran into Malcolm's room, locked the door and hid under the bloody bed! We heard them thumping on every single door – this was at about midnight – shouting all sorts of abuse, plenty of it racist. That must have been especially confusing to some of the guests who had been woken up. After about half an hour, things quietened down and I sneaked nervously back to my room and went to sleep.

When I woke up the next morning my hand was blue and about twice the size it should have been. I thought I could play through it but when I got to the ground I couldn't hold a bat. I was hopeless during fielding practice, too, at which point Mark came over and said, 'Judgie, what's the problem?' I told him the story and he said he didn't want to hear any more and that we'd sort it out after the game. Funnily enough, Kippy came into the team in my place and played a match-winning innings.

When I told Mark the full story he backed me, as did Hampshire when the Welsh rugby club threatened to press charges. Malcolm's story matched mine, so did the night porter's, and Gordon and Cardigan also explained just how intrusive and aggressive the blokes had been in the pub. Tony Baker, our chief executive, was great throughout and helped alleviate any problems. In the end, they didn't press charges and it all disappeared. I was out for over a month with a broken hand covered in plaster, but it didn't stop me practising on the bowling machine using just my left hand to hold the bat. The official line was that I'd broken my hand in the field against Combined Universities.

As I said, I'm not an aggressive person but I couldn't accept someone talking to Macko like that, and in that split second as I ducked the punch I felt I had to do something. I've got plenty of regrets in my life but that isn't one of them.

Despite my false start to the season, I received a letter asking about my availability for that winter's World Cup. I had three innings in the week before England announced a provisional squad of 25, all against Essex at Portsmouth – two in the County Championship and one in the Sunday League. I'd scored an unbeaten 209, the highest score of my career, against them a week earlier and thought one big score might get me in the squad. This time I didn't get 209, just nine. And that was in all three innings. A duck on the Saturday, a duck on the Sunday and nine on the Tuesday. I was disappointed as I'd have loved to go to a World Cup, but at that stage I probably didn't think I was quite good enough to bat with Gooch, Lamb and all those blokes.

My big breakthrough came when Hampshire won the Benson & Hedges Cup in 1988. The innings that opened all the doors was in the quarter-final against Worcestershire. They were probably the best team in England at the time – they won the County Championship in 1988 and 1989 and the Sunday League in 1987 and 1988 – and had a quality pace attack of Graham Dilley, Neal Radford and Phil Newport.

It was actually a three-day game because of the weather. We were 84–6 chasing 170 on a very uneven pitch, which a lot of people thought was too dangerous to play on. I got 87 not out and we won by three wickets. The next highest score was 18 not out from Nigel Cowley, who gave me brilliant support at No. 9. I was really proud and knew I'd played the best innings of my life up to that point. What I didn't know was that Micky Stewart, the England coach, was at the match, and that performance bumped me right up the queue towards England selection.

Mark was also starting to write some newspaper articles and had a reputation as a very good judge of players and characters. He spoke highly of that innings in the press – 'I don't think you could ever see much better batting than that in such conditions' – which didn't do any harm.

It was an exciting time for Hampshire, as the club had never reached a one-day final at Lord's before. I made a quick 20 not out in the semis, when we beat Essex, and went into the final against Derbyshire full of confidence. Steven Jefferies took five for 13 and we rolled them for 117. Low targets can be tricky sometimes and when I went in, at 44–2, I wasn't sure how to approach my innings. I asked Mark, who was at the other end, and he gave me some simple advice. 'Show off. Play your shots. Enjoy yourself, have fun and embrace the atmosphere.'

Whatever you say, captain! I blasted 38 off 27 balls before Steve Goldsmith took an unbelievable catch at fine leg. I played very freely and remember driving Michael Holding down the ground for four off the back foot, which is a dream shot for any batsman. He wasn't as quick at that stage of his career but it was nice to be able to say I'd played a stroke like that against one of the greats. It was an eye-catching cameo that sparked some nice comments from some great people like Richie Benaud, and Micky Stewart came into the dressing room afterwards to say, 'Well played.'

The timing of the innings was perfect, as a week earlier England had been bowled out for 135 and 93 by the West Indies in the third Test at Old Trafford.

The following weekend we were in Birmingham playing Warwickshire. As I was stirring on the Sunday morning, Kath called to say there was speculation in the papers that I'd been picked for the fourth Test at Headingley. I couldn't sit still until, 15 minutes later, the phone went again. It was Chris Cowdrey, the Kent captain. I wondered what he wanted as I hardly knew him, and I was desperate to get him off the phone in case somebody more important was ringing. He quickly explained that he was the new England captain and was calling to tell me I was in the squad. I was 24 years old and I was about to play for England. I told the press, 'I am so excited I just can't think straight.' I was so thrilled at how proud my family were – Kippy was with me, and Dad heard the news on the radio at Royal Lytham, where he was following Gary Player at the Open.

It's funny how things work out. For a few years, the media said the reason I hadn't been picked for England was that I got too many pretty thirties and forties, yet in the end it was a pretty 38 in a low-scoring cup final that clinched my selection.

Over the next few days, after that initial disbelief passed, one thing dominated my mind. It was a thought that was with me throughout my England career. Am I really good enough?

Chapter 7
Three Lions

At the age of 55, I still have one recurring dream about cricket. I'm at Lord's, a wicket has fallen and I'm the next man in. But I'm not ready. I haven't got my pads on, I'm scrambling round to find my gloves and I'm in danger of making history as the first man to be timed out in a Test match.

You don't need to be Freud to understand it. I used to get so nervous before batting, which is why at the very least I liked to be prepared well in advance of my innings. I hated feeling rushed, which is one reason why I didn't necessarily like batting at No. 3 in first-class cricket, even though many people felt it was the perfect position for me.

I preferred to have the bit of extra time you got at No. 4. I liked to take my time after fielding – go to the loo, have a shower, get my pads on slowly and get organised. Everyone has a different method of preparing to bat. Beefy would be watching anything but the cricket, he couldn't have been more relaxed. David Gower might sit reading the *Financial Times*. Apparently, Viv would have a nap and wake up when a wicket fell. He'd splash his face with a bit of water, swagger out and belt the bowling to all parts.

As I said, Viv's swagger inspired me to create a persona when I was batting. If you saw me strutting to the wicket like a gladiator, you'd think I was full of confidence. All those mannerisms, the furious blinking and the whirring of my arms like I was getting ready to chop a bloody tree down, were mainly bravado.

I had to work very hard to get myself in character and the two sides of my personality were always wrestling with each other. While the Judge was swaggering out to the middle, Robin Smith was seeking reassurance by thinking of the caption that would be appearing on the little TV in the dressing room – the one that shows the incoming batsman's statistics.

Look, you're averaging mid-forties in Test cricket, you're good enough to be out here. Don't feel too humble.

Those mannerisms were also a way of getting myself loose. I used to stretch my eyes wide to adjust to the light, and swing my arms around to get rid of any muscular tension. I wanted to wake myself up because I often found that I didn't have the right intensity at the start of an innings. Sometimes, if I felt sluggish, I'd deliberately let a fast bowler hit me to get myself going. Not on my head or on a bone – I'm not that stupid – but I enjoyed a little sharpener on the inside of the thigh to wake me up.

The nerves didn't really go away until I reached double figures. I was never concerned about getting out for a duck, because for me that was the same as getting 5 or 6 – it was still a low score. I know 11 or 12 isn't going to change the world but when I got to double figures I started to relax a bit. I felt like I was on my way.

I felt properly 'in' when my feet were moving nicely, when I was seeing the ball well and picking up line and length quickly. When that happened, it felt like it was me rather than the bowler who was dictating terms.

I had a few superstitions as well. My biggest was a four-leaf clover, which I had on my bat and later put on all the bats that were made by my business, Chase Sports. I wore a Christian chain around my neck for most of my career, and the clasp always had to be at the back when I went out to bat. I also had a silly superstition to bring my partner luck when I was at the non-striker's end. Before each delivery I would place my bat inside the return crease, then move it across to

Top left: Mom and Dad on their wedding day in 1955

Top right: Mom was South Africa's leading ballerina and instilled a love of ballet in me

Bottom left: She is tough, too, and posed for this photo soon after being shot at through a car window

Bottom right: My bike rides with Dad, with me on the saddle in front of the seat, were one of the highlights of my childhood

Top left: Proudly showing off my school trophies at the age of 12
You can even see the beginnings of the Judge's wig

Top right: Grooving my cover drive on the bowling machine at home

Bottom left: I was a very good rugby player at school, and at one stage
I thought that might be my chosen career

Bottom right: My second mum, Florence, a beautiful and sensitive woman who doted on me

Top left: 'Judge, I really think that as the junior pro, you should field at short leg'
'Bugger off, Kippy!'

Top right: One of the greatest cricketers of all time meets Sir Garry Sobers. Ha ha. Seriously, though, it was such a thrill to meet an absolute legend of the game

Bottom left: Malcolm Marshall, a dear friend and the greatest of all fast bowlers, at Kippy's wedding in 1987

Bottom right: Kath and me on our wedding day in 1988

Left: Batting with Kippy for Hampshire. We are so proud that the Smith brothers scored over 50,000 runs for the club

Below: Nailing a trademark square cut, and hearing that lovely rifle crack at the point of impact, during my maiden Test hundred against Australia at Old Trafford in 1989

Opposite page, top left: Lamby and I had so much fun in the middle. I wish I could have batted with him forever

Opposite page, top right: I was so flattered when David Gower said one of the reasons he joined Hampshire was so that he could bat with me

Opposite page below: Beefy is one of the most generous people I have ever met, and whenever I played with him he made me feel a million dollars

Top: Celebrating victory in the match of my life: Hampshire's wi over Surrey in the 1991 NatWes Trophy final

Middle: The 1992 World Cup fir was the biggest disappointment my career – I was left out of the and then watched England lose an inspired Pakistan

Bottom: Lifting the B&H Cup with Mark Nicholas, my Hampsl captain and mentor, after our wi over Kent in 1992

Top left: I was so inspired and moved when I met Mother Teresa during our tour of India in 1992–93. She was the soul of empathy

Top right: On the same tour I pulled Gatt along on a rickshaw, which wasn't such a bright idea

Bottom: Playing a classical off-drive during my 167 not out against Australia at Edgbaston in 1993. I've always loved a good technique

Top left: With my wonderful son, Harrison, during the New Zealand tour of 1991–92

Top right: And my gorgeous daughter, Margaux, who was born in 1994

Bottom: The Smith family posing for a photo at our home in Nomansland

the right and then back again. I felt it brought my team luck. No, I've no idea how that one started.

You probably think all this is daft. But honestly, it didn't matter whether it was a vital Test match or a charity game, whether I was the No. 2 batsman in the world or the No. 200 – I had the same fear of failure swirling round my stomach and my brain. I think the thing I worried about the most was letting other people down. It could be family, teammates, supporters, sponsors, even the bloke who paid £2 to watch me in a charity game with his kid.

I've always had this desperate, pathological need to please people and live up to their expectations, which has had both a positive and negative impact on my life. Just about the only time I ever said the word 'No' was when I was running between the wickets. Kippy said in my benefit brochure, 'If it's possible to be too nice then Robin would qualify', and I suppose I know what he means. I've always hated the thought of people saying, 'That Robin Smith isn't a particularly nice bloke.' During my career, I found it very hard to say no when I was invited to something.

Though failure troubled me, I never had any fear of success. I was hardly ever out in the nervous nineties playing a bad shot. My conversion rate of fifties to hundreds wasn't always as good as it should have been, but that was down to concentration, exhaustion or running out of partners, rather than any fear of getting a hundred. I wasn't particularly worried about getting out in the nineties. I know it's a cliché but I really did have the mindset that ninety was a darn sight better than a duck. If anything, the fact I could no longer fail – the thing that really worried me – meant I sometimes relaxed too much when I got to 50.

In cricket, failure and success are there in black and white on the scorecard. In reality you could do nothing wrong and get 0, or bat like a novice and get 50, but the person who looks at the scorecard in the paper the next day doesn't know that. In my head, the number of runs I scored was an absolute verdict on the quality of my batting that day, and that's probably why I fretted so much.

With all this worrying, you can imagine how I felt before my Test debut. Dad flew my mentor Grayson Heath over from South Africa, and he drove from Southampton to Headingley with me the day before the game so that we could chat about what might happen. This is someone who had trained me for thousands of hours, and it meant so much to have him there. That journey has stayed with me – and so has something he said during it: 'Robin, just remember one thing. We'll have a drink after you've batted for the first time and you'll say, "Grayson, it wasn't as hard as I thought it was going to be."'

Whenever I didn't back myself, which was a lot, I tried to remember those words.

It was very intimidating going to the team hotel. The England squad was full of people I'd admired or even idolised, like Lamby, Goochie and David Gower. I was also worried about how I might be seen by some players because of my South African background. But they all really embraced me. That evening, before the team dinner, Goochie rang my hotel room and asked if I wanted to go for a beer. We were staying at the Trusthouse Forte in Bramhope, and three or four of us went for a couple of pints in a lovely pub called the Fox & Hounds. I thought I should try Tetley's bitter as they were the team sponsor and we were in Yorkshire. After one pint it was straight back to the lager!

We then went back to the hotel for the team dinner. The debutants – in this case, Tim Curtis and me – had to sit next to the chairman of selectors Peter May, and we spent the meal trying our best to behave while everyone pelted us with bread rolls.

I have another priceless memory from that hotel. I think it was before my debut although it might have been before we played Australia at Headingley a year later. I was sitting in the bar with some of the other players and Laurie Brown, the physio who used to work at Manchester United, when Lamby made his excuses. About half an hour later he appeared with a big smirk on his face and ordered a pint. He'd managed to get the key to Laurie's room and decided to have a bit of fun. Lamby had opened the bay windows, which were in front of a pond that was full of wild Egyptian geese, and having stored a load of bread rolls during the meal, left a trail of breadcrumbs from the pond all the way into Laurie's room. When the geese followed the trail, he shut the bay windows, locked them in the room and went back to the bar. I'm no goose expert but it's fair to say they were thoroughly pissed off. When Laurie got back, his room was an absolute state: there were feathers everywhere and they'd left a number of deposits all over his bed. Laurie came charging down the stairs, with a couple of geese for company, and into the bar.

'Lambyyyyy! What the fuck have you done?!'

'What did I do, Laurie, eh?'

Laurie was a lovely Scottish bloke who normally wouldn't say boo to a goose, but he was bloody angry that night. And he said a lot more than boo to the geese. We were in tears of laughter. Lamby was so good for morale – always up for a joke, always accentuating the positive about the match we were playing.

On the first day I was waiting to bat at No. 6 when David Gower walked off having been the third man out. It was his 100th Test, he'd been caught down the leg side having an airy-fairy waft and he probably knew he'd get slaughtered in the press. Yet he took his pads off, plonked himself next to me and started having a chat to help me relax. This is the great David Gower, and I'm just some young bloke making his debut. It was such a thoughtful gesture and such a nice thing to do. The way I was treated during that match played a huge part in helping me settle into Test cricket so quickly. All I've ever wanted is to feel like I belong, and all these legends in the England team made an effort to help me feel that way.

I went into bat soon after with England in trouble at 80–4. I couldn't have asked for a better batting partner – Lamby, the bloke who sledged the hell out of me in South Africa six years earlier. We'd never batted together before, though I'd got to know him a bit through county cricket. I was so bloody nervous for the first few balls but a few one-liners from Lamby helped me to relax. I was crapping myself with fear one minute and wetting myself with laughter the next.

He also gave me some simple but important advice. After a while he came down the wicket and said, 'Judgie, what's up?'

'What do you mean, what's up?'

'Why aren't you playing with your usual flair? You haven't played an attacking shot!'

'Well, Lamby, this is a Test match.'

'Judgie, the reason you were picked to play in a Test match is because of the way you bat for Hampshire. I've played against you for Northants and our bowlers bloody hate having to bowl at you! I know these are better bowlers but they won't enjoy it either once you start expressing yourself. Play your natural game, the game that got you into the team.'

After a few overs, Malcolm Marshall dropped one short and I smashed a square cut for my first boundary in Test cricket. Malcolm was at the top of his mark, waiting to bowl the next ball, when Lamby put his hand up to stop him and walked down the wicket. I thought, 'Bloody hell, Lamby, what are you doing?!'

'Fuck, Judgie, that was a great shot!' he said, before pointing to the crowd. 'I can see Kath up there. She's just had an orgasm and slipped off her seat!'

'Oh, Lamby, please!'

'Come on, Judgie, you're going well. Just relax, china.'

And I did. My brain was starting to calm down. I thought, 'I've been out here for half an hour, I'm really enjoying it and the crowd is behind us. The West Indies are bowling well but I feel comfortable, happy, and I'm seeing the ball well. I don't think this Test match stuff is as hard as everyone makes it out to be.'

In other words, Grayson was right. From that moment on, I felt like I belonged on the big stage. I finished the first day on 23 not out and felt good that night when I had a drink with Grayson. The next day, Lamby and I extended our partnership to 103 before he pulled a calf muscle and retired hurt, the soft prick! In the next over I was caught behind off what Wisden called an 'evil lifter' by Sir Curtly Ambrose for 38. A score of 183–4 soon became 201 all out. I got 11 in the second innings, LBW to Malcolm, and we were well beaten by 10 wickets. I thought it was going past leg stump and said that to Malcolm when we were back at Hampshire. 'Middle stump, Judgie. Middle stump.' He loved getting his mates out. Dessie Haynes, his best friend, never heard the end of it if Macko dismissed him in county cricket.

That first innings with Lamby accelerated a great friendship on and off the field. I loved his company and sense of fun. I still remember my 21st birthday, when we were playing Northants at Southampton. Lamby decided to help himself to my presents, which included a nice new fishing rod. While we were in the field, Lamby put a sinker on the edge of the rod and cast it over the balcony.

My England debut was the first time I batted with him. We fed off each other – me more so than him, as his confidence was so infectious – and ran very well between the wickets. We prided ourselves on that. It was especially important against the West Indies, because the last thing you wanted to do was get stuck at one end. If you did that they would lock in and wear you down.

Batting in Test cricket could be such a trial, but Lamby made it fun. We had a great laugh out in the middle. As a young bloke I wondered what Lamby was talking to his batting partner about. The answer, it turned out, was very little! With some players you talk about the cricket between overs – how the bowler's trying to set us up, what the pitch is doing – but with Lamby I don't think we ever spoke about the state of play.

'Where are we going tonight, china?'

'Look at her in the crowd, she's sensational.'

Not that we followed through with anything. It was just a fun, throwaway line to relax the mood.

There were nine years between us and he really was like a big brother. A lot of statistics mean little but I think my partnerships stats with Lamby tell a story. We had five century stands in 16 innings and our average partnership of 79 is the highest for England in Tests since the Second World War. I told Lamby this and he thought I'd made it up, but it's true. I was really chuffed when I was told that stat, especially as most of our big partnerships were against the West Indies.

Lamby was the most important person I played with for England. I never really believed in myself but he did – and he told me so every day. He constantly pumped my tyres up, which was what I needed. Lamby would say to me, 'Come on, Judgie, these okes aren't good enough to get you out. You seem a bit quiet today, what's going on, Judgie, eh? Come on, perk up, we'll have some fun out there today.' It was simple man-management but it worked for me every time. He just made me unbelievably comfortable, and I love the bloke.

The other significant thing about Lamby is how unselfish he was. He probably knew that if I did well I'd eventually take his No. 4 spot, because I was a few years younger, and that's exactly what happened. Yet he encouraged me all the way.

I scored my first Test fifty in the next match, the last of the series at the Oval. I hit seven off my first two balls and then knuckled down to bat three and a half hours for 57. It was bloody hard work and I relished it. A lot of my innings against the West Indies felt like a war of attrition. I didn't plan it that way. My approach was always the same: Arrogance + Humility = Confidence. But batting against the West Indies took more out of you than any against other side. With their slow over rate you only faced around 40 balls an hour. You might have four down the leg side, maybe ten at your head, you might leave ten outside off stump, so you're only really playing 16 balls an hour. It wears you down because you just don't get bat on ball. You could be out there for 45 minutes and think, 'I'm playing nicely here', and then you'd look at the scoreboard and see you're 1 not out.

It meant you usually had to make ugly runs – a thick edge here, a glove to fine leg there, maybe a boundary off the pads or the occasional square cut for four. It certainly wasn't any less satisfying than scoring more fluently, it was just rewarding in a different way. That's one of the things I loved about batting – that every innings was slightly different, depending on the opposition, the pitch, your own confidence, the match situation and so on. You had a different puzzle to solve each time.

We lost that fifth Test by eight wickets to complete a 4–0 defeat. In the second innings I was out LBW for a third-ball duck to Winston Benjamin. He set me up a treat: I played and missed at two legcutters and then padded up to a big inswinger. It was the same way Malcolm used to try to get me out, and he also used the tactic against Mike Gatting.

I was annoyed, not because of the way I was out – it was excellent bowling – but because I shouldn't have been out there. It was nearly 7 p.m. when I went in, and the coach Micky Stewart asked if I wanted a nightwatchman. I didn't want to send a tailender out to face 90mph bowling as the light was fading, so I went in myself. I suppose I also wanted to be seen not to be showing any weakness. When I walked out to join Graham Gooch, he did a double take. Three balls later I was out and Neil Foster went in as nightwatchman.

It was stupid and throughout my career I probably didn't think about myself enough. If the team needed an odd-job man, I would volunteer – whether it was opening the batting or even standing in as wicketkeeper for a few overs. I did what was best for my team and best for my country, not always what was best for me. I learned far too late that if you don't look after yourself, nobody else will.

One of the few times I did try to look after myself led to a big row with Mark Nicholas. Sri Lanka were playing Hampshire in a tour game in 1988, and I was scheduled to face them again in the one-off Test at Lord's. Our left-arm spinner Raj Maru was bowling to Athula Samarasekera, who could give it a bloody good smack. Mark asked me to field at bat-pad, which I usually did.

'Mate, I don't really want to field there because he hits it bloody hard, I could hurt a finger and I've got a Test match coming up.'

'Hey, china, get in there and field bat-pad!'

'Oi, who's your fucking china … china?!'

We still laugh about that 30 years later. It was the only time I was disrespectful to Mark and the only spat we had in about ten years of his captaincy.

Fortunately, I didn't get a smack – from Mark or Samarasekera – and played in the Test match when we beat Sri Lanka. I made my one-day international debut a few days later as well and was instantly at home on the big stage. I'd had a small taste of Test cricket and I absolutely loved the atmosphere, the tension, the pressure, everything about it. I felt I was born for those games.

I got some nice praise in the press for my performances that summer. England had struggled so much for runs that even scores like 38 and 57 stood out, and people seemed to like my fighting spirit. Thanks to Dad's scrapbooks, I know now that *Wisden* said I batted like I'd 'been playing Test cricket for five years'.

Even at that early stage I noticed that almost every mention of me included a reference to my background. I was 'the Springbok', 'the South African-born batsman' or 'Durban-born.' It upset me because my parents were born in Britain and I cared deeply about playing for

England. Nobody called Colin Cowdrey 'the Indian-born batsman'. Lamby always said to me that, because of our background, we had to do a bit more than the other blokes to keep our place in the side.

I don't want to sound ungrateful. I always had a great relationship with the England fans and the media were very, very kind to me, particularly in the first half of my Test career. It just wore me down when I saw it in every single article – especially when it was still happening years later. I sometimes felt like I was seen as an England cricketer rather than an *English* cricketer.

Look, I'm sure the England cap meant a bit more to people like Graham Gooch and Alec Stewart. That's just natural. But I hope nobody ever doubted my commitment to England. I wasn't as gifted as the greats – at one stage my record suggested I was, but I wasn't. I was just a very good player who got behind the line and tried to do my best for England. I had absolutely no thoughts about playing for South Africa even when they were readmitted to international cricket. I was bloody proud to play for England.

There are a couple of bits of Titanium, one in my left hand and one in my head, which remind me how much I love England. The injuries I suffered playing for my country include a fractured cheek-bone, a broken jaw and a right index finger that was broken four or five times. I haven't been able to properly feel the left side of my face since being hit by Ian Bishop at Old Trafford in 1995. You don't give your heart and soul and get battered if you don't love the place.

My breakthrough season of 1988 ended in perfect style with my wedding to Kath on 21 September. It was a beautiful day, with the ceremony at Careys Manor in Brockenhurst. The vicar had told me beforehand that he would not marry us if I arrived with the smell of alcohol on my breath, so you can imagine my fear when Lamby announced we would be going to my local, the Three Tuns in Romsey,[1] on the morning of the wedding!

We had maybe 90 or 100 people at the wedding, and Jon Hardy was my best man. I didn't invite too many England players as I was

---

[1] A place I first started drinking at in 1983, just after my three centuries in the County Championship. I couldn't ignore somewhere with such an apt name!

new to the team, just Lamby. When the vicar asked if anybody knew of any lawful impediment to the marriage, I was mortified to see Lamby's hand go up.

'Yes, I do, vicar. I'm not sure the Zulu boy is worthy of Miss James!'

The whole congregation was in stitches. I'd secretly bought Kath an MGB sports car as a wedding present, so that we could drive to our hotel before flying out the next morning on our honeymoon to Grindelwald in Switzerland. We walked through a lovely guard of honour, Kath in her beautiful wedding gown, and I showed her the car. We jumped in, I started the ignition – and it coughed and spluttered for a few seconds before going dead. I turned around to see Lamby and some of my Hampshire teammates giggling like naughty schoolboys. The buggers had put potatoes in the exhaust pipe!

I was named in the England squad to go to India in 1988–89 but the tour was cancelled because of a row over sporting links with South Africa. Eight players were on a UN blacklist and were refused visas.[2] I sometimes wonder how much I would have benefitted from playing five Tests in spin-friendly conditions earlier in my career, when I was young and playing with freedom. When I did eventually play my first Test in the subcontinent I was 29 and it was harder to learn a slightly different technique.

But there are two sides to every story, and it's also possible I got a stroke of luck with the tour being abandoned. As I saw with Graeme Hick and other players, it can be difficult to claw back a Test career if you have a bad start, no matter how good you are. Had I gone to India and struggled, maybe been dropped, it would have affected my confidence. Instead, I started 1989 in the form of my life. Just in time to meet those friendly Australians.

---

[2] I wasn't on the blacklist, though I'm not entirely sure why. I think it's because I hadn't played sport in South Africa since renouncing my citizenship.

Chapter 8
It's not a fucking picnic

NEVER MEET YOUR HEROES: they might call you a little prick. Or something even stronger! I played against Allan Border for the first time in the 1989 Ashes, having admired him for years and heard what a great bloke he was. The reality wasn't quite what I expected.

In fact, the whole series was a shock to the system. I batted very well and scored my first two Test hundreds, yet we were stuffed 4–0. Cricket is strange in that it's a team game that involves 11 individual performances. When both come together successfully, as happened a few times against the West Indies in particular, it's the greatest feeling. But for a lot of my career I had the weird emotion of playing well without being on the winning side.

All four of my one-day international centuries came when England lost, including probably the most famous innings of my career – 167 not out against Australia at Edgbaston in 1993. Only two of my nine Test hundreds came in England wins. It happened a lot at Hampshire, too. And even in retirement, when I was playing for my buddy Patrick Trant's team at a local park, I couldn't escape it. In one final we were chasing 110 – I scored 82 not out and we still lost!

It's such a deflating, confusing feeling. I know cricket can be a selfish game, because a load of great individual performances make up a great team performance. But it's more complicated than that. Team success was absolutely paramount and far more important than me scoring runs. That sense of a shared experience, especially in victory, meant everything to me. I'd be very surprised if not all players felt that way. I picked up that attitude from Grayson Heath, my mentor. Goochie and Mark Nicholas were also big on the whole 'no I in team' philosophy.

Overall, I was on the winning side in 14 out of 62 Tests. Mind you, more than half those games were against Australia and the West Indies, the two best teams in the world at the time, and we weren't going to win too many of those.

I wasn't originally picked at the start of the 1989 Ashes series. I had begun the season in cracking form for Hampshire, with nearly 600 runs in my first six Championship innings and an unbeaten 155 against Glamorgan in the Benson & Hedges Cup (yep, we lost). But England went for an experienced middle order of Gatting, Lamb, Gower and Botham. They were all legends but I was disappointed when Micky Stewart rang me to say I was being left out. I thought I'd done well enough the previous summer to keep my place.

I was so disappointed that I went down to Lynmouth in Cornwall for a break with Kath. While I was there, I received a call to say that Gatt and Beefy were injured and that Kim Barnett and I had been called up. Actually, I owe my Hampshire teammate David Turner for that. We were playing Middlesex in a Sunday League game when he edged a ball to second slip. Gatt took the catch but damaged a finger in the process. I didn't think much of it at the time and assumed it was just bruising, but it turned out he was unfit for the Test. I bought a painting during that trip to Lynmouth which we hung in the house as a reminder that the bad times don't last for ever.

There was no consistency of selection in those days. When I made my debut in 1988, England dropped *nine* players from the squad for the previous Test. We had four captains in five Tests that summer: Mike Gatting, John Emburey, Chris Cowdrey and finally Graham Gooch. In fact I had three different captains in my first four Tests – Cowdrey, Gooch and then David Gower in 1989.

We used 29 players in the six Ashes Tests that summer – good luck trying to name them all[1] – and in my first nine Tests I played with 37 different players. Contrast that with my Hampshire mates Malcolm Marshall and Sir Gordon Greenidge, who only had 39 different West Indies teammates throughout the 1980s. Here's an example of how things were. When we toured in the Caribbean in 1990, I saw somebody in a hotel lobby wearing an England T-shirt and asked the guys why some random bloke was wearing official team gear. It turned out it was Chris Lewis, who had been called up to the squad as cover. I had never played against him before, never mind alongside him, so I had no idea what he looked like.

The first Test at Headingley set the tone for the whole Ashes series in 1989. We put the Aussies in and they got 600, with Steve Waugh, who was a flamboyant player in those days, smacking 177 not out. He'd never scored a Test hundred before but we didn't get him out until the third Test at Edgbaston, by which time he'd scored almost 400 runs. We should have saved the game comfortably but collapsed on the final afternoon. I got 66 and 0 and made the acquaintance of Merv Hughes, who said only one word to me for most of that summer. Arsewipe.

Actually, that's unfair on Merv, as there were usually two words.

Fucking arsewipe.

If I saw Merv on the outfield before the start of play, I'd greet him with a cheery, 'Good morning, buddy.' He'd usually respond with a grunt and then the inevitable 'Arsewipe!' I don't think Merv is a morning person.

He went for me straight away at Headingley, both with verbals and short stuff, and we had a great battle all series. I loved it. In the second

---

[1] In alphabetical order: Mike Atherton, Kim Barnett, Sir Ian Botham, Chris Broad, David Capel, Nick Cook, Tim Curtis, Phil DeFreitas, Graham Dilley, John Emburey, Neil Foster, Angus Fraser, Mike Gatting, Graham Gooch, David Gower, Eddie Hemmings, Alan Igglesden, Paul Jarvis, Allan Lamb, Devon Malcolm, Martyn Moxon, Phil Newport, Derek Pringle, Tim Robinson, Jack Russell, Gladstone Small, yours truly, John Stephenson and Chris Tavaré. How many did you get?

Test at Lord's, when I was trying to get us back in the game with David Gower,[2] I played a loose shot and was beaten outside off stump.

'You can't fucking bat, arsewipe.'

Later in the over he bowled a short ball and I smashed it through the covers for four. It bounced off the advertising hoardings and rolled back down the Lord's slope towards Allan Border at mid-off. He walked over to pick the ball up and threw it to Merv, who was grunting as he marched furiously back to his mark. I couldn't resist saying something. I ran down the wicket, knowing it was always going to be a boundary, and said, 'Oi, Merv!'

He spun around. 'What do you want?'

'We make a great fucking pair, don't we?'

'What do you fucking mean?'

'I can't bat and you certainly can't fucking bowl.'

Merv paused for a second and digested what I'd said.

'Fuck off, arsewipe!'

I had a good record against Merv and I think that wound him up. He had one of those actions which I enjoyed facing. He seemed a bit quicker than he actually was because of his bravado and everything – I'm sure he grew that big, hairy moustache as a form of intimidation. One thing he did very well was swing the ball away from the right-hander – he didn't get always get credit for that. But he definitely made the most of his ability. I quietly respected Merv for his energy and effort. He ran in so hard and, no matter how many times I panned him to the pickets, he always came back for more.

At tea on the fourth day of the Lord's Test the players on both sides were introduced to the Queen. During the afternoon session, Her Majesty would sit in the MCC Committee Room and be told about the current situation of the game by the president of the MCC or the secretary. Then she would meet us on the red carpet at teatime. That day David and I were trying to rescue England and Merv was

---

[2] This was the game when David walked out midway through a bad-tempered press conference on the Saturday night because he was going to the theatre to see the musical *Anything Goes*. I was waiting in the taxi for him with a glass of champagne, as I suspected he might be a bit dry in the palate after facing the press.

running in and giving me the usual heap of shit. She witnessed all this, and you didn't need to be a body language expert to realise what was going on. When I was introduced to her, she said, 'It appears that you don't have many friends out there.'

The Aussies were right in my face all series. One story gets told every time people talk about famous Ashes sledges. It happened on the third day of the fifth Test at Trent Bridge. They batted throughout Thursday and Friday, getting over 600 again. The forecast for the Saturday was shocking and none of us thought there'd be any chance of play, so we went out and had a few beers on the Friday night. I might have had a few too many, but I thought I was very professional about the whole thing. Every time I ordered another beer, I checked outside to see if it was still raining. It was teeming down. Same again please!

The following morning I woke up to see clear blue skies. I felt slightly seedy but assumed the ground would be waterlogged. A quick session in the indoor nets, an early lunch and then back to the hotel for a siesta.

What I didn't know was that the rain had all been on one side of the River Trent and the ground was on the other. Trent Bridge was bone dry and the sun was out all day. Shocker. They batted on a bit more and then I was in pretty early. After one over, in fact, with England 1–2 in reply to Australia's 602–6. So much for getting a bit of extra time to prepare at No.4!

A few pints of water and a couple of Panadol seemed to do the trick and I felt fine as I walked out to bat. But after a while I started to get a bit dry in the mouth. You were allowed to call for a drink at the end of an over or at the fall of a wicket, so long as you didn't hold up play. Through courtesy and sheer respect for Allan Border, I thought I'd ask his permission. They had just taken another wicket and were celebrating. As he ran past me from mid-on to join the huddle, I said, 'AB, do you mind if I call for some water?'

He said nothing and continued running. After about five yards, he abruptly stopped, turned around and walked back to me.

'What d'ya say, mate?'

'I said, "Do you mind if I have a glass of water?"'

He looked me in the eye and said, 'No, you can't have any fucking water! What do you think this is out here, a fucking picnic or what? You'll wait for a fucking drink like the rest of us, you little prick!'[3]

I was shell-shocked. I stood there and said, 'Um, okay.' And Captain Grumpy just walked off! I had to wait for the next break, I was bloody gasping for a drink. 'Be strong,' I thought. 'Don't let that little shit get the better of you.'

Though I was happy to give plenty of verbals back to Merv, I said nothing to Border. I suppose that ties in with my upbringing, and the respect for elders and superiors that was ingrained in South African culture. I saw Border, the great Allan Border, as my superior, whereas Merv was my equal and therefore worthy of the odd reciprocal F-bomb.

Border didn't sledge very often, so when he did it had a real impact – a sudden, savage burst of abuse from an absolute legend of the game. It unsettled you, which is what good sledging should do. In the second innings at Lord's, he was fielding at leg gully when Merv was bowling. I wanted to leave my crease and prod down a small divot in the pitch. Again, out of courtesy and respect, I turned around and said, 'AB, do you mind if I leave my crease.'

He walked up and looked in my face. 'Whatd'yasaymate?'

'I was just asking you if I could leave my crease.'

He considered my request for about half a second.

'Mate, we're not here to run you out. We're here to fucking knock you out, you little prick!'

And that was it, he just walked off!

Goochie and Lamby, who knew him well, were disappointed with his attitude during the series, not so much with his aggression on the pitch but with his attitude outside the game. He'd just had enough of losing to the Poms. He decided to be extremely hostile to everyone, and you can't really argue with the result.

I never really got to know AB during our playing career, as he was always a senior player and I was just making a name for myself. In

---

[3] When this does appear on the list of great sledges, it's usually written that Allan Border said, 'It's not a fucking tea party', but I'm pretty sure he said, 'It's not a fucking picnic.' Either way, the message was the same.

2007 I bumped into him when we were playing XXXX Gold Beach Cricket in Australia. All the teams were staying at the same hotel in Scarborough, Perth, and one morning I saw him milling around in the foyer when I was heading off for a walk. He came over and asked me what I was up to, and I said I was going for a stroll along the beach. I was pleasantly surprised when he asked if he could join me and we spent the next couple of hours chatting as we walked up the beach. He showed a lot of interest in me and my family and what I was doing. We really enjoyed each other's company, and he was so, so nice. If I hadn't played in that beach cricket match I would still think of him completely differently. He was a real gentleman. Turns out it is okay to meet your heroes.

It's the same with Merv, who is the nicest bloke you could ever wish to meet. Seriously. I didn't realise this for a few years either, though at the end of the 1989 series he did come into the dressing room to shake my hand and growl, 'Well played.' I thought that was nice. We had a beer together and it was great to chat to him – I think he even called me Judgie. The next time I played against him, in Australia 18 months later, he called me by my proper name, Mr F Arsewipe.

The level of hostility was like nothing I'd experienced, and that includes the Currie Cup. During the first Test of the 1990–91 Ashes, Lamby and I wandered into their dressing room at the close of play with a beer. The reception we got was even colder than the beer. We drank our cans in record time and left. As we did so, Lamby said to me, 'That's the last bloody time I go in their dressing room.'

Merv, Geoff Lawson, Terry Alderman and occasionally AB were the biggest sledgers in the Aussie teams I played against. The wicket-keeper Ian Healy tended to speak indirectly, the Norman Gifford approach, with a subtle comment to one of the fielders that he knew you'd hear and would unsettle you. He was different from someone like Pakistan's Moin Khan, who called you every name under the sun.

In my time, the Aussies were generally the worst sledgers around – though Pakistan ran them close – and I think that's why they've often been so unpopular. They go too far, though that might be changing after what happened in South Africa in 2018. Some of that was ridiculous, even before the ball-tampering stuff. I couldn't believe it when I saw David Warner doing the haka when AB de Villiers was run out in the first Test. What was that about?

As that 1989 series went on I took the sledging as a compliment because I knew I was playing well and that they respected my ability. I got 96 in the second innings at Lord's, despite pulling a hamstring early on, and was so close to my maiden Test hundred when Alderman bowled me with an unbelievable delivery that straightened up the slope to hit off stump. Dickie Bird, who was umpiring, said to Alderman it was the best ball he'd ever seen. It was certainly the best I received in my career. Honestly, have a look at it on YouTube, it was an absolute jaffa.

It was normal for umpires to chat to players during a match, especially a character like Dickie. Their only allegiance was to the game and they liked to see players on either side do well, so they were usually up for a chat. There was always a really good rapport between the players and umpires. Most of them were ex-players and they had the best possible view to spot if you were slipping into bad technical habits – if you were playing across the line or weren't using the crease as well as usual. I also figured it couldn't hurt to buy them a drink and have a chat after play. If there was a tight decision and they liked you, maybe you'd get the benefit of the doubt. More than anything, it was an extension of those friendships that I loved to make in the game.

The day after my 96, after Australia had completed their victory, I read a report in the *Daily Telegraph* which said I'd 'lost concentration and missed a straight one'. As I said, journalists were generally very good to me but that upset me. In fact, it pissed me off. There were times when I lost concentration, but why the hell would I do so when I was fighting to save an Ashes Test at Lord's, and I was four away from my maiden Test hundred?

The hamstring injury meant I missed the third Test, a rain-affected draw, and returned to the team at Old Trafford. We were 2–0 down with three to play and in all sorts of trouble. It was the first time I'd played in a Test match with Beefy. On the first day, we were struggling again when he came to the wicket to join me and decided to take control of the game. Before he'd scored he charged down the wicket to the legspinner Trevor Hohns, tried to deposit him over the Pennines, missed and was bowled.

That evening I said to him, 'Beef, what the fuck was that?'

'The sun got in my eyes, Judge.'

I love Beefy to bits – he's one of the best, most generous blokes you could ever meet – but my God he had an excuse for every dismissal. He'd look suspiciously at the wicket and trudge off. What I eventually realised was that it was all part of his invincible persona – he never showed weakness, never admitted a mistake, and that amazing level of self-belief allowed him to do such astonishing things on a cricket field. He believed he could climb Everest every day.

That was the same day I climbed my own Everest by making my first Test century. I was 112 not out at the close and eventually got 143 out of 260 before a soft dismissal when I was with the No. 11 Nick Cook, caught at third man trying to hit Merv for six. Whatever happened after that, I could always say I'd scored a Test century.

I don't remember that much about the innings though. It's strange, as I could probably tell you more about a load of innings that didn't matter anywhere near as much as my first Test hundred. I know Mom and Dad were there, which meant a lot, and I remember not being nervous in the nineties. That's about it.

We were eventually beaten by nine wickets, despite a fantastic maiden hundred from Jack Russell in the second innings. Australia regained the Ashes with two matches to spare, yet that wasn't the big story. On the last day of the game it was announced that 16 players had signed up to a rebel tour of South Africa.

We knew something was going on because there seemed to be a load of secret meetings throughout the Test. The rebel squad, led by Gatt, included seven guys who had played in the series and three who were in the team at Old Trafford: John Emburey, Tim Robinson and Neil Foster.

I thought it was a bit strange at the time as we were still involved in a Test, trying to save the Ashes, and it seemed like a lot of people didn't really give a toss about that. They were coming and going all the time, clearly distracted by something. It was only afterwards that it all made sense.

I think the people who went on rebel tours to South Africa should have been banned from international cricket for much longer than three years. That includes Graham Gooch, who went on the first tour in 1981–82. We never really spoke about it, and I don't like to criticise him because he was such an inspiration to me when he was my England captain. But I do think it was wrong that they came back into the team so quickly after both tours. Imagine how much David Gower and Sir Ian Botham could have made had they gone on that tour. I think Beefy was offered US$1 million for that tour in 1989–90, with David not far behind, and yet when Gatt was recalled after his three-year ban for the tour of India in 1992–93, it was David who lost his place.

It's nothing personal, but I do feel very strongly about the principle. I'm not saying the players who went over there believed in apartheid – everything I know about their characters tells me they didn't – but if you go over there then you accept it to some degree. In those days, cricketers didn't really think much about politics. I suspect that most of the players saw an opportunity to earn very good money and look after their family, without thinking of the wider implications.

The West Indies players who went were banned for life, although those bans were later lifted, so I didn't quite understand why Australia and England players were allowed back so quickly. If the rebel tourists knew they'd be banned for life I'm convinced they wouldn't have gone. These are complicated subjects, I appreciate that, and there isn't always a simple answer. I've read more in recent times about aboriginal apartheid, for example, and I sometimes wonder why Australian sport was never sanctioned in the way that South Africa was.

Goochie and Gatt later became England selectors, and David Graveney, who was player/manager on that 1990 rebel tour, became chairman of selectors for a long period. I'm not sure you can preach about fighting for the Three Lions when you've given it up yourself. Where was that attitude when you guys went off and turned your back on English cricket? What about when England needed you?

Look, it's a very difficult decision, especially when you've got a mortgage and a young family. It was reported that someone like Paul Jarvis was paid £80,000 after tax, and apparently he worked out that he'd have had to play every Test home and away for six years to earn the same amount. It takes a strong and brave man to turn down a lump sum like that. I can see both sides of the story. Make up your mind, no problem, but you can't have it both ways. You can't go on a rebel tour and then walk back into the England team.

In the summer of 1989, the announcement of the rebel tour left us in disarray. We were 3–0 down with two Ashes Tests to play, and half the people who had played that summer were unavailable. The next Test at Trent Bridge was another fresh start for English cricket; there were a few of those in my time. The first day of our new era ended with Australia 301–0. Yes, Geoff Marsh and Mark Taylor batted all bloody day. We bowled 102 overs and didn't take a single wicket. At the close of play I walked off with Devon Malcolm, who had just had a miserable first day as a Test cricketer. Beefy was in front of us, having bowled 20 overs himself without success, and I pointed to him and said, 'Mate, that old bugger must have been a decent bowler in his prime – he's got more than three hundred and fifty Test wickets and we've just gone a whole day without taking one between us!'

Eventually, Australia scored 600 and we were hammered by an innings, a result that took the shine off my second Test hundred.

At the time, anyway. I look back on it with a lot of pride because technically this was without doubt the best innings I ever played. I didn't know until recently that Allan Border – who refused me a drink during that innings – called it one of the best Test hundreds he'd ever seen. I'm not sure I could have hit the ball much better. I may have played better overall against the West Indies on one or two occasions, but they were different types of innings, more of a scrap for survival.

This was different because Australia gave me the opportunity to get forward and play those classical drives I'd been practising every day for about 15 years. They had very attacking fields as they were so much on top, so I got full value for my shots. I don't know why but, even though I had a slight hangover, I felt supremely confident about my batting that day from the moment I got to the ground. I played some scintillating front-foot drives and absolutely murdered a few square cuts. There were five fours in ten balls at one stage and overall my 101 came from 150 deliveries, which was a cracking rate in those days. I was a bit surprised at how comfortable I felt while wickets were tumbling at the other end and I can't remember playing and missing much, if at all, though I do remember being very thirsty.

I pulled one ball straight into the helmet of David Boon at short leg. He had to leave the field, and when Geoff Marsh came in to replace him he said, 'Ah, mate, please don't, I've got two kids!'[4]

I was playing so well, and feeling so sharp, that I took off my helmet and batted in a cap, even against the quick bowlers.

When I reached my hundred there was a voice in my head telling me, 'Don't throw it away.' I tried to consolidate, when I should have carried on attacking and playing on instinct, and I was out moments later playing a nothing shot outside off stump. I was furious and had my head in my hands in the dressing room. I'd been playing so well, and having so much fun, that the personal milestone of a hundred was absolutely no consolation. I'm not sure I was ever more annoyed with myself after a dismissal.

Trent Bridge quickly became my favourite ground. Sometimes you just have a good feeling about a place and I liked everything about playing in Nottingham. I liked the dressing rooms, the ambience, the pitches – and I loved the nightclubs!

It was also the venue for some of Lamby's more memorable pranks. One day at the close of play, I had a shower and walked out onto the balcony, in all my naked glory, to grab my towel. Lamby shut the door and locked me out, and I had to sit there covering myself and shivering in the rain, while thousands of people were funnelling out of the ground. During the same Test, when I was on the toilet, Lamby shoved a burning newspaper through an overhead window into my cubicle. It landed on my back, and I jumped up in shock while I was in the middle of … well, you probably don't need to know the rest.

Lamby was always up to something. At Lord's, he and I, along with Beefy, would discreetly throw grapes at the members to wake them up if they were having a post-prandial nap. We thought they should be watching the bloody cricket! They would wake up, coughing and

---

[4] Shaun, who went on to play Test cricket, and Melissa, who played basketball for Australia. Geoff's second son, Mitchell, was born in 1991.

spluttering and looking around, while we were laughing our heads off up above.

I scored my 101 on the Saturday afternoon of the Test. That night, with a rest day scheduled for the Sunday, Kath and I were invited for dinner at Beefy's. He was effectively out of the game, having broken a finger in the field. It was organised in advance, so on the Saturday evening Kath was waiting in the car to drive us up there. Beefy disappeared for a bit and then arrived with this huge coolbox on his shoulder. The Aussies were sponsored by XXXX that summer – quite appropriate given their vocabulary on the field – and Beefy had been in and helped himself.

It was about a two-and-a-half-hour drive from the ground to his place in North Yorkshire, and in that time I had maybe eight cans and Beefy put away a dozen. That might seem a lot now but that's the way that it was, that's what we did. I was very intense during a day's play, very focused, so I needed a release in the evening. It didn't affect my game so there was never really a problem.

We had a lovely dinner that night, with his 11-year-old son Liam waiting on us, and spent a great Sunday with the Botham family before travelling back in the afternoon. Beefy had a trout pond and was trying to grow the biggest trout fish in England, so he proudly showed them off while he was feeding them. The hospitality of Beefy and his wife Kath is phenomenal – they're such a kind couple, and great company. Beefy is one of the most loyal, generous and thoughtful people you could ever meet, and the work he has done in support of leukaemia research is inspirational.

I went on three of his walks – not the whole lot, just three or four days, which is enough. The first time I walked with Beefy, I thought I'd take in a few of the sights as we strolled through the beautiful villages. No chance! He really motors. After the first day I was so stiff, because I was exercising muscles I hadn't used before. And Beefy does this for 25 days, 25 miles a day. His willpower is phenomenal. At the end of each day, his feet are blistered and in an awful state. It helps that for the last hour and a half of each day, Kath will give him a lovely big water bottle filled with orange and tequila. That keeps the pain at bay.

I never once saw Beefy pissed, no matter how much he'd had to drink. He built up this monumental resilience to alcohol. We had a chat about it once and I asked him if he thought he could have taken 450 Test wickets and scored 6,500 runs if he'd had a few more early nights.

'I'll never know but I don't think so,' he said. 'What you see out in the middle is my character. I'm not a light switch – I can't be this brazen attacking player out in the middle and a meek and mild pussycat off the field. I need to go out and enjoy myself to keep up that energy, that positivity, that arrogance – because that's what I carry onto the field. What do you want me to do, go back to my hotel early and wake up at 5 a.m. worrying about the game?'

It was the same with Sir Garry Sobers, the West Indian who most people suggest is the greatest all-rounder ever to play the game. I spoke to the great Sir Everton Weekes and he said he'd often come into the West Indies dressing room to find Sir Garfield sleeping off a bottle of brandy. That was good for him. If that's not your style, fine, you don't do it. Other players lived a quiet life and were better for it – like Jack Russell, who would go back to his room and paint. Peter Bowler, who was captain of Somerset, used to study in the evenings and eventually became a solicitor. Elite sport takes all sorts. It needs all sorts.

Bloody hell, I wish I'd seen Sobers play. He sounds like an outstanding batsman. In the last year or so I've had dinner with Dennis Lillee and Ian Chappell and on each occasion I asked them who was the best batsman they ever saw. Not the best all-rounder, just the best batsman. They both said, without a second's thought, Sobers. The thing that set him apart, they said, was that when he was in the mood he could hit your best ball for four, never mind the bad ones.

A lot of players think too much about the game, they get too deep into it and then they can't get out. Beefy and Sir Garry didn't do that. They knew how their minds and bodies operated. You shouldn't treat great players like everyone else.

Beefy and Lamby had a confidence and a healthy arrogance that seemed to lift me, and I fed off their bubbly, upbeat attitude. They were always so positive and full of energy. During a Test I'd usually go out for a few beers with Lamby and, when the conversation occasionally turned to cricket, he filled with me positive thoughts. If I was on my own in a hotel room, the negative, invasive thoughts would run riot.

I was a great worrier and I didn't want to spend time on my own. I only went to bed when I knew I could put my head on the pillow, be asleep within 30 seconds and get my eight hours. I hated, almost dreaded, going up to bed if I knew I wouldn't sleep straight away. My mind was so active that it was better to keep it occupied until I was ready to sleep. I'd rather have those extra couple of beers with the journalists or the players to make me sleep.

If I was waking up every day with a pounding hangover I wouldn't have done it, but I was lucky – or unlucky – that this never happened. I'd feel a bit grubby now and then but I never, ever suffered from major hangovers.

Sport has changed so much, and the players of today don't drink anywhere near as much as we did. That might be a very good thing. I do believe I played in the best era to be a cricketer, though – we didn't earn that much money compared to now but there were a lot of characters in the game, we had a lot of fun and I made many lifelong friends. I had a lovely balance between earning some good money and playing with legends who were allowed to express themselves on and off the field. It was a fantastic life and I loved every minute of it.

Back in 1989, we scrambled a draw in the last Ashes Test at the Oval. I got 11 in the first innings and was worried that a second low score would end the summer on a low note, so I really didn't want to bat again. I should have looked at it the other way, that 24 more runs would take me to 500 for the series. With the form I was in, I should have been itching to get out there, but I often had a tendency to focus on the worst-case scenario. We still almost lost, but I helped save the game with 77 not out to finish with 553 runs at an average of 65. I felt I'd won the respect of the Aussies, which is all any young cricketer wants. But we lost 4–0, so what did it all mean?

At least I felt secure in the team. That sense of belonging, which I desperately needed, was strengthened when the chairman of selectors Ted Dexter invited me to his home in St John's Wood. He told me I was one of the first names on the teamsheet and that I was a fabulous attacking player – but that he thought I could become even better by having more belief in myself. We sat down and watched some videos over a cup of tea and he gave me a few bits of advice. I can't remember specifically what he said – it was 30 years ago now – but I remember being really touched that he was so interested in and supportive of me.

Around that time, whenever I walked out to bat, I felt loved by the chairman of selectors, the coach and the captain. That was a really important phase in my career.

Ted could be a bit out there – when we lost the Ashes he blamed the juxtaposition of Venus – but at his core he's a true gentleman. He had such warmth and magnificent manners, such an amateur spirit. Between Test matches he'd dash off to Paris and come back on his motorbike. For a young, naïve bloke like me, meeting all these different characters was fascinating.

There were a few in the dressing room as well. Somebody I really liked touring with was Derek Pringle. I roomed with him when we went to India in November 1989 for the Nehru Cup, a kind of mini-World Cup.[5]

It was an otherworldly experience, a really powerful assault on the senses. I felt bombarded – by the noise, by colours I couldn't have imagined, by textures I didn't know existed. And the spices in the food were like nothing I'd tasted. I can vouch for the awesome rogan josh, chicken biryani, basmati rice, mango lassis, and the unbelievably accommodating hospitality and manners of the locals.

Pring was a walking encyclopedia of history and architecture. As a relatively uneducated South African who grew up isolated from the rest of the world, I found Mr Cambridge to be an inspiration. He made me realise there was so much more to India than food and cricket.

One afternoon I was lounging by the pool, about to enjoy a nice frosted glass of lager, when Pring wandered over.

---

[5] It was staged to celebrate the centenary of the birth of Jawaharlal Nehru, who was India's first prime minister when the country became independent in the 1940s.

'Judgie, what are you doing?'

'Ah, just taking it easy for the day.'

'Come on, Judgie, don't be like the rest of them! We're here in India, we've got to embrace the country. I'm taking you on a cultural tour.'

That become our routine – every time we had a day off, Pring would take me somewhere. One of the days he had me up at 6 a.m. and we went off to see the Taj Mahal. We got this rickety old taxi that took two hours to get us there. He'd read up about it and he was like a tour guide for me. Pring said we needed to stay there all day because he wanted to be there at sunset. At one point we were sitting watching a piper play his flute. He had a cane basket next to him, and a cobra popped its head up to say hello. I jumped a mile! 'Relax, Judgie,' Pring said, 'it's tame.' We also went to see the Red Fort in Delhi. 'It's not far,' Pring said. Not far?! It was an eight-hour round trip!

Another time he took me round the slums in Mumbai, which I found really hard, but I'm so glad he took me out of the five-star touring bubble to see the real India.

I know empathy is a good quality but too much of it can be damaging, and throughout my life I have found myself horribly, disproportionately affected by the plight of others.

When we were in Kolkata a few years later, on the 1992–93 tour, I had the opportunity to be introduced to Mother Teresa when Phil DeFreitas, Neil Fairbrother and I went to her convent.

She was a tiny little woman in her eighties yet she had such immense energy and it was so inspiring to see somebody who had devoted their life to helping others. She was the soul of empathy. It was a bit of an epiphany for me and made me realise how unimportant cricket was in the wider scheme of things.

On the same tour I dragged Mike Gatting around on a rickshaw in Kolkata. That wasn't such a bright idea.

I had a good time with the bat on my first tour of India in 1989–90. I was England's top-scorer in the Nehru Cup, and we got to the semi-finals before losing to the eventual winners Pakistan. The next trip was the toughest of all – the Caribbean, to face the all-conquering West Indies.

Goochie had replaced David Gower as captain and the selectors decided on another fresh start. David and Beefy were surprisingly left out, with a load of inexperienced players picked including Alec Stewart, Nasser Hussain, Devon Malcolm, Keith Medlycott and Ricky Ellcock. It meant that Goochie and Lamby, his vice-captain, were the only players with any kind of Test experience. All of a sudden, I was an important player. It also meant that, for the opposition, I was a target.

One thing was clear – it wasn't going to be a picnic.

Chapter 9

Pace like fire

At the start of *Fire in Babylon*, that brilliant documentary about West Indies cricket in the 1980s and 1990s, there is thrilling footage of some poor bloke getting a fearsome blast of chin music from Courtney Walsh and Ian Bishop in the Caribbean. You can hear the home crowd baying for blood as a beautiful bouncer roars past his face. 'That is a *quick* ball,' says Geoff Boycott, commentating on TV, with relish. 'Oh yes, that is a fine, aggressive, nasty delivery.'

The second ball is the same, coming within a whisker of the batsman's nose as he sways dramatically out of the way at the last second. 'This is pace like *fire*,' says the other commentator Tony Greig.

The next ball, from Walsh, is on a similar length. This time it follows the batsman as he tries to move out the way. At the last second he instinctively turns his head to the side and the ball slams into his face. 'Oh, he's hit him!' screams Greig. 'That may have broken his jaw!'

As you've probably worked out, the poor bloke getting worked over was me. It was during the Antigua Test of 1990, and it was one of the most exhilarating 15 minutes of my entire life.

It's often said that anyone who says they enjoy facing fast bowling – proper fast bowling – is a liar. I can say, hand on heart, the same heart that has been bruised by many a short ball down the years, that

I absolutely loved it. I'm an adrenalin junkie, and nothing has ever given me a hit as good as that.

That tour of the Caribbean in 1989–90 gave me a reputation as somebody who relished facing the quick stuff. Dad even has a cutting from *Cricnet* magazine which listed me as the No.1 player of fast bowling in England's history. Mind you, I'm aware there's probably another magazine article that has me very high on the list of England's worst players of spin!

I wasn't one of the all-time greats, but if people remember me as a good player of raw pace bowling then I'm chuffed with that because it's something I worked so hard on. I'm very happy if I'm remembered as somebody who stood up against the best and nastiest bowlers around, and who was never intimidated. I still think I got off quite lightly, because West Indies were not at their peak when I played against them, but it was still pretty hot in the kitchen.

Despite that heat, I never wore a grille on my helmet. When I started my career there were no grilles, just basic helmets, and I became used to wearing those, though I added side pieces to protect my temple and earlobe. When I tried wearing a grille I felt claustrophobic and maybe a bit complacent as well because of the extra facial protection. Having no grille meant there was an added sense of danger, which added to the appeal – but not necessarily because I was trying to be macho. I loved the challenge, the enormous adrenalin rush, the test of my technique, reflexes and courage. Seriously, the quicker the better. I genuinely believed that if you watched the ball, you wouldn't get hit, and I never wore a grille because I fancied my reflexes against any pace. I was very conscious I was playing with fire, not to mention my jaw, cheekbone and eye socket, but honestly, it was the most spectacular experience.

I batted long periods on that West Indies tour and had an amazing time on and off the field. The Caribbean was always my favourite place to tour. I worked hard in the middle and took my punishment. At the close of play I'd run from the ground to the hotel, grab a rum and dry ginger and sit under a palm tree on the beach with Lamby or whoever as the alcohol gently relaxed my body and took the edge off the bruises.

Before the West Indies tour I did a bit of technical work with Geoff Boycott, who called and asked if I wanted to travel to Headingley for a few net sessions. It was a great opportunity to work with him and pick his brain, even if it meant a ten-hour round trip each time I went to see him. It wasn't practical to drive because of the rush-hour traffic, so I'd park my car at Southampton train station and head into London Waterloo. Then I took the underground to King's Cross and a train up north. Not the easiest journey with an oversized cricket coffin! He got some young Yorkshire bowlers – including Paul Jarvis, who was rapid and had already played a few Tests for England – to bowl at my head from 18 yards. Paul actually apologised at one point. He was worried about hitting me but he said Boycs had given him firm instructions to bowl everything as fast as he could at my head.

I suggested to Boycs that it wasn't an entirely fair contest, being peppered indoors under artificial light and on a shortened pitch. 'Well, you can pack your things and go home,' he said. 'Because this is the sort of treatment you'll be getting for the next three months.'

I spoke to Boycs a lot during my career. It's such a shame he wasn't asked to be an official batting consultant with England, because when he stops talking about his own achievements he's an absolute wizard at analysing the game. And he was totally honest. I didn't always agree with the things he said on air or to my face, but I always respected his opinion.

I'd tried to pick his brain a bit earlier in my career. We played Yorkshire in 1985 on a dodgy wicket at Middlesbrough, and Malcolm Marshall was charging in. Boycs, who was 44 years old, got 110. They had a great big bath tub where both teams piled in at the end of the day's play. Boycs was in there on his own at one point so I thought it was a great chance to learn from a legend. I asked if I could jump in and he grunted something, which I assumed to be yes. He sat on one side of the bath, I sat on the other and we didn't say a word to each other. Great chat, Boycs!

I'm ashamed to say he got me out once – *c Illingworth b Boycott* – in a match at Southampton in 1983. They had a combined age of 94, which was almost five times my own at the time. Oh, Judgie!

England were given absolutely no chance in the West Indies, and most thought we'd do well to lose 5–0. You can understand why people felt that way. The West Indies only lost one Test in the Caribbean throughout the 1980s and we'd only won one Test in three years.

Graham Gooch was captain of a really young side – with eight caps, I was the fourth-most experienced player for the first Test at Sabina Park. When Gordon and Desmond Haynes added 62 for the first wicket, it was business as usual. I still can't quite get my head round what happened next. Devon Malcolm ran out Gordon and they collapsed to 164 all out. We had an all-pace attack – Dev, Gladstone Small, Gus Fraser and David Capel – and they bowled beautifully. Gus, who was emerging as a captain's dream, ended with five for 28 from 20 overs.

We had to battle hard that night, and the next morning I came in to join Lamby with the score on 116–3. We batted for nearly four hours and added 172, with Lamby hammering a spectacular hundred. We did so well in that partnership that at one stage they resorted to bowling their part-time spinners, Carl Hooper, Sir Viv Richards and Carlisle Best. We agreed that we'd milk them professionally for three or four singles per over so that Viv kept them on, and did that perfectly for half an hour. Then – bang, bang, bang! – Lamby blasted three fours in one over. At the end of the over I walked up to him.

'Lamby, what are you doing? What happened to professionally milking them?'

'Ah, Judge, man, I couldn't help myself!'

Lamby didn't mind them bringing the quicks back anyway as he was such a brilliant player of fast bowling. He wasn't that tall so he had a low centre of gravity; he picked up length brilliantly and was straight onto anything short. He cut and pulled very well, and his height meant he could avoid the bouncer more easily. Another thing about Lamby is that he was an absolutely exquisite timer of the ball, especially for someone with such limited feet movement. He was also physically and mentally tough, a real fighter who loved the battle and was a positive player in every sense. He always went out to score runs rather than bat time.

As a team, however, our plan was the opposite. Goochie and Micky Stewart decided that we should sell our wickets dearly and try to wear the West Indies down both with bat and ball. If you went toe-to-toe with them, there was only going to be one winner, so, with the exception of Lamby with the bat and Dev with the ball, we played a more attritional style of cricket.

I was an attacking player and, perhaps because of that, I took a lot of pride in playing my unnatural game and batting for long periods of time. It feels like that is a dying art. Look, I know I played some shit shots at times, and I understand the adrenalin surge you get when you hit boundaries – but even allowing for the modern culture of instant gratification, it does surprise me that there are so few people in world cricket with the ability to bat all day.

With Lamby bashing it everywhere I was happy to play a supporting role and give him the strike whenever I could. I made 57 from 161 balls, one of a handful of hard-fought innings in the Test series. In the fourth Test in Barbados, I scored 102 runs in the match from 396 balls, and overall I batted almost 17 hours in the series for only 186 runs. Geoffrey must have been proud of me! It was different to the Ashes, when I scored very quickly against Australia, but an average of 37 was decent. I ended up as second highest run scorer behind Lamby, who got more than twice as many runs as the rest of us.

My concentration wasn't always as good as it could have been – my brother was far better – so I tried to break my batting down into small, manageable sections. I aimed to bat short periods, usually half an hour, and not worry about the score. The way I played meant the scoreboard usually took care of itself if I stayed at the crease. As long as I was looking to score runs (Arrogance + Humility = Confidence), I didn't mind if I was stuck on the same score for an hour.

I tried to improve my concentration by constantly barking at myself between deliveries:

'Be strong, Judgie!'

'Get forward! Head straight, over the ball.'

'Stay confident, Judgie. This is your stage, you belong here.'

We took a first-innings lead of exactly 200 in Jamaica, and at the close on day three they were eight down and only 29 runs ahead.

It poured down on the rest day and then again on the scheduled day four, with no play possible. After two days of solid rain we were starting to panic, thinking we'd be denied, but thankfully it all worked out fine. The sun shone on the last day and we won by nine wickets. Wayne Larkins, who at the age of 36 was playing his first Test for nearly a decade, scored the winning runs. Two weeks earlier, Buster Douglas had beaten Mike Tyson in one of boxing's greatest shocks. This was the cricket equivalent, and without doubt the best England win of my career. I'd be surprised if there has been a more unexpected victory in English cricket history.

The second Test in Guyana was washed out without a ball bowled. There was an old-fashioned structure to the tour, with one-day internationals dotted in between the Tests. We had a tour match before the third Test against a really strong President's XI. An unknown 20-year-old called Brian Lara laced 134 and we were in trouble in the second innings. I fought so hard to reach 99, and had eked out some priceless runs with our No. 11, Devon Malcolm, at the other end. He had four balls from Patrick Patterson to survive before I could get my hundred. He played the first two perfectly. 'Beautiful, Devvy!' I shouted. 'Absolutely beautiful!' Then a switch went off in his head. He had a huge heave at the third and his middle stump went a mile. He walked off, shaking his head. 'Judgie man, I'm so sorry.'

I said, 'Dev, that's a first-class hundred gone!'

Everyone expected a murderous backlash from the West Indies in Trinidad for the third Test. In fact, we should have won that match too. We had them 29–5 on the first morning and, though they fought back, we were always ahead in the game. After another volcanic spell from Devvy, who took out three top-order batsmen in one over, we needed 151 on the last day to go 2–0 up in the West Indies with two to play. It felt too good to be true.

And it was. It rained heavily for part of the day, Graham Gooch had his hand broken by Ezra Moseley, which put him out of the rest of the tour, and the West Indies time-wasted shamelessly. At one stage they took nearly half an hour to bowl two overs. Look, we'd probably have tried something similar – if not quite as extreme – but the umpires should still have been stronger. We ran out of time, or rather, of light. In the end, David Capel and Jack Russell couldn't see a thing and we had to call off the chase at 120–5, 31 runs short.

With Goochie out of the tour, Lamby was captain for the last two Tests. The next game was in Barbados, but before that we had a tour game in the same place. Malcolm was playing and on the first night of the match we had dinner together. He told me he'd get me out the next day, LBW playing no shot. I laughed and asked him how he intended to do this. 'Simple, Judgie,' he said. 'Two awayswingers and an inswinger should do the job.'

When I came out to bat the next day he was bowling and had a smile on his face. 'Judgie, don't forget our conversation last night.' I got a single at the other end and then took my usual middle and leg guard to face his first ball, a lovely awayswinger at good pace. At the end of his follow-through he said, 'Judgie, that's the first one.' The second ball was the same; I came forward and offered no shot.

He smiled again and said, 'This is it.' He changed the field and placed mid-on at second gully. I thought it had to be another away-swinger with a field like that. He ran in and bowled one well wide of off stump. I moved forward to leave the ball, as I didn't want to get caught behind playing at a wide one, and then it started to swing back towards me. It was far too late to do anything about it. Macko was appealing almost before the ball thudded into my pad.

Smith LBW b Marshall 1

He never let me forget that moment.

We knew a win in the fourth Test would give us a series victory and possibly the greatest achievement in English cricket history. That's how close we were. But the West Indies were on top from the start and we were fighting to save the game. I had another big partner-ship with Lamby in the first innings, when he made another great hundred. I made 62 from 246 balls, a battling and slightly strange innings. I was dropped four times yet I never really felt like I was struggling as I hardly played and missed at all. It just happened that almost every false stroke was an edge. On another day you might play and miss ten times and not edge one of them.

We eventually started the last day three wickets down, needing to bat all day for a draw. Jack Russell, who'd gone in as nightwatchman, fought like a demon and I joined him at 97–5. We batted throughout the afternoon session, willing each other on after every over. I put almost all my attacking shots away as runs were not important. Generally I was better when I played positively but this was an obvious exception.

They took the new ball almost an hour after tea, and then Sir Curtly Ambrose produced the first of his many match-winning spells. He bowled Jack with a shooter and ran through the lower order to finish with eight for 45. We lost Nasser Hussain, David Capel and Phil DeFreitas in less than half an hour, all LBW to Ambrose, which meant it was just me and Devvy trying to save the game. I did everything I could to farm the strike, encourage him and see us through to a draw. We batted together for 29 minutes and then Ambrose finished us off with another LBW. Dev was out and I was left on 40 not out from 150 balls. I'd batted almost ten hours in the match, been dismissed once, but it counted for nothing.

The scorecard says West Indies won by 164 runs but it was so much closer than that. The sun was setting and there were shadows across the wicket. It was just starting to get dark, and the umpires were looking at each other. Another over and I think we would have been off. Devvy, bless him, he did his best. Maybe we should have tried to waste time by calling for a new pair of gloves, stuff like that. To be honest, the thought didn't really come into my head.

It was the most phenomenal bit of bowling from Ambrose. I don't remember us scoring a run in front of square off him all day. He found this incredible rhythm and landed everything just back of a length; it felt like every ball was thudding off the glove or the top of the bat and going down to third man. He was the most accurate bowler I faced, which along with his steepling bounce made him so hard to score off. He was just relentless.

We were shattered physically and mentally, yet had only a one-day break before the series decider in Antigua. The Barbados Test finished late on the 10th of April and we were batting again in Antigua on the morning of the 12th. I was the only person to play in every game on the tour and I was running on empty. The whole team was, to be honest, and we were beaten by an innings inside three and a half days.

We started the game well enough, actually, and I came to the crease on the first afternoon with England on 143–3. For some reason, perhaps because they were sick of me hanging around in Barbados, the West Indies decided to launch a serious assault on me. I suppose they knew, with Goochie injured, that the key partnership was Lamby and me. If they could break that, or break one of us, they would win the series.

Twelve of the first 13 balls I received were at my head, all bowled with extreme intent. Walsh's penultimate ball before tea hit the seam and jagged back, and as I tried to get out the way I realised it was following me. At the last moment I instinctively turned my head and it smacked me in the face. My jaw wasn't broken but it started swelling immediately.

I read once in a book about fast bowling[1] that you have 0.44 seconds' reaction time against the really quick stuff. I suspect that, because of the exhaustion of a long tour, my reactions were fractionally slower than usual and that's why I was hit.

I was a little bit dazed. Desmond Haynes beckoned straight away for the physio, and Viv came up and put his arm round me. 'Judgie, man, you'll have to go off, it's swollen.'

Lamby, our captain, was a yard away.

'Hey, Viv, he's not going anywhere! I'm the captain of this ship and he's staying out here with me. We've lost enough players already. Judgie, put your helmet on and let's get going, china!'

Yeah, thanks, Lamby!

I was never going to retire hurt. No chance. I wasn't going to give Courtney Walsh or any other bowler the pleasure of seeing me walk off unless there was absolutely no alternative.

I also knew that showing toughness was how you earned the respect of these great cricketers. Viv used to give me a lot of support out in the middle when we played against the West Indies. Between overs, he'd nudge me on the shoulder and say, 'Keep going, Judgie, you're playing well.' He was my hero and always will be, so it was a serious thrill to become friends with him. I loved playing against the

---

[1] *Letting Rip: The Fast Bowling Threat from Lillee to Waqar* by Simon Wilde.

West Indies because they had the perfect balance between playing tough and playing fairly. I think they liked players who showed a bit of fight, and Viv adored Lamby. It's strange – we're two blokes who were born in South Africa, but apart from Beefy I think we were his best mates in the England team.

When play resumed in Antigua after I'd been treated, there was time for one more ball, another short one from Courtney. I avoided that, and walked off 0 not out from 13 balls, and with a jaw like a golf ball. The exhilaration was like nothing I'd experienced.

Mom was in the stadium, and when I was hit in the face she burst into tears and left her seat to walk around the ground. She bumped into Gladstone Small, who held her hand and walked with her for a bit. They always had a special bond after that because he was there for her when she needed a bit of reassurance that her little boy would be okay.

She should have known I'd be fine – because I got my toughness from her and from Dad. Mom used to refuse an anaesthetic before operations; that's how tough she is. Once, she was driving through a dangerous neighbourhood in Durban when she was shot at. The bullet missed her head by a foot, but she was fine and when she got home she cheerfully posed for photographs by the car with a bullet hole in the rear window.

I've never been frightened of pain. Sometimes it doesn't register in my brain, and if it does, I find I can usually ignore it. To me, pain is what my former Natal teammate Rob Bentley experienced. He was in the Rhodesian Bush War when he was a teenager. His squadron were ambushed and most of them were shot and killed. Rob's only hope of survival was to play dead by lying face down in the mud. But the people they were fighting checked everyone was dead by plunging bayonets into the backs of their thighs. Had Rob flinched even one little bit as the bayonet burst through his skin, he would have been shot dead. *That's* pain. *That's* courage.

I was quite lucky that I wasn't hit very often in my career. Simon 'Yozzer' Hughes pinned me on the sidepiece of my helmet with a bouncer, which skidded off the wicket, at Uxbridge early in my career. That shook me up a bit, I suppose, because it was the first time it had happened. Apart from that, I think I was hit on the head or in the face only three or four times. Funnily enough, one of the few times I was really hurt was against a slow bowler, I forget who it was, when I top-edged a sweep into my face and needed a load of stitches in my eyebrow.

I always thought being hit on the body by a cricket ball was fine. A bee sting on the arm or the inside of my thigh would wake me up, and so long as I didn't break anything that would cause me to miss the rest of the game, I had no problem. You see people with major injuries and you complain about having three or four bruises on your ribs. For me, that doesn't cut it.

If I was in the right zone of concentration – and nothing focused the mind quite like serious pace – I would be willing the bowler to bowl faster. I was swept up by the adrenalin rush and felt like a boxer dancing round the ring, desperate to be tested. *Come on, fucking give it to me! Hit me all you like. Hit me harder! I don't feel pain, so give me your best. You won't break me. Come on, what are you waiting for?*

Sometimes, especially with someone who sledged a lot like Waqar Younis, I told them so. 'Come on, Waqar, is that all you've fucking got?' Those battles with a fast bowler were the ultimate for me.

In Antigua, Courtney came to see me at tea and ask if I was okay. The West Indies were much friendlier than the Aussies – it was nothing personal, just business. They were pretty much all delightful blokes but they could be really nasty on the pitch and that was fine with me. It was their job to intimidate batsmen.

Having come to see how I was doing, Courtney then broke my hand straight after tea. I bloody wish I'd made a hundred that day, with a fractured hand and a busted face, but I was out for 12. In the second innings I tried to bat with a bad hand but reluctantly retired hurt after an hour because I could hardly grip the bat. When you can't grip the bat it's different, especially if it's your bottom hand because you need that to play the cut and the pull. And you need those shots because, as the West Indian bowlers told me on many occasions, 'Judgie, if you want a drive, go and hire a Mini Moke down the road.'

The match was effectively lost and the county season had already started, so I knew if I batted on I was in danger of doing a lot of damage and missing maybe a month of the county summer. I hated retiring hurt and the only time I ever did so was for practical reasons or, as at Old Trafford in 1995, if I was away with the fairies and the physio took me off for my own protection.

I do think you need more than just blind courage to face the quickest bowling. I was a strong square-cutter and good on the pull, though I didn't use that shot so much and I hardly ever hooked because I didn't think the potential reward justified the risk of being hit or caught. I was a good judge of length, better than I was of line, though I don't know why. I was quite supple and I think I had good reflexes, particularly when it came to snapping my head out of the way at the last second so that I'd end up looking like a limbo dancer. I regularly practised avoiding the short ball and also did a lot of skipping, which made me lighter on my feet. You look at boxers, who are huge blokes but very nimble around the ring, and I wanted to be like that.

Okay, I know what you're thinking. Who was the fastest?

I remember a spell by Patrick Patterson on a quick, bouncy wicket at Old Trafford in 1986. He was the most feared fast bowler in the world at the time and had just butchered England in the Caribbean. Graham Gooch said that facing Patterson on a corrugated pitch in Jamaica was the one time in his career that he feared for his safety.

He bowled like fire at me and Sir Gordon Greenidge. I battled for ages to make 21, mainly at his end, before he got me out. Kippy came in next and faced about two balls from Patterson before they put on the medium-pacer Steve O'Shaughnessy. Kippy mauled him and got 70-odd. The next day the paper said R A Smith 21, C L Smith 70, and everyone praised Kippy for taking on Patterson!

Allan Donald was seriously fast, especially in Johannesburg, where he was helped by the altitude and bounce. Waqar was *quick*. He hated me, so whenever I came into bat he always bowled viciously. Courtney Walsh's angle from wide of the crease made him really awkward, especially when he upped his pace like he did that day in Antigua. He bowled a brutal spell to Mike Atherton in Jamaica in 1994 as well.

Courtney bowled slightly within himself, which is one of the reasons he was able to bowl those incredibly long spells, but every now and then he really cranked it up. When he did, things got very serious.

One name that might surprise you is Ezra Moseley, who played a couple of Tests for the West Indies when we toured there in 1989–90, and broke Graham Gooch's hand. He wasn't a great bowler overall, but he had one of the qualities of a great bowler, which is that he could generate pace off the pitch. Very few bowlers can do that. Sir Richard Hadlee was another. When Moseley got it right the ball really zipped off the pitch and he was as quick as anyone. Type 'Ezra Moseley Jimmy Cook' into YouTube and you'll see what I mean.

But the best fast bowler I faced, and the one who was consistently quickest, was Ian Bishop. The others could be awkward but he was *fast*. He had a magnificent, classical action, which allowed him to swing the ball away from the right-hander. His action also meant his bouncer was really hard to pick up. We didn't have speedguns back then, so speed was in the eye of the beholder. Some bowlers seemed slightly faster or slower because of the way you lined them up. You learned to pick up cues from certain fast bowlers, in the same way you try to read a spinner.

Here's an example. With some bowlers, like Waqar Younis and Garth Le Roux, you knew the short ball was coming because they would really put their shoulder into it, but with Bishop there were no tells, no apparent increase in effort. But I bet there were other batsmen who knew when Bishop's bouncer was coming and had no idea with Waqar. We all read body language in different ways.

I thought Bishop was a sensational bowler, and but for his back problems he would be recognised as one of the all-time greats.

I doubt you'll be surprised to hear the two most skilful fast bowlers I faced were Malcolm Marshall and Wasim Akram. Malcolm swung the ball both ways, intimidated you with the short ball and probed your weaknesses. And Wasim was just magnificent. He and Waqar didn't get me out much and I'm proud of my record against them. It's strange that I often felt more comfortable against great fast bowlers like Donald or Waqar than some of the dibbly-dobblies in county cricket. There was a guy called Martin Weston at Worcestershire, a typical county medium pacer, who had me on toast in the summer of 1988. Thankfully I managed to see him off in that B&H quarter-final, when my 87 not out pushed me to the brink of England selection.

The bouncers I often found more difficult were from shorter blokes. Malcolm, Darren Gough and the New Zealander Danny Morrison when he bowled quickly. There were a couple of others, Terry Alderman and Paddy Clift, who bowled around 80mph and swung it away from the right-hander. Then, all of a sudden, a much quicker bouncer came along and took you by surprise. I thought they chucked their bouncer, as I couldn't understand how they were able to go up 10mph whenever they bowled it.

There were a few wildcards, too. One young Zimbabwean called James Carse, who played for Eastern Province and later Northamptonshire, was seriously fast. And there was a Dutch guy called Andre van Troost who was at Somerset in the early 1990s. With bowlers like Ambrose and Glenn McGrath, they are so good that at least you know what's coming next. Van Troost was the opposite. The bloke was *lightning*, but he didn't have a bloody clue where the ball was going, so as a batsman you had even less idea.

If Bish was consistently the quickest bowler I faced, there's no doubt who was the most sinister. Sylvester Clarke. I reckon 90 per cent of people who played county cricket in the 1980s would say the same. I know Steve Waugh regards him as the most intimidating bowler he ever faced. I tried everything I could to humanise him when he played against Hampshire for Surrey. I always offered him a whisky or a double rum and Coke at the end of a day's play to be friendly, thinking he'd go a bit easy on me the next day. Did he heck!

I should have gone the whole hog, like Beefy. One year, during a Somerset versus Surrey match, when Somerset knew they would be batting in their second innings the following day, he took one for the team by setting up a drinking contest with Sylvester. It ended in the early hours with Sylvester passing out on a pool table. Beefy did a job on him and the scorecard shows that ST Clarke did not bowl in Somerset's second innings. Apparently, he spent the whole day asleep in the dressing room and nobody dared wake him up.

Sylvester wasn't exactly a classical fast bowler. He often wore plim-solls rather than spikes and he didn't have much of a run-up, maybe 10 or 15 yards, but suddenly the ball would start to rear at you from a length. It was always angling in from wide on the crease, which made it even more awkward, and it would really thud into your body. The number of times he hit people in the ribs was amazing. He was a breathtaking fast bowler, all right.

I did eventually see a softer side to Sylvester, but that was long after he had retired. On the field he was a nasty piece of work, as mean as anyone I've ever known. He didn't bother with sledging, he just looked at you with an expression that suggested he wouldn't lose a millisecond of sleep if he rearranged your face. He wanted to hit you and hurt you, and if he got you out it was a bonus. It could be pretty unsettling. And, hand on heart, I loved every minute of it.

Chapter 10
Sinning and confession

I'D LIKE TO THINK I'm a good person, but I know for sure I've done bad things. I vowed to tell my story warts and all, so here goes. One of the things that shames me most, and which gnaws at my conscience pretty much every day, is my infidelity. It was totally out of order and I so wish I could change it.

I don't believe in excuses, only explanations. I've tried to analyse my behaviour, good and bad, while writing this book, and on reflection I believe my infidelity stemmed from my adrenalin addiction. I'm not being flippant when I say it felt similar to facing the West Indies fast bowlers. I loved the challenge of trying to chat somebody up and I suspect on some level I was stimulated by the fact it was illicit. With one lady in the Caribbean, for example, I knew her husband was in the marines and she told me that, if we were caught, we would both be dead. A sensible person would find that a turn-off.

The lifestyle of a professional cricketer was conducive to infidelity. That's not an excuse, just an observation. The temptation often came when I wasn't looking for it, and I wasn't strong enough to resist. 'It's hysterical,' Kath said once. 'You put the players in whites and it's an instant aphrodisiac.' That was the start of the problem. From early on in my professional cricket career, sex was easily available, and that didn't change when I settled down with Kath.

Kath has since said that I committed myself and settled down too early, and I agree with her. I was 20 when we started going out and it got serious very quickly, but I realise now that I hadn't got the bachelor lifestyle out of my system. I should have been stronger and said it was too soon to settle down, but then I've always been someone who is happy for people to make decisions on my behalf. I was used to having my life mapped out by others, and I've always tried to live up to external expectations of me. Kath was older, stronger, more decisive and the one who initiated everything: moving in, getting engaged, getting married, having children. On the other hand, I was very happy for the relationship to snowball.

I remember one winter when she came over to Perth in the mid-1980s. There were times when I realised the enormity of what I was promising her, emotionally, and felt like I needed my own space for a bit. Had we been in England, I might have said, 'Look, let's take a break for a couple of weeks and see how it goes.' But because we were 7,000 miles away, I didn't do that. Had I done that, maybe both our lives would have turned out very differently. She might have gone home, met somebody else and still be with him today. It's not easy being married to a professional sportsman – especially a cricketer – as they spend so much time travelling.

When I had one-night stands or affairs, a big part of me was searching for a chemistry and an intimacy that wasn't there in my marriage. Don't get me wrong, I was very happy most of the time and Kath was a good wife. We got on very well and I loved her company. She was never demanding, she didn't spend hundreds of pounds on designer clothes or things like that. And though I knew something was missing, I thought it might evolve as the relationship became more serious. I was trying to do the right thing by staying with Kath. I didn't realise this at the time, but I see now that I was doing things backwards: I got married and had children in the hope they would make me fall in love. At the time, in my early twenties, I had no idea what being in love really meant.

It was easy for me, especially as somebody who avoids confrontation and likes to go with the flow, to drift along in the hope things would work out fine. I didn't address the problem and that's been an issue throughout my life. I've been too soft. I look at life through rose-tinted glasses, thinking that things will miraculously change. I learned too late that, if nothing changes, then nothing will ever change.

I think Kath knew about my infidelity, if not, at that stage, the scale of it. I became a seasoned liar, something that bothers me greatly to this day. I was ducking and diving as I built a web of deception, addicted both to the quick fix of casual sex and the danger to my marriage that went with it. I wasn't playing a laddish game or looking for an ego massage. The reason I was doing it was because something had broken down in my marriage.

If Hampshire were playing away from home, we might have a couple of beers in the dressing room with the opposition and then a few of us would go to a wine bar. When we were there, the alpha male came out. I was a natural flirt, so there was often a very thin line between me chatting to someone and trying to chat them up. I have always enjoyed female company, and after being surrounded by blokes all day I liked to get a different perspective on the world. The problem was that I often struggled to leave it at that.

Once I got over the psychological hurdle of the first extra-marital fling, they became a regular occurrence. One indiscretion was effectively the same as a hundred. That's how I justified it. The fact it was always alcohol-induced also helped me rationalise it. Robin Smith knew what he was doing was wrong and was racked with guilt, but the Judge didn't give a toss.

I can't stress enough that none of this is an excuse. I take full responsibility for my behaviour, but I also want to understand and try to explain it.

I really did make some shocking adulterous decisions. On one occasion I had two mistresses at the same time, both assuming I was being exclusively unfaithful with them. I determined that if they were happy to sleep with me knowing I was married, it wasn't such a huge misdemeanour to cheat on them as well.

In 1992, Hampshire were playing away from home one weekend. The team went out on the Saturday night and I met a lady, went back to her place and stayed the night. I left in the early hours so that I could go back to the hotel and have a few hours' sleep before our Sunday League game. I was woken by a phone call from the woman; I had one of those early mobile phones and must have given her my number.

'I didn't really appreciate you getting up and leaving while I was asleep. You will see me tonight, won't you.'

An alarm went off in my head. I tried to placate her. 'Of course I'll see you tonight. What do you think it was, a one-night stand?'

I didn't want her to feel aggrieved or used, so decided to see her again – one more night to smooth things over before I left. We were going back to Hampshire the next morning so I took her out for dinner.

When I got home, however, she kept hounding me.

I said, 'I told you I was married. Please, this has to stop.'

'No. I'll decide when this stops.'

Her tone was so cold, and I knew straight away I was in trouble. At first she threatened to tell Kath. Every time I tried to finish it, she would say, 'You'll continue seeing me until I have met somebody else and want to move on.'

She later said that if I stopped seeing her she'd go to the newspapers. She had a tabloid lined up – she'd told them it was a current England cricketer, without naming me, and said they were willing to pay her £30,000 for the story. The thought of what it would do to my family terrified me. I was also selfishly worried that it would impact on my England career. I was caught in the web of a black widow spider, and those creatures always kill their mate. I was petrified of her. I had no choice but to see her whenever I was anywhere near that part of the country, which was every three weeks or so.

This went on for almost three years. She even demanded that I call her on Christmas Day. I said, 'I'll be with my family, how am I going to do that?'

'You'll find a way.'

So, one Christmas morning, while Kath was opening presents with our young son Harrison, I had to discreetly pour a litre of milk down the sink and make a big song and dance about someone drinking all the milk. It was desperate. There was a BP garage always open so I said

I'd drive there and get some milk. While I was out, I was able to fulfil my miserable obligation.

When England toured the West Indies in 1993–94, she made me fly her out to Jamaica. I can still remember Graeme Hick and me spending an age looking for her ring when she dropped it in the pool. You probably think I deserve everything I got for being serially unfaithful, and I wouldn't argue with that, but it was such a stressful experience.

Eventually I thought, 'Bugger this, this can't go on.' I bought a Dictaphone and recorded some conversations on speaker in the car. I spoke to a friend in the Hampshire constabulary, who said they couldn't do anything unless there was evidence of blackmail. He suggested they tap my home phone and get her to call there, but I couldn't do that because Kath would find out. He put me in touch with the Home Office, who said the same – to tap the phone at home, as the Dictaphone tapes were not strong enough evidence.

In the winter of 1994–95 I was left out of the England squad to tour Australia. I figured if I couldn't play for England, watching them would be the next best thing. I set up Judge Tours, a little travel business that specialised in taking small groups of cricket-lovers abroad to experience international cricket in different countries.

During the last Test at Perth I was staying at the Burswood Casino Hotel with Rod Bransgrove, a pharmaceutical entrepreneur who I met through Paul Terry and who would later become Hampshire chairman. One night we came home after a good night out and the phone rang in the early hours. Rod picked it up, looked very serious and handed the phone to me.

It was Kath. She'd gone to pick up my post at Hampshire and found a letter from this woman. Kath said, 'If you want to save your marriage and see your children grow up, you'll get on the next flight back to England and come and explain yourself.'

There was nothing I could do until the morning. The next few hours were absolutely awful – I could barely lie still, never mind get to sleep. I sorted the first possible flight home: Perth to Harare, Harare to Johannesburg, Johannesburg to London, then a taxi from

London to Hampshire. The journey took 33 hours, during which my mind ran wild with worst-case scenarios.

I spoke to Kath to give her my flight details. She told me she was so upset that she had to call a friend to come round and console her. This led to another major problem, as I was having an affair with her too.

Not such a nice guy now, am I?

I was beside myself when I got to the airport. I bumped into Dennis Lillee and his lovely wife Helen, who could see I was in a state. I told them what had just happened and they said, 'Come and join us in the executive lounge.' Dennis wasn't surprised – he knew what professional cricket was like – but he and Helen were lovely. They didn't take sides, they just listened and comforted me. She said, 'Look, if you explain everything to Kath, I'm sure it'll be fine. She'll give you a second chance.'

And a third, and a fourth. I'm not proud of any of this.

I was so nervous because I thought Kath was going to chuck me out, and I knew I deserved whatever was coming my way. When I got home, I told Kath the full story. She didn't believe that I'd been blackmailed, so I played her the cassette that I'd kept from the recording in my car. I kept it in my locker at Hampshire because I thought, 'One day I might need this.' When I played that she softened slightly. It was a huge relief once Kath knew, so I could call the woman – in front of Kath – and say that I no longer wanted to see her. That was the end of that, and I never really heard from her again. Nothing happened with her selling the story to the papers, so maybe it was an idle threat, who knows.

You would think I'd have learned my lesson from such a horrible experience, but I didn't and I continued my covert infidelity.

It's easy to say with hindsight that Kath and I should have split up. But there was never one moment in the relationship when it was now or never. You go with the flow and, before you know it, 15 years have passed and you're married with two children.

Most of the time, we were happy. We didn't argue, there was no physical abuse or shouting and screaming. And we had two beautiful children who we wanted to bring up in a stable, loving environment with their mother and father present. We decided to stay together for the children. It was very selfish of me to have had affairs so I'm not going to pat myself on the back.

I became very good at rationalising or justifying my behaviour in self-serving ways. For example, if I made it clear I was never going to leave Kath, or I never hid my wedding ring, then on some level I felt like it reduced the severity of my cheating. It's complete rubbish – cheating is cheating and I was totally out of line – but those were the tricks I sometimes played on myself.

I'm a psychological contradiction. My mother is religious to the core. My most ardent beliefs, my compassion, patience, loyalty and empathy for others have been passed down from her. So how did I become such a sinful idiot?

Chapter 11
Down Under

I'VE NEVER HAD MUCH confidence in myself, and probably never will. Despite my interest in the power of the mind, and the success of certain techniques like visualisation, self-belief has often been frustratingly elusive both in cricket and the world beyond.

Let me give you an example. At the start of the 1990–91 Ashes tour I was talked up as one of England's bankers. I averaged 54 in Test cricket, I played well on hard, bouncy wickets and I'd scored lots of runs against Australia in 1989. But I had a shocker. My confidence evaporated when I went cheaply in the first innings of the first Test at Brisbane and things got so bad that I almost had to learn how to bat again. It was the first real crisis of my career and I didn't know what to do.

It all came as a bit of a shock, especially as I'd had a very good summer in 1990, when I scored ten hundreds for England and Hampshire. We'd arrived back in the country on 19 April after the West Indies tour, mentally and physically shattered. Within a week, most of the squad was playing in the first County Championship match. I missed that but returned for the first Sunday League game, just over two weeks after Courtney Walsh broke my hand.

There was a lovely moment for the Smith family at the start of the summer when I was named one of *Wisden*'s Five Cricketers of the Year. Kippy received the award in 1984 so we became only the ninth brothers, and the first since the Chappells in the mid-1970s, to both be on that prestigious list.[1] We'd come a long way from all those sessions in the back garden in Durban.

It was a good summer for England. We built on the promise of the West Indies tour and won both Test series, beating New Zealand and India 1–0. They were our first series wins anywhere since the 1986–87 Ashes, and two of only four series wins in my England career. But please don't think I'm telling you a hard luck story – we had two 2–2 draws with West Indies which felt like triumphs, especially in 1991. Those were England's best results during my Test career.

At Hampshire, 1990 was a season of near misses. We finished third in the Championship and lost to Northants by one run in the semis of the NatWest Trophy, despite cruising at one point. Our squad was strengthened by the signing from Leicestershire of David Gower, who said one of the reasons for moving was to bat alongside me and therefore avoid fielding at square cover when I was batting! The other reason he gave, and I reckon this was a much greater motivation, was that he would no longer have to face Malcolm Marshall in county cricket. I know he needed a change in his life anyway, as he had split up from his long-term girlfriend and wanted a new challenge in his career, but, as someone who grew up watching him, it was so nice to hear him say that.

Even though I was becoming an established England player, I was still star struck if I received praise from my idols. The biggest of all, Sir Viv Richards, said some nice things when I hammered 153 in the Championship against his Glamorgan side in June – and then he trumped me with an awesome 164 not out to win the game in the fourth innings. What a legend.

That match was typical of the 1990 season, when thousands and thousands of runs were scored. The size of the seam on the balls was

---

[1] The brothers were: Harry and Albert Trott, 'Tip' and Henry Foster, John and George Gunn, Johnny and Ernest Tyldesley, James and John Langridge, Graeme and Peter Pollock, Mushtaq and Hanif Mohammad, Greg and Ian Chappell, and Kippy and me. Steve and Mark Waugh joined the list in 1991.

reduced – that, along with a very dry summer and the beginning of four-day cricket meant batsmen had the chance to book in for bed and breakfast. Graham Gooch had a Bradmanesque summer both with Essex and England. He started the Test summer with a golden duck, then scored over 1,000 runs in the last five matches. The New Zealand series was the one time I played against Sir Richard Hadlee in international cricket. He was nearly 40 but still a master craftsman, who landed it on the seam just back of a length every bloody ball. You never got an easy run off him.

I had a quiet series, with a top score of 64, and even managed to get out hit wicket at Lord's. But Goochie and Mike Atherton, who looked the part in his first full Test series, scored tons of runs. I so enjoyed watching those two bat together and loved seeing them doing well – especially as it meant I could put my feet up for a few hours! Devon Malcolm was in great form too and won the series for us by taking eight wickets in the final Test at Edgbaston.

The India series was a feast of run-scoring, with 15 centuries in three Tests. I got a couple, both unbeaten, and ended the series with an average of 180.50. That's the power of the not out! I'm more than happy to say mine weren't the most memorable centuries in that series. In the first Test at Lord's, Mohammad Azharuddin made a magical hundred and Goochie hit the small matter of 456 runs in the match.

At the time the world record score was 365 by Sir Garry Sobers and I was batting with Goochie on the second afternoon as he approached the mother of all milestones. He was 299 not out at tea and in the last over I kept trying to nick a single. He seemed more relaxed than I was and was happy to go off on 299.

By the end, he was struggling. He was 36, he'd been batting nearly two days and he was genuinely exhausted. I kept saying, 'Goochie, keep going, not long to the record.'

'Judgie,' he wheezed, 'I'm buggered!'

'Mate, you are so close to the record. Don't give up on me, Goochie!'

He was on 333 when he was bowled having a weary drive at Manoj Prabhakar. It was his match though: he took an important wicket, scored another hundred in the second innings and sealed our win with a spectacular run-out.

In the second Test at Old Trafford, I was on 76 when the last man came to the wicket. Devon. I had visions of that match in the Caribbean a few months earlier, when I was left stranded on 99 not out after he had a slog at Patrick Patterson. He must have been able to read my mind. The first thing he said when he got to the middle was, 'Judgie, I've learned, don't worry. I'm a better player now, better technique. I'll see you through to the hundred. I've been working hard at my game.'

I said, 'Devvy, mate, I've heard it before! Fantastic. Show me.'

As it turned out, he batted beautifully and I got my hundred. That match was saved on the final day by the most brilliant century from a 17-year-old Sachin Tendulkar. In those days you knew very little about the opposition – there was no video analysis or anything like that – so we hadn't heard of him. When he came out to bat in the first Test, we all said, 'Who's this little toothpick? We'll see the back of him pretty quickly.'

We did at Lord's, where he had a modest game, but at Old Trafford he made 68 and then batted nearly four hours in the second innings to save the match. He was so composed. I walked past him and saw his thin little arms holding this huge bat. I thought, 'How on earth do you lift that? It's almost as heavy as you!'

He played one shot at Old Trafford that's among the best I've ever seen. Devon was bowling really quickly and got one to kick from a length towards Tendulkar's chest. He got on the back foot, kept his left elbow nice and high and drove it back past Dev for four. You usually pull or cut off that length. You certainly don't get on your toes and hit it back from where it came for four. Not unless you're a genius, that is. Barry Richards used to do exactly the same thing in our back garden in Durban.

At the end of the season we were asked to play a couple of exhibition matches against the West Indies in Toronto and New York, where there were loads of expats who wanted to see a game of cricket. The TCCB[2] wasn't happy but we all went along for a jolly. The matches

---

[2] The Test and County Cricket Board, which was later replaced by the England and Wales Cricket Board (ECB).

were fun, in front of huge crowds, and we had a heck of a night out in New York.

The West Indies weren't bowling at full tilt and I hit some strong pulls and cuts. I didn't know at the time but there was a scout for the New York Mets there who had played cricket for Jamaica. A few of us were given a baseball bat and told to have a bit of a swing, and I was lucky enough to smack a few that went a fair distance. I suppose somebody who plays like I do, with those square cuts, has a chance of being fairly successful. The way I hit the ball impressed the scout and when we got home I received a letter offering me a trial as a rookie with the New York Mets. The contract was for $300,000 for nine months, which was much more than I was earning at the time. In 1991, for example, my yearly earnings were £112,000, and that included various sponsorship deals. I think I was the highest earner in England at the time.

I was very flattered to be approached and it could have been fun, but there was too much for me to give up. Kath was pregnant with our first child, Harrison, and we had bought a nice home. I'd also just signed a new contract with Hampshire and I was a regular in the England team. Had I been single, had I been more adventurous – maybe a little bit more ambitious and confident in my own ability – I might have gone for nine months because I could always have come back and started my career again. Who knows what might have happened?

A month later we went on the tour to Australia that quickly became a total nightmare. I started with a flawless performance – and I didn't hit a single ball. The tour began with the usual curtain raiser, a one-day match at Lilac Hill against an Australian XI. Their team was usually a mixture of past, present and future stars, and on this occasion Dennis Lillee was down to play. We got wind that he'd been working really hard on his fitness and was desperate for one last crack at the Poms. We knew that, even at the age of 43, he could still bowl well with that beautiful action. We also knew the press in both Australia and England would slaughter us if he ran through us at his age.

The night before the game, Goochie told me I wasn't playing but that as 12th man I had to do a lot more than just *carry* the drinks. 'Go out with Lamby and Dennis and get him as pissed as you can, so that tomorrow he's all over the place.'

Dennis organised a boat trip along the Swan River in the afternoon, and then Lamby and I took him out afterwards. Lamby stayed for a while and then made his excuses – he was playing the next day – before I continued to selflessly perform the task my captain had asked of me. By the end of the night Dennis was so pissed that I had to get him in a cab and take him home. His wife Helen came to the door, saw the state he was in and said, 'Have you no shame?!'

I'm still not sure whether she was talking to me or him.

The next day Dennis struggled through nine overs without taking a wicket and went for a lie-down in the dressing room. For some reason, he wasn't too keen on a post-match beer. 'Very good job, Judgie,' said Gooch. 'I had every confidence in you.'

I still see Dennis now. I live about five minutes down the road from him and have dinner occasionally with him and Helen. I see him walking along the river quite regularly, and I almost chinned him last year. I was sitting doing some emails, with my bike behind me, and the next thing I knew some bloke was making off with my bike. I grabbed him and he turned around. It was Dennis, laughing his head off.

Goochie wasn't so pleased with me at the start of that Ashes tour when I accidentally put him out of the first Test. We were playing a practice match at my old club Nedlands and Goochie was bowling to me. I drove the ball straight back at him, he tried to take the catch and split his finger open. It looked awful – he later described it as being like a sausage that has split in the frying pan. It needed 30 stitches but still turned septic and spread to his hand. He was in hospital for ten days and missed the first Test, which given his inspirational form in 1990 was an enormous blow.

So was losing Lamby for the second and third Tests. He'd been in unbelievable form in the tour games, smacking effortless hundreds everywhere we went. When we played Victoria in Ballarat, he wanted to drop down the order so that others who weren't in such great form could get some practice in the middle. The management said no, and Lamby was so pissed off that he belted six sixes in a quickfire 143. He decided to get rid of some more of his frustration that night. 'Judgie, put your running shoes on, we're running back to the hotel.' It was something we often did, but on this occasion he pulled a hamstring.

The absence of Goochie and then Lamby put even more focus on me as one of the senior batsmen, and I went into the first Test playing really well. On the first day, I lost sight of a swinging yorker from the tall left-armer Bruce Reid, which came from over the top of the sightscreen, and was bowled. For some reason, my confidence just completely went.

Looking back, I suspect the expectations that I would score a bucket-load of runs compounded my natural fear of failure. The fact I did so well early in my career put more pressure on me rather than less, because I'd set a standard and when I dropped below it, people asked questions and I asked questions – even though my lower standard, on reflection, was still better than most.

For the next two months my head was confused and I really struggled in the international games. My brain started playing tricks on me and I began to imagine the opposition were bowling better than they actually were. It was also as if they had 13 or 14 fielders. The gap between fielders – say at point and cover point – would look smaller than it actually was. My game felt paralysed and I was pushing at the ball more in hope than expectation. I wasn't worried about where the next big score was coming from; I was more concerned where the next run was coming from.

The difference between batting when you are high or low on confidence is like night and day. I swear that time slows down when you are playing well and feeling confident. You seem to pick up the line and length earlier and have more time to play your shots. When I was confident, my shots were so much more positive and decisive, whether I was attacking and defending. Everything – even leaving the ball – was done with intent and intensity. It was also very important that I was happy with my balance and how my feet were moving. If they were, I felt much more secure.

Players are usually put into two categories – mentally tough and mentally weak. In my experience, most players are both at different times. Even someone like Mike Atherton, who was as tough as anyone

I played with, wrote in his autobiography that he was shot mentally against Glenn McGrath by the end of his career.

There were times in my career when I was really tough mentally, and others, like in Australia, when it all got on top of me. The structure for the tour was typical for those days: the first Test, then a block of one-dayers in a triangular tournament, then Test, ODI, Test, ODI and so on. There was a month between the first and second Tests, and in that time a blip became a crisis.

I had confidence issues against spinners later in my career but this was different. Australia's slow bowlers were Greg Matthews and Peter Taylor, and New Zealand had Grant Bradburn. They were all decent offies but nothing to worry about, and I hardly got out to a spinner all tour.

I had a few other distractions that might not have helped my form. I needed regular injections for a groin injury, and more importantly I was fretting about the birth of my son, Harrison. There were times when I was distracted, not in the matches but certainly in practice. The birth was scheduled for early December, in between the first and second Tests, and I wanted to fly home. In those days it was almost unheard of for sportsmen to miss a match for the birth of a child, never mind fly halfway round the world. So even though I wasn't going to miss any of the Tests, I got a lot of criticism in the press, with Geoffrey Boycott saying I was a 'big baby'. I love Boycs but that disappointed me. We were from different generations and he saw the world differently.

It was agreed in advance of the tour that I could fly home for the birth, as it was scheduled for between the first and second Tests. But the England management changed their mind at the last minute and said I couldn't fly home. They wanted me to play in some one-day matches because my form wasn't great. Maybe a break would have done me good, and I'd have returned with a clear head and enjoying the buzz of fatherhood. Who knows?

Kath was in labour for a long time and it was very stressful. I really hated not being there. I knew how much Kath was looking forward to me coming home and so, stupidly, I delayed telling her until the last minute. It was heart-breaking when I finally told her.

Family has always been so important to me and I hated missing Harrison's birth. We were in Canberra for a tour match at the time. All the England boys stayed up with me so that we could wet the baby's head, but Harrison took his time and at midnight they decided to call it a night. I stayed up, of course, with Mom giving me a running commentary on a mobile phone from Kath's bedside, and eventually he came into the world at around 4 a.m. Canberra time. The first time I saw my son was a photograph in one of the tabloids. We had really good relations with British Airways at the time and they brought over a load of newspapers for me. The first time I saw him walk was on a video in the team room when we were on tour in India. It's one of the sacrifices you make as a professional sportsman, but I did so with a pretty heavy heart.

At first, things got no better on the field. I suppose I could have tried to read Kippy's books more, but my way of dealing with it was to work and work some more in the nets. One thing I'm proud of is that, throughout my career, I often ended difficult series or tours on a personal high. No matter how low I was, I never gave up or threw the towel in. If anything, I worked even harder.

I had phoned Kippy, my brother and mentor, to ask for his advice. He then arrived in Sydney for the third Test as part of a tour group, so we did some technical work. We went right back to basics and I put my technique back together bit by bit. No matter how grooved your technique is, you can easily develop bad habits without realising.

He observed that, although we both liked to look to get forward, I was committing myself too early and falling over to the off side. He suggested I continue to press forward but not move too early and watch my head position, with my eyes over the ball and not my pads. In those days it was harder to correct technical faults that crept into your game. Split-screens, which allow you to compare your technique when you're playing well with when you're playing badly, weren't available then, so you couldn't really see yourself. Kippy was my most reliable pair of eyes. I think if I was playing now I'd spend a lot of time analysing my technique on an iPad. Probably too much.

It's maybe no coincidence that my form started to pick up after that. I got a hundred in a tour match against Queensland just before the fourth Test – I was going to ask to be left out, for the first time in my career, before that game, until Lamby pumped my tyres up again – and it was like I'd rediscovered the old Robin Smith. I ended the tour with a couple of decent fifties in the Tests. Nothing spectacular, but a big improvement on where I'd been. By the last Test at Perth, on that bouncy wicket, I was in my element and hitting it sweetly. I nailed a few square cuts, hearing that lovely rifle crack every time I made contact, and I remember uppercutting Craig McDermott for six over third man. I had another really good partnership with Lamby in the first innings of that game, when I made 58, and I felt good for a lot more than 43 in the second innings when I fell to a dodgy LBW.

It didn't matter in the grand scheme, as we were well beaten to complete a frustrating 3–0 series defeat. Goochie, who was really weary by the end of the tour, said it was 'a fart competing with thunder'. The annoying thing is that, unlike in 1989, we were competitive for parts of every match. We took a first-innings lead in the first two Tests only to collapse in the third innings each time. In the second Test at Melbourne we were 103–1, 147–4 and then 150 all out. That's an outrageous collapse even by our standards.

Bruce Reid took 13 wickets in that Test and our right-handers, me included, had lots of problems with him. He was really awkward to face because he was both a left-armer and tall, which is quite a rare combination. He was another one, like Ian Bishop, whose career was sadly curtailed by back problems.

The tour is best remembered for the Tiger Moth incident, when David Gower and John Morris got in all sorts of trouble for hiring two planes and then flying them low over the ground in Carrara while we were playing a tour match. In a way it was my fault – they did it to celebrate my century and return to form.

Lamby quietly told me what was going on, so when these Tiger Moths buzzed the ground we waved and pretended to shoot them down with our bats. Lamby lay down on his back like he was in a war film and started firing at the sky. Nobody knew except Lamby and me, and it was all pretty harmless. Team spirit was low at the time, so we needed a bit of fun and a bit of a boost. The management didn't agree and both Gower and Morris were fined.

I didn't think that was good management at all. A big rift started, which wasn't always pleasant. A few days later, in the Adelaide Test, David fell into a leg-side trap right on the stroke of lunch while Goochie silently fumed at the other end. It looked lazy – but then everything David did looked effortless. Sometimes, like with Mark Waugh, you can confuse elegance with not giving a toss. David cared enormously and gave everything every time he batted for England – and he'd been our best batsman on the tour, making two lovely centuries at Melbourne and Sydney. It was the ball before lunch so it didn't look great, but we all make mistakes. Why make such a big thing of it?

I loved playing under Goochie, because he was an inspiration, a really good man and a lot of fun. We'd often go out for something to eat, a few of us, and he had this amazing ability, especially in New Zealand for some reason, to fall asleep at the dinner table after a couple of glasses of red. I hope it wasn't my company.

He was the perfect captain for me, because he was disciplined and he set a magnificent example with his run-scoring, focus, determination and fitness. I loved running back from the ground to the hotel with him and Lamby. I learned a lot and it was a privilege to bat with him. I don't use that word lightly. But though he always had good intentions, I think he'll reflect that he could have managed some people slightly differently. Maybe he was brought up in the old school, where the same rules worked for everyone.

The problem with that is that I'm not the same as David Gower, Devon Malcolm, Philip Tufnell or Eddie Hemmings. If David didn't want to go for a net or naughty boys' fielding practice, then so be it. Just because Devon can't field and Tuffers can't concentrate for 90 overs in the field doesn't mean David Gower needs to do more practice. Don't drag him out at 9 a.m. when his family have just arrived in Sydney. That approach just didn't cut it with Gower, Lamby and the other senior players. We were all individuals.

I felt like I was stuck between the two different schools, both of whom I had such respect for. I wasn't comfortable getting involved in any of the arguments. During the tour, Tuffers enjoyed a late night out – so late, in fact, that he wasn't back at the hotel for breakfast.

Micky was on the warpath and, because I was Tuffers' roommate, asked if I knew where he was. I panicked. I wasn't going to dob Tuffers in, but I had to say something. Before I knew it, some words were coming out of my mouth.

'He's already gone, coach. He likes to run to the ground some mornings.'

Bloody hell, Judgie.

Tuffers, run to the ground? He didn't like running from fine leg to third man, never mind seven or eight miles. It was another reminder to me, not that I needed it, that I am a truly dreadful liar. About 30 seconds later, to compound my misery, Tuffers swanned through the hotel reception wearing the kind of attire that wasn't exactly suitable for running to a cricket ground.

We did have the odd bit of fun on tour. One night, during a tour match in Adelaide, a young larrikin[3] called Shane Warne showed me and Lamby the sights. He'd been bowling to us in the nets and played a couple of one-day games against us for an Australian Cricket Academy team that included Justin Langer, Damien Martyn, Greg Blewett – and my future England teammate Jason Gallian. We had a great night out with Warney and I've been friends with him ever since. We share a birthday and get on famously. Apparently, Warney was a great AFL player as a kid. Unfortunately, he chose cricket.

Lamby was also good friends with Eric Clapton, as they used to go fishing together, and Eric gave us tickets for a show in Adelaide. At the start he said, 'I've got a few friends in tonight – the England cricket team!' Everyone started booing, at which point Eric pretended he was going to pack up his gear and go offstage. 'Right, that's it, I'm walking offstage unless you cheer my buddies.' We then received what must be one of the biggest cheers ever for a group of England cricketers in Australia.

Lamby and I weren't playing in the next day's game and Eric invited us up to his hotel suite for a private afterparty – just him, his PA, Lamby and me. I didn't realise he was a fan of mine and he asked if he could have one of the cricket bats I was using during the Ashes

---

[3] An Australian word for a boisterous young rogue.

series as memorabilia. He offered one of his guitars in exchange, but I told him not to worry about it and that he could have the bat anyway. Lamby said, 'What are you doing, mate?! You've just turned down the offer of one of Eric Clapton's guitars!'

I was lucky to meet some brilliant characters in the celebrity world. Rod Bransgrove, the Hampshire chairman, is a friend of the Zeta-Jones family as his wife Mandy used to dance with Catherine in some West End shows, so we had dinner with her a few times. And Ollie Reed often came along to watch Hampshire games and enjoy the hospitality.

I also became friends with Rod MacSween, a rock promoter who was, among other things, Ozzy Osbourne's promoter and Jon Bon Jovi's best man. He introduced me to some legends of the stage and screen. I used to leave complimentary tickets at Lord's for the actors Peter O'Toole and Ronnie Fraser, who would come and sit in the Compton Stand. What I didn't know is that, once he had settled in for the day's play, Ronnie didn't like the idea of getting up and going to the toilet, even though he would drink industrial quantities of alcohol throughout the day. When I say he didn't like the idea, I mean he couldn't be bothered.

He developed a habit of discreetly relieving himself towards the vacant seat next to him. Eventually there were complaints, and the ECB checked who had given him the tickets, so I had some explaining to do. When I asked Ronnie, he said, 'Judgie, I'm a superstitious man, we were going well and I didn't want to leave my seat in case we lost a wicket.'

'That's fine, Ronnie,' I said, 'but what's your bloody excuse when we're in the field?'

Chapter 12

My perfect summer

ONE OF THE BIGGEST regrets in my career is that I didn't spend long enough smelling the roses. The failures lingered a lot longer than the successes. Take the summer of 1991, which was undoubtedly the high point of my career. I won two Man of the Match awards as England drew 2–2 against the West Indies, a huge achievement against the best team in the world. I played the innings of my life and took part in the game of my life, both in front of a full house at Lord's. Yet I spent most of the summer thinking about the next game and the next innings. It's only now, almost 30 years later, that I have looked back and thought, 'Jeez, I could play.'

It's probably no coincidence that I had such a brilliant season when I felt at peace on and off the field. Harrison had been born a few months earlier and I was still buzzing from that. It also helped that I had a father figure of my own in the England dressing room. I cannot speak highly enough of Micky Stewart, my England coach from 1988–92. I adore that man.

Throughout my career I had to work very hard on being positive and getting this humble attitude out of my mind. Micky and Allan Lamb in particular were so good at pumping my tyres up and giving me the confidence I needed. Micky was a very good man-manager, especially with the younger players, and took into account the different personalities and characters in the team. He was soft and gentle with me and understood that I had very little confidence of my own – that I was living off the swagger of others in the dressing room. I needed him to tell me I was the best No. 4 in the country. I'm soft, and Micky understood that. He knew how to make me feel happy about my game.

But he was tough too. If I didn't do something right, he came down hard on me. If I was loose in the nets and played a bad shot he'd say, 'Judgie, shit shot, tighten up.' I loved that side of him. I'm one of those people who needs to be bollocked from time to time. If Micky had said that to someone like Ramps, he'd have thrown the toys out. That's the point: everyone needs different treatment. Micky had the lovely habit of saying the right thing at the right time.

If I saw Micky in the evening he'd put his arm round me and say, 'How's my best player going?' I'm sure he said the same to most of us, but he just made me feel great. He instinctively got the balance between the carrot and the stick just right. I could take a deserved bollocking, but I struggled when I felt I was being singled out, which became a problem after Micky retired.

Thankfully, that wasn't an issue in 1991. We knew we had our work cut out against the West Indies, who had just beaten the same Australia team that had thrashed us. Yet unbelievably, as in 1989–90, we won the first Test. It was the first time England had won at home to the West Indies since 1969. Goochie played a legendary innings, 154 not out in a total of 252 in the second innings. It was a dodgy Headingley wicket, with movement and uneven bounce, and he was up against Ambrose, Marshall, Walsh and Patterson. It's one of the greatest innings I've seen.

That Test also saw the debuts of Graeme Hick and Mark Ramprakash, two awesome players who weren't quite as successful as everyone expected at Test level. They had such a difficult series to start with, against a very good West Indies attack on some bowler-friendly pitches, and they were always playing catch-up after that. The culture of English cricket in those days was such that if you didn't get off to a good start, you were under pressure straight away.

Ramps actually got off to a brilliant start, but you wouldn't have known it from looking at the scorecards. In that first series against the West Indies he played so well, fighting incredibly hard for a succession of scores in the twenties before getting out, probably through sheer exhaustion. He played beautifully and showed great mental strength and toughness, and they were very important runs as the games were usually low-scoring. But then he got a duck in the last Test of the summer against Sri Lanka, he lost his place to Dermot Reeve during the winter and after that he was under pressure every time he came back into the team.

Ramps had the best technique of any England batsman I've ever seen – it was as close to perfect as you could realistically get. I was surprised that, because he was such a pure batsman, he wasn't able to recover and do at least as well as Ian Bell, another player with a classical technique. Perhaps Bell, as I found out later in my career, was a bit more resilient.

I liked Ramps a lot but sometimes he had a scrambled mind at the crease. I first played against him for Hampshire, when he was 17. There was a lot of hype about him being the best young batsman in the country, and he was facing Malcolm Marshall, the greatest bowler in the world at the time. From his second or third ball Ramps charged down the wicket, tried to smack it over the top and was caught. Charging Macko? Nobody did that. As he walked off, Macko said to us, 'What was that about?' What he was really saying was, 'Where's his respect?'

If Macko didn't like you, he could make life very difficult. Ramps barely got a run against us for the next few years.

There was another game, a Test against Pakistan at Headingley in 1992, when I had a chat with Ramps during the lunch break. We'd lost a wicket to the last ball before the interval so he was starting his innings. He told me that, whatever happened, he was going to defend his first two balls and sweep the third. He missed the sweep and was LBW to Mushtaq Ahmed for a duck.

He and Hicky were absolutely bombed in that West Indies series. Poor Hicky was under immense scrutiny before a ball was bowled. He was the saviour of English cricket, the new Donald Bradman, who would average 50 in Test cricket without breaking sweat. Nobody should be put under that kind of pressure. You can imagine Sir Curtly Ambrose and the other Windies bowlers thinking, 'We'll see about that.' Through no fault of his own, Hicky had a huge target on his back. I honestly believe that when he came out, the opposition fast bowlers kicked up a gear or two. It was the same against Pakistan the following summer, and then Merv and Australia the year after that. His career might have been very different if he had started his Test career with a few big scores against weaker opposition.

Instead he was given a torrid time by Ambrose especially, and averaged 11 before being dropped for the last Test. It was difficult for him to come back from that, especially with all the expectations that people had. That's the only real explanation I have for the difference between his Test and first-class average because he was a fantastic player. But to be honest it still doesn't really make sense to me. People say he couldn't play fast bowling but, while there were times when he could be a bit leaden-footed, he got a big hundred against West Indies in a tour match in 1991. I also saw him score a thrilling counter-attacking hundred against Donald and Pollock on a lively pitch at Centurion in 1995.

He's another one who needed careful management because he's not a naturally confident person. He's a beautiful bloke – shy, sensitive, very humble. He didn't have that killer instinct, that bit of nastiness. When he came into the side in 1991, he wasn't embraced in quite the same way as I'd been three years earlier. I was essentially shy and quiet but I could also be outgoing and I liked a few beers, whereas he didn't really lend himself to being one of the boys.

He had this astonishing record, he was a big physical presence, and we didn't really know what to say to him. It's easy to think someone is aloof when in fact they're just shy and that happened with Hicky. If I knew him then as I do now, I'd have embraced him a bit more.

Hicky played spectacularly for England at times, particularly in the mid-1990s. There were times when I wondered about his preparation, though. I remember once we were playing the West Indies at Lord's, so the day before the game I got Devon Malcolm and Phil DeFreitas to bowl at my head from 18 yards. I didn't like it but I knew I needed to do it – as Dad taught me all those years earlier, if you make practice as tough as possible, then the real thing will feel a little easier.

I looked across to the other net and Hicky was getting throw-downs, punching these half-volleys beautifully through the off side. I thought, 'You won't be getting any of those in the morning, Hicky!' He wasn't the only one, though. When we played the West Indies, I'd often look around the nets and be surprised that nobody else seemed to be practising against the short ball.

I suggested to him once that he should try skipping because he got caught on the crease a lot and I found it really helpful when I played fast bowling. But I didn't say much apart from that. Who am I to tell Graeme Hick how to play? He's far better than I am.

We drew the second Test at Lord's, when I helped us avoid the follow on with 148 not out. All things considered, this was the greatest innings of my life. I played better attacking knocks, like against Australia at Trent Bridge in 1989, but overall I think this was better for a few reasons. The ball swung throughout the Test and there was a bit of variable bounce; it was against a serious pace attack; and most of all it helped save the game and keep us 1–0 up in the series. I got a lovely ovation from the Lord's crowd when I reached my hundred, and I think they recognised what an important innings it was for me after my struggles in Australia. A moment like that – when you have played really well in tough circumstances, and you hear 25,000 people applauding you – is almost like an out-of-body experience.

I had a quick look at the video before writing this and my cele-bration was modest, almost sheepish. That was always my way. I rarely, if ever, lost it when I reached a milestone. Like most human beings, I have a bit of an internal struggle between humility and pride. I suppose, when I was celebrating, Robin Smith briefly took over from the Judge.

A few days later after the Lord's Test, I played for Hampshire against the West Indies in a tour game. Although central contracts would have been better for us in the 1990s, I absolutely loved going back to play for my county. I loved the club, the players, my captain, Mark Nich-olas, and the supporters. I understand why they don't do it these days as there is so much international cricket but back then we were really lucky.

There were other benefits, too. If I was out of form, it was a chance to get some runs; if I was in form, it was an opportunity to keep that going. That was very important to me, because I've always been at my best when the innings have come thick and fast and I've had a good rhythm. That might be one of the reasons my Test record was much better in England than overseas.

The downside of playing for Hampshire was the risk of injury, and in this match Ambrose broke my finger. I can't help wondering whether he did it deliberately. I'd just pulled him for two fours and a big six – straight into the block of flats I used to pepper in my 2nd XI days – in one over, and he didn't like it. He didn't say anything, he never did, but the next thing I knew there was a beamer homing in on my face. I put my glove in the way instinctively and it smashed my right index finger, the same one Courtney Walsh had broken a year earlier. I carried on for a bit and then retired as a precaution with the next Test match in mind.

I had a few problems with that finger, and 30 years later it's still a mess. I'm unable to bend it – but hey, if that's my only problem after twenty-five years of professional sport, I can count myself lucky.

Curtly was a good enough bowler to hit a dinner plate nine times out of ten, so for him to bowl a beamer and miss his length by that much was highly unusual. It wasn't wet and he didn't suggest the ball had slipped from his hand. I felt he was just too good to get it wrong like that – he rarely bowled a full length, never mind a full toss. It seemed too much of a coincidence that I'd just spanked him for a few boundaries. He said, 'Ah, sorry, man.' I felt like saying, 'Like fuck you're sorry!'

The fact he bowled another beamer later that day at our No. 11 Kevin Shine, who had also just hit him for six, only heightened my suspicions. We all have bad days, I suppose, and I'll never know for certain whether it was deliberate. I do like Curtly and it's not something I hold against him. He's a top bloke and I always enjoyed the music he played in his band with Sir Richie Richardson.

I refused to have the finger X-rayed, because I didn't want to know whether it was broken or not. If the X-ray showed a fracture,

I wouldn't be allowed to play anyway. I had a cortisone injection in the joint, which made me realise I was definitely capable of feeling pain. Yep, that really hurt.

After that I had no pain but I couldn't feel my left hand at all. I played in the third Test and got runs even though we lost but the finger deteriorated and I had to miss the fourth Test. Until the morning of the game I was convinced I'd make it. Goochie told the quicker bowlers to really give it to me in practice, and I could feel myself flinching just slightly. I knew I couldn't do myself and the team justice. It's hard enough facing the West Indies at full fitness, never mind when you're struggling to grip the bat. I wouldn't have been any good to anyone. I was very honest with them, and I was the one who made the decision that I should miss the game. I was pretty emotional because I don't like missing any match, never mind when it's 1–1 with two to play against a team that hadn't lost a Test series for 11 years.

We lost by seven wickets and went into the last Test at the Oval needing a win to square the series. The pitch was a trampoline, just what their fast bowlers wanted. And just what I wanted. I loved pitches like that – quick but not lightning, with a nice consistent bounce and a very fast outfield.

In the first session they gave our batsmen, especially Hugh Morris, an awesome barrage. There was a virus going round our dressing room and I wasn't feeling great, but there's no medicine like the adrenalin of facing the West Indies and I couldn't wait to get out there. Beefy had also been recalled and was in great form around the dressing room, which meant I was in a lovely, relaxed mood.

When I came in they had a deep extra cover, just behind square, and a third man straight away. I suppose it was a compliment, but it meant some of my best shots were only going for one. I had to be patient and pick my attacking shots carefully.

I'd reached 98, having fought for almost six hours, when Malcolm walked up to me. 'Judgie, man, leg stump.'

'What's that, Macko?'

'Next ball, leg stump.'

'Are you sure, Macko?'

'Leg stump, half volley.'

He made a big song and dance about moving square leg to gully. I didn't know if it was a set up, and kept thinking back to the tour game in Barbados a year earlier when he told me how he was going to get me out. Was this a double bluff? I was half expecting a short ball that I might fend to second gully, or an inswinger. He ran in and bowled a beautiful non-swinging half volley on leg stump which I clipped through square leg for three. I raised my bat and Macko said, 'Well played, man.' Viv walked past, tapped me on the shoulder and said, 'Nice present, man. You deserve it, well played.'

Malcolm got me soon after, LBW for 109, but at least he gave me the hundred! We were dismissed for 419, our first 400+ score against the West Indies in 15 years, and we went on to win a thrilling match by five wickets. It meant England had drawn a series with the West Indies for the first time since 1974. I suppose that was our equivalent to the 2005 Ashes win.

I was made Man of the Match for the second time in the series, which completed a happy recovery from my Ashes misery. The adjudicator was full of praise.

'Robin Smith has become a tremendous Test player in this series and I was delighted to make him Man of the Match … it was the manner in which he scored his runs that was so vital. He is a superbly positive batsman, always trying to take the game to the opposition and never be dominated. That's the secret behind his success.'

Ray Illingworth always said nice things about me in those days.

Goochie said some lovely things in his book, *Testing Times*, about that Oval innings as well. 'Robin's got the game for the Windies and I've nothing but admiration for his power. He thrives on the big occasion; I've seen others, just as talented, intimidated by nerves and the pressure. All it does to Robin is inspire him.'

I use Goochie's quote not to blow my own trumpet (well, not that much), but because it's an independent view on something that was really important to me. The ability to deliver in big games became my badge of honour.

I suspect it's also one of the reasons I was quite popular during my career. This is a hard thing to talk about but I was always very grateful for the amazing goodwill I received from fans around England. I have a bit of a strange relationship with praise. It means so much when people say nice things about me, especially as I am painfully insecure, but it's also pretty embarrassing and uncomfortable.

However, my editor has told me that I need to at least *attempt* to blow my own trumpet, and discuss why people seemed to like me, so here goes. If I was popular, it might be because I always tried to have time for fans and supporters who love their cricket. I suppose I treat people as I'd like to be treated, and I've always loved the social side of cricket, which is maybe why I've made so many friends. Supporters probably liked my fighting spirit and the fact I took on the fast bowlers.

Right, that's enough of that.

The international summer ended when we beat Sri Lanka easily in a one-off Test at Lord's. My performances against the West Indies meant I was now ranked the No. 2 Test batsman in the world behind Goochie. I didn't know until I saw it in the official programme during the Sri Lanka Test, but it meant a lot because in my insecure head it felt like hard, statistical verification of my ability. I might have had doubts but if a sophisticated computer programme said I was No. 2 in the world, that had to count for something. And when I saw some of the legends who were further down the list – Javed Miandad in fourth, Martin Crowe in eighth, Allan Border at ten and Viv at 12 – it made me even prouder.

I was back at Lord's ten days later, playing in the NatWest Trophy final against Surrey. I'd been in strong form throughout the tournament, but now I had to face the new sensation of world cricket: the Pakistan fast bowler Waqar Younis. He took 113 wickets for Surrey at an average of 15 in first-class cricket that season, and a few days before the final he flattened us with 12 wickets in the Championship. He also broke Mark Nicholas's hand, which meant he was out of the final.

We were without Kippy, too, as he had left to take up a job in Perth. He was only 32, and still one of the best openers in the country, but he had been offered the job of sales and marketing manager at the Western Australian Cricket Association in Perth. It was a huge job, far too good to turn down. Word had spread about how successful his various marketing initiatives with Hampshire had been. He accepted that position, and the following year, aged 33, he beat over 135 applicants from around the world to become chief executive of the WACA.

Kippy has a lovely photo of the last time we ever batted together. It was in the quarter-final of the NatWest Trophy against Nottinghamshire at Southampton, when I made 67 and Kippy was Man of the Match for his 105 not out. The memory of that day means a lot to us both.

When it came to the final, my battle with Waqar was built up like a heavyweight boxing contest. He loathed me, and every time I played against him he threatened to kill me. The match was a thriller. Waqar nailed David Gower – our captain for the day – LBW, and we were in a bit of trouble at one stage. I knew if he got me out, we'd probably lose. He was brought back into the attack, with the game in the balance, and I barely saw his first ball as it whistled past the outside edge. Waqar's speed could be awesome. That ball sharpened me up and after that I took him on. I'll always remember one shot, when I hit a reverse-inswinging yorker through mid-off for four. It scorched along the turf. When you consider the context – fading light, a really intense moment in a huge game against the hottest bowler in world cricket – that might be the best shot of my career. It was a real statement and it changed the momentum of the game.

We edged towards our target and, though I was run out for 78 with victory in sight, our No. 6 Jon Ayling hit a big six out of nothing and saw us home in an unbelievably tense finish. I was given the Man of the Match award and put the champagne to good use. We had a few drinks in the dressing room then went back to the hotel to join our wives, partners and the supporters.

To me, that was the ultimate. When I became a regular in the England team, I stopped setting targets for run-scoring with Hampshire because I didn't know how many games I would be available for. Instead, I set myself a target of playing a major role in Hampshire winning a trophy. That was another of Grayson's tips: if you are struggling to find a target or motivate yourself, make it your objective to win the game for your team. Scoring runs didn't make me nearly as happy as the sound of champagne corks popping and everyone in the dressing room whooping with joy.

I look back on that day with such pride. It meant so much to play an important innings, share the victory with blokes I'd grown up with over the past decade, and to see the joy it brought to so many Hampshire supporters. It also came at the end of the best summer of my career and involved the kind of bare-knuckle duel with a fast bowler that I relished. Yeah, I reckon that was the game of my life.

When you win a match like I reckon that you think of the glory, not the money, but there was an added financial bonus. The prize money meant all the players could go on a lovely end-of-season holiday with our partners, and was probably the difference between a weekend in Cornwall and a fortnight in Greece. It was fine for me, who earned a good wage, but some of the squad weren't on a huge amount of money so I was chuffed to be able to help out in that way.

You'd think that an end-of-season holiday would be the time to reflect on what a great season I'd had, but it wasn't really like that. I had far more important things than cricket to think about – Harrison was approaching his first birthday, and I took so much pleasure from being able to spend every day with him, playing by the pool and reading to him or teaching him to walk.

Although there was no time to pat myself on the back, I did at least think I'd proved again that I was a big-game player. The sort of bloke you'd want on the teamsheet, for example, in a World Cup final. I was wrong.

Chapter 13

World Cup misery

I WAS A BIG-GAME addict. I lived for the chance to play on the grandest stage, whether it was for Hampshire or England. The adrenalin rush of those matches allowed the swaggering persona of the Judge to completely take over from the shy, humble Robin Smith. So when England left me out of the XI to play in the 1992 World Cup final, it was the biggest disappointment of my career – and it came completely, horribly, out of the blue.

We'd started the winter with a tour of New Zealand, where we won the Tests 2–0 and the one-dayers 3–0. We were the first team to win a Test series there in 13 years – not even the great West Indian side of the 1980s did so. It's the forgotten success of English cricket in the 1990s. You'd think, given how few series wins there were, that none of them would be forgotten.

I also bowled my legspin for the only time in Test cricket, a miserly spell of 4–2–6–0 on the final day of the first Test in Christchurch. We were battling to win the game but struggling to take wickets, so Goochie decided it was time for something completely different. Martin Crowe, someone I had formed a really close friendship with over the years, was in the middle of a rearguard innings when Goochie walked up to me. I assumed he was going to ask about field placings.

'Warm up, Judgie.'

'Warm what?'

'Warm up. Bowl to your mate Crowe.'

'Bloody hell, Goochie, he'll smack me everywhere!'

'We need to try something. Go and sledge him, tell him you're coming on to bowl.'

For the next few overs I started loosening my shoulders in a really exaggerated way. Crowey keep looking quizzically at me.

'What are you doing, mate?'

'I'm bowling in a minute. And if I get you out, china, I'll phone you every day for a year to remind you.'

I was a decent legspinner when I was young and once took nine wickets in a school match. Before I seem too boastful, you should know those nine wickets cost me 165 runs! I also took a few wickets early in my career, usually when there was some declaration bowling going on. The list of people who fell to my demon legspin includes some decent names – Alec Stewart, Mike Gatting (stumped at Lord's!), Wilf Slack, Matthew Maynard, John Morris, Alan Butcher and Monte Lynch. Those days were long gone by 1992. Yet when I came on to bowl, Crowey treated me with so much respect. It was like I was Shane Warne and Abdul Qadir rolled into one. Almost every ball was met with a perfect forward defensive. We had a bit of a mutual-appreciation society going and always encouraged each other when one of us was batting, so I thought I'd carry that on.

'That's beautiful, Crowey. That's the perfect forward defensive. Jeez, you could put that in a textbook. Oh, and by the way, I know your home phone number.'

He didn't play a single attacking stroke off me and I was taken off after four overs. That was it for my Test career, so I retired with an economy rate of 1.50 an over. I'm officially one of the most economical bowlers in English history!

We won that game in a dramatic finish, when Crowey tried to hit Tuffers over the top and was caught by Derek Pringle at mid-off. If the ball had gone for four it would have guaranteed a draw because there would have been no time for a change of innings. Instead we won by an innings and four runs. Tuffers had one of his golden days, taking seven for 47 from 46.1 overs. Around that time he was a proper match-winner – this was the third consecutive Test in which he bowled us to victory – but he was one of many individuals who weren't particularly well managed as the decade went on.

The ultimate match-winner, Beefy, wasn't with us at the start of the trip because he was doing pantomime in Bournemouth. I suppose that seems a bit odd, given I wasn't allowed to fly home for Harrison's birth a year earlier. But there were a couple of differences – he had made himself unavailable in advance and, more to the point, he's Beefy! He could do and say as he pleased, and quite right too. I won't hear a word said against the man.

He flew over halfway through the tour and played the third Test, which was also his hundredth for England. We had practice the day before, and I was just getting changed when Beefy popped in and said, 'Judgie, you're with me this afternoon.'

I knew what an afternoon with Beefy entailed.

'Ah, no thanks, Beefy, it'd be nice to chill out and relax, we've got a big game tomorrow.'

'That's okay, it'll be nice and relaxed, you're coming with me.'

'Where are we going?'

'Don't worry about that.'

He'd never tell you where you were going but he always had something planned for an afternoon or a day off, particularly in New Zealand as he loved the country. This time it was me, Beefy and Lamby. We went down to Wellington harbour where there was a helicopter waiting for us. It was about 1.30 p.m., we had a team meeting at 6 p.m., and now we were flying over the bloody Cook Strait, the body of water between the North and South Islands! Beefy had his road map out and we were flying so low that he could read the signs on the road.

Eventually Beefy instructed the pilot to drop us by the Cloudy Bay vineyard. He knew the owner, Kevin Judd, who put on a magnificent spread. We had a tour of the vineyard, then settled down for the most amazing Chateaubriand with all the different wines to sample. It was a brilliant afternoon, but by 4.30 p.m. I was getting slightly edgy.

'Lamby, mate, it's half four, should we b—'

'No, no, Judgie, all good, mate, all good. Just have another little dessert wine here. We've got *plenty* of time. Don't worry about it.'

Fifteen more minutes passed. By now Lamby was well into his dessert wines and didn't give a shit what day it was, never mind what time it was. I looked pleadingly across the table and said, 'Beef, it's coming up to five, mate. Bit close?'

'One more, Judgie, all good. We'll just try this Cabernet Sauvignon. You should try some.'

'No, no, Beef, I'm all good.'

All of a sudden, Lamby chimes in. 'This is a beautiful drop here, Judgie, a great vintage, you've got to try it.'

Eventually, at about quarter past five, I got up and said, 'Beef, please, mate, we really have to go.'

I didn't mind if they wanted to miss a team meeting but I was young and I wanted to do the right thing. We said our thank yous and goodbyes to our wonderful hosts and jumped in the chopper that was waiting for us at about twenty past five. Beefy looked at his watch and said, 'We're running a bit behind here.' I said, 'Bloody hell, thanks, Beef. I know we are!'

On the way back, over the Cook Strait, he phoned the chauffeur who was waiting to pick us up. We landed at about five to six. I felt like running back to the hotel, I was bloody hysterical. There was no traffic so it was two minutes back to the hotel, through reception, into the lift and up to Micky Stewart's room for the team meeting. We walked in right on six o'clock; it was like something out of a film. I was white, sweating, and Lamby said, 'Well, where's the fucking problem, Judgie? I told you we'd be here on time.'

That's the way they were. There was a big game the next day, but rather than sitting in your room and building the game up into something it isn't, why not take your mind off the game and do something enjoyable? It also gives you a great opportunity to explore wherever you're touring and what these wonderful countries have to offer. And to drink some extremely good wine!

The match was a high-scoring draw, sadly memorable for one of the most horrible things I've ever seen on a cricket field. And it's definitely the worst I've heard. Syd Lawrence, the big paceman from

Gloucestershire, was charging in and giving everything even though the game was meandering to a draw. In his delivery stride his kneecap fractured, making the most sickening noise. I heard the crack and was one of the first on the scene. Syd was a real powerhouse – his ability to bowl fast came from sheer strength rather than rhythm – and he was in absolute agony. I knew instantly it was incredibly serious, because you just don't see a bloke who's six foot three inches and 18 stone cry with pain like that. I can still picture him banging his fist on the pitch with such force that you could see the ground move. *That's* pain. It was just awful.

A few of us helped him onto a stretcher and off the field. Syd never played for England again. He worked so hard to get back for Gloucestershire, a rehabilitation that took five years. He bowled at me on his comeback in 1997 and I was so happy for him that I could have cried. But his knee just wasn't right and he had to retire a year later. It was so sad. Syd was such a nice bloke, the definition of a gentle giant, and I had so much affection for him.

The World Cup, which started a fortnight later, was co-hosted by Australia and New Zealand. I started with a cracking 91 in a tight win over India at Perth – I just loved batting on that pitch – and as a team we were on fire. We won five of our first six games and the other, against Pakistan, was a moral victory when we bowled them out for 74. The match was washed out, which meant a point each. That point ultimately got Pakistan into the semi-finals.

We were winning games so convincingly in the first half of the tournament that there wasn't much chance to bat – I got a few middling scores, including 30 not out when Beefy gave Australia one last beating,[1] but lost a bit of momentum. So, eventually, did the team. The format for the 1992 World Cup was the same as 2019 – everyone played everyone and the top four went through to the semi-finals. We were starting to fade by the end of the group stage, with a lot of

---

[1] After that game, I stayed behind in the dressing room to have a beer with Beefy, Lamby and Allan Border. It was a day–night game, and we ended up getting locked in the MCG, so we had to ram one of the gates to get out!

players picking up injuries, and after we'd secured qualification we lost our last two games to New Zealand and Zimbabwe.

I was preparing for the semi-final against South Africa, always a big game for me because of my background, with the usual fielding practice. Micky hit a ball towards me, and as I dived to pick it up I felt a sudden, sharp pain. The next thing I remember is Chris Lewis shouting for our physio Laurie Brown to come and help me out. I'd pinched a nerve in my back and couldn't play in the semi-final. I couldn't even watch it at the ground. I was barely able to move so I had to stay in bed at the hotel and watch the game on TV. Dermot Reeve came in for me and batted really well, pumping Allan Donald round the park in the last few overs.

We beat South Africa, aided by those strange rain rules,[2] and had three days until the final against Pakistan. I did everything I could to get myself fit: cortisone injections, sleeping pills, a special rock-hard bed. I batted in a corset in the nets and had a local anaesthetic, and by the morning of the match I knew I was okay to play. It was a day–night game, so I did a fitness test in front of Goochie and Micky at the MCG on the morning of the match and it went well. They said nothing afterwards so I assumed I was in.

We were doing our last warm-ups as the crowd started to funnel in. The capacity at the MCG is 90,000 and the atmosphere was electric, like nothing I'd experienced in my career. A few minutes later I saw Goochie walk up to Gladstone Small. You could tell from the body language of both men that he was giving him the bad news. I really felt for Gladstone as he was such a good mate, but it was a nightmare decision for Goochie because Derek Pringle was fit again and had to play.

After that Goochie strolled towards the rest of the group. And then everything started to slow down.

Hang on, is he walking towards me? He is. What the f—

'Judgie, I'm sorry, we've decided not to pick you today.'

---

[2] If overs were lost due to rain, the target was adjusted by subtracting the least productive overs of the side batting first. It meant the team chasing were heavily disadvantaged.

I asked him why and pleaded that I was fit, but I was in such a daze that I can't really remember what he said. I've wondered for twenty-five years whether Goochie believed I was fit. It turns out he did, and I didn't realise that at the time he said it was 'the hardest decision I ever had to make'. I don't know whether that makes it easier or harder to bear.

Gladstone and I embraced and then walked off the field together, and the next hour or so is a blur. I vaguely remember us sitting on the podium, both in tears. It was so tough to take and I couldn't stop thinking about what I was missing out on.

This is what I practise for. This is why I got up every single morning at 5 a.m. in Durban. This is what I love: the biggest crowd, the biggest pressure. This is a test of character, mental strength and power. This is what I need in my life. This is what I was born for – and I can't have it, not today anyway.

And, as it turned out, not ever.

Once there were no more tears left inside us, Gladstone and I put our game faces on. You always try to keep your pecker up in those situations – we had to make sure we didn't mope around the dressing room because we had the responsibility to be good 12th men and keep spirits high.

To be honest, I still struggle to accept I wasn't picked. We did have a very strong batting line-up – Gooch, Botham, Stewart, Hick, Lamb and Fairbrother – but I still felt I should have played. You've got to trust your big players, surely. I was Man of the Match in two of the three major finals I played for Hampshire, and in the other I played the innings that got me into the England team in the first place. Goochie even said himself in his book, published a few months earlier, that I was a big-game specialist.

Goochie said they went for the extra experience of Lamby, who had returned to fitness after missing most of the tournament. Lamby was a genius finisher and I had no problem with him playing. But if they weren't going to pick me anyway, why make me do a fitness test?

We had Dermot Reeve at No. 7. He was a good, competitive cricketer but he hardly bowled in the match – three overs – so maybe we could have played me as a seventh batsman and used Gooch and Hick as the sixth bowler. Dermot made 15 from 32 balls when we batted and we eventually lost by 22 runs. It was a tight game and I do wonder whether I could have made a difference. We'll never know.

Pakistan were brilliant but I honestly think we were the best team in the tournament. They were lucky to qualify for the semis and then peaked at the right time. Even then, there were some big moments that went their way in the final. Pring had Javed Miandad stone dead LBW twice in the same over, both not given by the umpire Steve Bucknor, and then Goochie dropped Imran Khan. They could have been 50–4 but instead those two made runs and then Wasim batted and bowled brilliantly. His consecutive deliveries to Lamby and Chris Lewis, which derailed our chase, were astonishing.

It was a day–night game, so when their innings finished at around 7 p.m. I knew I couldn't take any further part in the game as a substitute fielder. I thought, 'Bugger it, it's the end of a long tour and I can't take part any more.' I've never told anyone this before, but after both teams had dinner I discreetly filled my water bottle up with Bundaberg rum and Coke to drown my sorrows. There were certainly sorrows to drown, even more so as the game slipped away from us. Beefy later said I took defeat worse than any of the XI who actually played. The whole day was the worst of my career. I always felt confident that it would happen again – maybe I was naïve, but in those days England nearly always got to the World Cup final.

Looking back, the feeling was one of sheer disappointment. It would be wrong to call it devastation – that's what happens in far more important walks of life than cricket. We want to win, but we'll live and breathe whatever happens. It's a game of cricket. So what?

I wish I could have seen that at the time. You realise that it's just a game as you get older, when it's often too late. You gain perspective when life starts to bite you, or take your best friends away prematurely. In cricket, two deaths hit me the hardest: Malcolm Marshall in 1999 and Martin Crowe in 2016.

When I was 12, I had a new sports coach at school – Terry Mehrtens, a former rugby player and the father of the great All Black fly-half Andrew, who was actually born while Terry was in Durban. He loved rugby and cricket, and one day he said to me, 'Robin, I have to tell you, you are so similar to another young man I've coached. Believe me, you will meet him one day because your paths are destined to cross. Remember the name Martin Crowe.'

We became really close and during the 1992 World Cup we had a bet who would score the most runs – he was the top scorer in the whole tournament, so I bought him a very nice dinner and a top-shelf bottle of red wine.

I used to love going out with Crowey. We shared the same sense of humour and would often be in tears of laughter, but he also saw beyond the bravado of the Judge and recognised the real Robin Smith. Maybe it was because of our backgrounds, both being talked up as sporting prodigies from an early age, but we gravitated towards each other. We had a lot in common: sensitivity, work ethic, athletic ability, even the same star sign. And our old men got on famously. I remember one day we were chatting in a corporate box and turned round to see them having a rugby scrum with each other. Thanks, dads!

We were both emotional blokes and could say things to each other that wouldn't cut it in the macho world of the dressing room. We always hugged and said how much we loved each other. It was like we had a biological connection.

Crowey was truly a great man and I was devastated when he died. He had so much insight and wisdom. His Cricket Max idea was a forerunner of Twenty20,[3] and he foresaw what would happen with David Warner as well. In 2015, three years before everything exploded in South Africa, he wrote an article on Cricinfo stressing the need for yellow and red cards in cricket.

'Watching from the luxury of my couch and after hearing numerous accounts from respected cricket people, there is a growing concern that David Warner's thuggish behaviour has gone too far. Soon one day it will lead to an incident that will sully the game for good.

'Warner can play, but he is the most juvenile cricketer I have seen on a cricket field. I don't care how good he is: if he continues to

---

[3] Cricket Max, which started in 1996, involved each team having two innings of a maximum of 10 overs each, with various tweaks to the laws of the game to increase the entertainment – free hits and things like that. Each match lasted three hours in total. Sound familiar?

show all those watching that he doesn't care, he must be removed, either by Cricket Australia or definitely by the world governing body.

'The more he gets away with it, the more others will follow his pitiful actions. Already we see one or two of his teammates enjoying being close to his hideous energy.'

How prescient is that?

Towards the end of his life, Crowey had a peace and spiritual wisdom that I found so inspiring. I've saved every one of the emails he sent me in his last few years, and they continue to lift me when I am struggling. 'We are blessed with second chances in life, and to take it and master it better than before is the best thing we can do.'

One day he sent me an email, and you could tell he was ready to move on.

'We've always had a special bond, hand-picked too early in hindsight, and now trying to piece it all back together – which we will, even if I don't live as long as you.'

A couple of days later he sent me a picture message with no text. It was the two of us, laughing hysterically during a game of XXXX beach cricket in Perth. When I arrived at work the next morning, one of my colleagues told me that he had passed away during the night. That picture was his last goodbye, his way of saying, 'Remember me like this.'

I should have spent more time communicating with him, even on email, because in his final moments we seemed to really connect again. It just shows the strength and the love we had for each other. Don't leave things to the last moment, which I did with Crowey. By the time he was close to death it was too late to give him the love and support he needed. How long does it take to write a few more fucking emails? I didn't and I should have done.

His wife Lorraine said something beautiful at his funeral. 'I recently asked him, "What is the most important lesson you've learned?" He said, "I have learned many lessons, but the most important of these is to only hold onto the truth, removing all that is untrue and false." I asked Marty how he wanted to be remembered. He said, "For being authentic, loving and full of prayer".'

Authentic, loving and full of prayer. That phrase will live with me for ever. It's how I'll remember him, and how I'd want people to remember me.

He's probably laughing his head off at me right now, because he's brought me to tears while I'm writing my autobiography! Crowey, I love you, I'm proud of you and I miss you being in my world.

Chapter 14

Yorkers and death threats

I WISH I'D PLAYED more against Pakistan, and I'm not just talking about the World Cup final. I played only one Test series against them in my career and it was utterly exhilarating. I loved the challenge of facing reverse swing, I loved the edge and animosity between the teams. I even loved Waqar Younis threatening to kill me on a daily basis.

The summer of 1992 was one to remember. We beat Pakistan 4–1 in the one-dayers, a small bit of revenge for the World Cup final, although one match later became the subject of match-fixing allegations. And they beat us 2–1 in a brilliant Test series that was bursting with controversy.

At the start of the season I received the England Player of the Year award, which was flattering but also bittersweet given I'd just been left out of the World Cup final. I wanted to prove a point in the one-day series, and I was Man of the Match in three of the five games. My editor tells me I ended that series at No. 2 in the ODI batting rankings, the highest position of my career.

Those one-dayers were played either side of the Tests – two in May and three in August – and I was in great form each time. But I had a really rough spell in between when I struggled in the middle of the Test series, particularly against the legspinner Mushtaq Ahmed.

I played him comfortably when I made a century in the first Test at Edgbaston, even though I couldn't really pick his googly. But when he bowled me round my legs in the second Test at Lord's I started to lose confidence and question myself. He was such a clever bowler. I'd been getting across to the off side, reasoning that if I didn't pick his googly it didn't matter as it would hit the pad outside the line of off stump and therefore I couldn't be LBW. He noticed this and started to attack my leg stump before slipping one round the back of my pads.

This is where all the stuff about me being poor against spin bowling really started. It's probably worth pointing out that many of the greats – including Peter May, Graham Gooch and Kevin Pietersen – have been bowled round their legs in a Test match. But there's no doubt I had problems against Mushtaq, who at that stage was comfortably the best spin bowler I had played against.

The struggle started to affect my mood, which was unlike me. Usually I was able to stay outwardly upbeat no matter what was going on in my head, but around that time I was irritable at home and a little withdrawn in the Hampshire dressing room.

It was the first summer since Kippy's move to Perth, and I missed not having him around to boost my confidence and keep an eye on my technique. He knew my game as well as I did, if not better. I'm pretty superstitious so I did a few ridiculous things – I tried a different Gray-Nicolls bat and even had the Judge's wig clipped.

A little pep talk from a great man helped me get my form back. Hampshire played Glamorgan at Portsmouth after the third Test at Old Trafford, a high-scoring draw in which I made 11 in my only innings before falling to Aaqib Javed, and on the first day Viv asked if I would have a drink at the close of play. I couldn't make it, but he asked again on the last day whether I had ten minutes for a chat before he drove back to Glamorgan. We sat in the dressing room and he said, 'What's wrong? You look despondent.' He reminded me how positive my body language had always been when I played against the West Indies, and told me to stop worrying about the Pakistan bowlers and focus on my abilities. It wasn't the specific advice that lifted me so much as the fact such a great man cared about me and went out of his way to try to help. Great support like that has always been important to me.

We were 1–0 down in the series with two to play, which meant Jack Russell was dropped and Alec Stewart took the wicketkeeping gloves so that we could play an extra bowler. A knock-on effect was that I moved from No. 4 to No. 3, ending the longest run of my career in one position – eight whole Tests. As I mentioned earlier, being that odd-job man probably didn't help me at times. I batted everywhere from No. 1 to No. 7 in Tests and was often moved to fill a problem slot. I never complained but in hindsight it would have been nice to settle in one position, ideally No. 4.

Alec had it even worse. One day he was a specialist opener, the next he was in the middle order and keeping wicket. And there were times when he was asked to keep wicket and open, which is a ridiculous burden.

I kept wicket myself for a few overs in the final Test at the Oval when Alec was off the field. I can tell you now, it's not as easy as it looks! Devon Malcolm was bowling fast with the new ball and I've no idea how I didn't let any byes through.

Although it took me a while to work out a method against Mushtaq, I ended the series with a determined unbeaten 84 at the Oval. I was a bit down after the first innings, when I fought really hard for 33 before being bowled through the gate by a googly as I tried to go down the track, and I had a chat with Goochie about it as he was such a masterful player of spin. He suggested I watch Mushtaq through the air and play him from the crease. I was worried that I wouldn't score a run off him this way unless he bowled a rank bad ball, but in the end I thought, 'Bugger it', and gave it a go. I decided to treat anything that pitched outside off stump as if it was a googly, even though most of them weren't, because if it turned the other way it would miss the off stump.

It worked fine. I sat on Mushtaq and got most of my runs off the faster bowlers. I think there was also some mental relief that, whatever happened, a difficult series was now almost over. I started to relax and played my best Test innings of the summer, even better than the hundred in the first Test. This was another example of me not backing myself enough. When I got to the ground on the third day it was overcast and the covers were on, and I secretly hoped it would pour down for three days so that a difficult summer would be over.

My return to form wasn't much consolation as we lost the match and with it the series. We just couldn't handle Wasim and Waqar. On the last morning of the final Test, Tuffers walked nervously to the crease and came over to talk to me.

'Are they fast, Judgie?'

'Don't worry, Tuffers, you'll be fine.'

He was bowled first ball.

There were rumblings in the media about the Pakistani bowlers tampering with the ball – they denied it, and nothing was ever proven – but that takes nothing away from their skill. Reverse swing is a great art and they were geniuses. To be honest, most of our complaints were sour grapes. One of the reasons we got so annoyed is that we tried to create the same reverse swing but couldn't exploit it like they did as we didn't have bowlers with the same pace. They were bowling 95mph toe-crushers.

The hardest thing with reverse swing, especially against Wasim and Waqar, was how late the ball moved. It went straight and then, out of nothing, it started to home in on your toes. They were very accurate as well, which they didn't always get credit for.

In pure cricket terms, it was much more devastating than playing against the West Indies. When you first went in they were unbelievably difficult to face, which is why they would often pick up three or four wickets in 20 minutes. We had some astonishing collapses that summer. The biggest was in the fourth Test at Headingley: 270–1, 292–2, 320 all out. And that was the Test we won!

When I played against them I treated the inswinger as the stock delivery, even though it wasn't, because I knew that was the danger ball. It was similar to the way I eventually treated Mushtaq's googly. I also knew I was good off my pads and could punish them if they got it slightly wrong. They did swing it away but that was less of a threat, because the ball would usually move earlier from the arm. Waqar also swung it away much less after the back injury that kept him out of the 1992 World Cup.

Wasim was in the top two or three bowlers I ever faced. He had such variety – over the wicket, around the wicket, swinging it both ways, holding the ball across the seam or seaming it away. He could change his pace, too. He was a really difficult customer, but the greater the challenge, the greater the satisfaction if you succeed. With Waqar you knew exactly what to expect: yorkers, bouncers and death threats. You had to concentrate so hard, though, because you knew the yorker would be coming any second. If your focus wasn't perfect you'd almost certainly lose your middle stump or break your big toe.

Believe it or not, I enjoyed facing Waqar. He was quite easy to line up, and although he bowled a seriously good bouncer, I at least knew when it was coming because he opened his shoulders slightly. You feel comfortable against some bowlers, no matter how good they are, and he was one of them. Allan Donald was another.

The opposite is also true – you have bowlers who you just can't get a handle on. I always found Derek Pringle hard to face; he hit the seam a lot and had the ability to get uneven bounce. Gus Fraser was the same – down the slope at Lord's, nipping it back. He was an outstanding bowler. I thought Craig White from Yorkshire was underrated too.

I had a pretty good record against Waqar and Wasim. Waqar only ever got me out once in international cricket, at Headingley in 1992, but that dismissal hurt because getting out to him was unthinkable. I'm still not sure how it started but on the field we detested each other. During the summer of 1992 he abused me every single day. By the end of the summer, even some of his teammates had had enough. When I walked out to bat in the last ODI at Old Trafford and we exchanged the usual unpleasantries, Wasim Akram said, 'Why don't you two just make up? You're beginning to piss me off.'

Later in that innings Waqar bowled a short ball and I swayed out of the way.

'The next one,' he said, 'will fucking kill you.'

'Yeah, good luck, fuckface.'

The next ball was short outside off stump and I nailed a square cut for four.

'By the way, Waqar, if you want to kill me you'll have to get a bit fucking quicker.'

When you get on top in a battle against a fast bowler, it's the most thrilling feeling. You know you're in control and they're not. If someone was sledging me and bowling short, I knew they'd lost it. Their focus had gone and they were trying to hit me rather than get me out. I had them where I wanted them – and where I wanted them to bowl. Perfect.

Javed Miandad used to say to me, 'Robin, always try and get the bowler to bowl to where you want them to bowl.' At first, I thought, 'What the hell do you mean, Javed? Shall I walk up and ask them to bowl short and wide?' After a while it all made sense.

The thing that confused me was that, even though he was vicious on the field, Waqar would smile and say hello in Urdu before play every morning. When Wasim came to play for Hampshire a decade or so later I asked him about it.

'Why were you guys so friendly in the morning and then so abusive on the field?'

'Do you know what they were saying to you?'

'Good morning?'

'No, they were calling you a motherfucker!'

They'd been doing that and I was smiling and waving at them like an idiot.

There was so much bad feeling in both the Test and one-day series. While sections of the media accused them of ball-tampering, they accused the home umpires of cheating. They even got shirty over a jumper, when Aaqib took offence to the way the umpire Roy Palmer gave him back his sweater at the end of an over.

It was incessantly nasty. Although I was really never sledged out in terms of losing my temper, I found it hard to concentrate against Pakistan because the abuse was constant. It was a never-ending blizzard of bullshit. Moin Khan, Waqar, Aaqib Javed; it came at you from everywhere. There were some players I really liked, including Javed Miandad, who is as nice a bloke as you could ever meet, and I've since become friends with Waqar and Wasim, but at the time it was all too much. Moin, the wicketkeeper, would basically call you the C-word every ball and leave it at that. I know I swear a lot but even I don't like that word.

Aaqib, now he was a nasty piece of work. He played with us at Hampshire in 1991, when Raj Maru, our left-arm spinner, took him under his wing. Raj adored Aaqib and they got on brilliantly, or so it seemed. A year later, when Pakistan played Hampshire in a tour match, Aaqib bowled him bouncer after bouncer. This wasn't done in a jokey way, he was really trying to hurt him. Raj couldn't bat to save his life either. It was totally out of order.

One day I asked Stewie, who played with him at Surrey, about Waqar.

'Come on, what's he really like?'

'Mate, Waqar is one of the nicest blokes you could ever wish to meet.'

'Nah, you are joking.'

'I know what you're thinking, Judge, but you have him in the dressing room and he is such a good bloke and team man.'

He went to play for Glamorgan and I asked the same thing of Matthew Maynard, who gave me the same reply as Stewie. I met Waqar after I'd retired, and it's true – he's a fantastic bloke. It's fascinating. There are very few people in cricket who I've disliked once I've actually got to know them.

We finished off the one-dayers after the Tests. In that last game at Old Trafford, I had a big partnership with Graeme Hick as we chased down a target of 255. I couldn't believe how often they were bowling short and wide to me. At one point I said to Hicky, 'What's going on? They are bowling shite!' I didn't think much of it at the time but when the match-fixing scandal broke in 2000 I reflected on that game and the one at Trent Bridge a week earlier, when they bowled poorly and we scored what was then a world record total of 363–7. Evidence was later given to an inquiry into match-fixing allegations[1] surrounding the team that at least one of these matches had been fixed, but they were denied and unproven.

Maybe their bowlers just had a couple of bad days, I don't know. We do all have them, and mine came at the end of that summer when I was playing for Hampshire. I'd had another good summer in county

---

[1] This was chaired by a high court judge, Justice Malik Mohammad Qayyum.

cricket and top-scored with 90 when we beat Kent in the Benson & Hedges Cup final at Lord's. The win brought me particular joy because it was Malcolm Marshall's first in a Lord's final. He'd been away on international duty when we won in 1988 and 1991, and he was on the losing side with the West Indies in the 1983 World Cup final. It was a really big ambition of his – the day before the game he refused to do any fielding practice in case he broke a finger – and I was chuffed to play my part.

When I returned to Hampshire for the last couple of championship games after the Pakistan one-dayers, however, I felt totally flat, devoid of focus and motivation. I was out for 1 and 3 against Durham at Darlington, and I was lucky to get that many. I had no energy and fell asleep in the dressing room before I went out to bat, which I had never done before. Our next game was against Essex and I was desperate to do whatever it took to get my concentration back, so I decided to go out to bat without a helmet.

The Essex attack included the left-armer Mark Ilott, who went on to play a few Tests for England. He could be really brisk when he wanted to be, and when I walked out with my cap on, I think he thought I was taking the piss. He soon sent down a bouncer that went straight past my face – I knew it was close because I heard the air whistle – and I started to wonder whether I'd made the right decision. I was far too proud to call for a helmet, so I rode out the storm before getting out for 23. I doubt I would have got that many if I had worn a helmet. My concentration still wasn't quite right but it improved once I felt the breeze of the ball going past my face. A bit of fresh air always sharpens you up.

One of the reasons I was so tired was that there had been a few end-of-season parties. The saddest was a farewell for Micky Stewart, my second father, who had decided to step down as England coach after six years. His last game in charge, the fifth ODI against Pakistan, also turned out to be the last time Lamby and Beefy played for England. I was at the non-striker's end when Lamby was out and felt really empty, because I had a hunch it would be the last time I was at the crease with him for England. I wish I could have batted with him for ever.

David Gower had made what turned out to be his last appearance for England in the final Test a couple of weeks earlier. Gower, Lamb, Botham and Micky Stewart all gone – it really was the end of an era, and it meant my dressing-room support network had disappeared at a stroke. Though I didn't know it at the time, I would never quite be the same player again.

Chapter 15
Slow torture

THE GREAT INDIAN LEGSPINNER Anil Kumble had a single season with Northamptonshire in 1995. He took 105 wickets and almost inspired Northants, captained by my old mate Allan Lamb, to win the County Championship for the first time in the club's history.

We played them towards the end of July on a turning pitch at the County Ground in Northampton. I came out to bat at No. 4 on the first day and it took Lamby about two seconds to open his mouth. His sledging was a bit more playful than when he made me cry all those years earlier in South Africa. 'Hey, Kumble!' he shouted, knowing full well I could hear every word. 'Warm up, china! Your bunny's coming in, eh? He can't play spin, he knows he can't play spin, so come and have a bowl and get a cheap wicket, eh?'

Cheers, Lamby!

In the second half of my career, my problems against spin were a regular talking point. Even my best mates were making a joke of it. Even *I* was making a joke of it. I had a look at my benefit brochure from 1996 before writing this and it's full of comments from me about my ability against spin. ('Ambitions: To hit Shane Warne for six!') I suppose it was partly self-deprecation and partly an attempt to show it wasn't bothering me, even though it was.

Look, I'm not silly – I know I was a much better player of fast bowling. I know I played with hard hands against spin, and I suppose I felt a bit emasculated when there was no pace on the ball and I was surrounded by fielders. But I also think my struggles against slow bowling were overplayed and cost me a lot of international caps.

There are many reasons why the second half of my England career was not as productive as the first, and the revival of mystery spin bowling is only one of those. There was also confidence, burnout, poor man-management, injury, even blackmail. When my confidence was low I was poor against spin – but when my head wasn't right I struggled against any type of bowling. I had difficult tours of Australia in 1990–91 and the Caribbean in 1993–94, when I hardly faced a ball from a slow bowler, yet nobody said I couldn't play pace. When I was confident and playing positively, I felt comfortable against any spin bowler in the world with one exception: Shane Warne. I freely admit I struggled against him. Who didn't?

You don't just have to take my word for it. There's plenty of evidence in *Wisden* to suggest that, when I was in the right frame of mind, I could play spin bowling just fine. I scored Test hundreds against Kumble, Muttiah Muralitharan and Mushtaq Ahmed. I never played against Abdul Qadir in a Test but I top-scored against him in the Nehru Cup semi-final, and I had a higher Test average against Pakistan, India and Sri Lanka than any other country. You can't average 44 in Test cricket, batting in the middle order, without scoring runs against spin. I also averaged 49 in ODIs in Asia. I'm told Joe Root, James Taylor and Ben Stokes are the only England batsmen with a higher average than that.

There was a spell in my career of around two years when I batted poorly against the slower bowlers. I'm still not sure which came first, the loss of confidence or the negative coverage. I do know that once you are written off by the press, it can be hard to recover. Even a great like Graham Gooch suffered during the 1989 Ashes, when people said Terry Alderman could get him out whenever he wanted. By the fifth Test, Goochie asked to be left out of the team.

I've been learning about an interesting thing called 'stereotype threat'. Basically it means that, once you are negatively stereotyped, you become anxious and unconsciously act in ways that reinforce the stereotype. The anxiety plays tricks with your brain and affects your ability to defy the stereotype.

Early in my career, apart from when I supposedly lost concentration at Lord's in 1989, the media were always really supportive. But latterly they perpetuated the idea that I was frail against spin bowling. I probably didn't help myself by talking honestly about my difficulties in the press. During the India tour of 1992–93, for example, I said, 'Give me Ambrose on a quick bouncy pitch any day to these guys.'

There's an old line from Henry Ford that I came across recently – 'Think you can, think you can't; either way you're right.' For maybe a two-year period, it was embedded in my subconscious that I couldn't play spin. Even when I was batting in charity games, some smartarse would shout, 'Hey, skip, put me on, I can bowl spin.' It started to get to me. It didn't help when my England coaches started ridiculing me in the media, either.

Some people like negativity, having their glass half empty. I prefer talking about the positive things in life, seeing the good in people. Everyone jumped on the bandwagon and said I was crap against spin and I became obsessed with what the media were writing. I never thought it was personal, not with the press, but I also knew that people believe what they read.

I tried to only read some of the more influential and knowledge-able writers like Christopher Martin-Jenkins and Mike Selvey, but I had a quick look at every paper and if I saw a negative headline about me I couldn't resist reading the story. Although it was a form of psychological self-harm, I couldn't help myself. Thank God there was no social media back then. I was more likely to read negative publicity than positive stories – I'd get embarrassed if people were saying wonderful things about me.

With my personality and character, I can lose confidence so quickly. As I became less secure I struggled against average county spinners, people I should have been smacking everywhere, never mind the greats. My opponents sensed that and started to bowl better, and the whole thing perpetuated itself.

I'd experienced the reverse of this – stereotype boost – when it came to fast bowling. I was perceived as one of the finest players of fast bowling of my generation. Bowlers knew I was good against pace and maybe some of them were intimidated when they bowled at me. I also played well because the reputation I had gave me confidence.

The more I got out to slow bowling, the more I lost my confidence. The gremlins started multiplying in my head in the dead of night. I'd go to bed and struggle to get to sleep, which was never usually a problem. I used to hate nights like that. It's quiet and dark and you start imagining what you're going to be confronted with the next day. Reality doesn't come into it, everything is blown out of proportion. You toss and turn, look at the clock, flip the pillows round, and none of it works.

The harder you try to get to sleep, the more likely you are to stay awake. Then if you do nod off, you might dream about playing spin and wake up feeling a bit tired and subdued.

This isn't an attempt to rewrite history. I know playing spin was my weaker suit but I also know I wasn't as bad as people make out. Middle-order batsmen are going to get out to spin bowlers, just as openers will get out to quick bowlers. Mike Atherton got out 19 times to Glenn McGrath and 17 to Sir Curtly Ambrose and Courtney Walsh. Was he a bad player of fast bowling? No, he was a bloody brilliant player. You wouldn't dream of leaving Athers out against Australia because he struggled against Glenn McGrath. Yet when England picked the squad for the 1994–95 Ashes tour, I wasn't even considered because of Warney.

It's no surprise I wasn't as effective against spin, as I hardly faced any growing up in South Africa. It was a constant diet of pace bowling on hard, fast pitches – and on the bowling machine at home, too. I didn't play a sweep shot until I was 18. There were a few good spinners, like the leggie Denys Hobson, but there wasn't much mystery spin and the pitches didn't encourage slow bowling. It was the same in county cricket in the 1980s. There were some fine spinners like John Emburey, Phil Edmonds and Derek Underwood, but they were all orthodox and the pitches didn't exactly turn square.

I was always a little confused about how to play spin. Early in my career, when Procky was bowling some offspin, I used to practise against him in the nets at Natal. He turned it a long way and sometimes I'd get hit on my pad, playing with my bat and pad close together. He told me to take off my left pad so that I would be forced to use my bat if I didn't want to be hit on the shin. That meant I learned to play with my bat in front of pad rather than alongside it, but as time went on I was criticised for playing too early and pushing at the ball. Mike Gatting was one of the best players of spin bowling around and he played it very late, usually behind his pad. Now, if he plays like that but the great Mike Procter has told me to play a completely different way, you start thinking, 'Well, what do I do?'

The first time I came up against mystery spin in a Test was Mushtaq in 1992. It was like a foreign language, and for the next couple of years I could barely speak a word. But steady exposure made me a better, more confident player. And while I never became truly fluent, by the mid-1990s I was more than able to get by.

There's one other thing about that Northants game in 1995, when Lamby told Kumble to warm up so that he could get an easy wicket. Kumble got 13 wickets in the match, including mine in the second innings. But in the first I smacked him round the park and made 172.

I also scored a hundred against him in the Old Trafford Test of 1990, but he was all over me when we toured India in 1992–93. He got me four times in six innings, hence Lamby's comments. I was out to a slow bowler in 13 consecutive Test innings around that time. I was so paranoid about getting out to a spinner – about being *seen* to get out to a spinner – that all I did was focus on survival rather than scoring runs. There were a few grim struggles: 8 from 74 balls in Kolkata, 17 from 84 in Chennai, 18 from 65 against Australia at Old Trafford in the first Test of the following summer. That's not me. I was generally more vulnerable when I was hesitant and defensive, which is maybe why my record against spin was very good in ODIs.

I was definitely at my best when I played on instinct. With spin bowling there was always too much time to think while the ball was in the air, and when I start to think I become a danger to myself!

Around that time, without realising, I stopped following Grayson Heath's formula for batting (Arrogance + Humility = Confidence) against the spinners. I had the humility but not the arrogance and therefore no confidence. Against quick bowling I always felt comfortable that I had a number of get-out shots, and that I could punish bad balls, so I never panicked even if I only scored one or two runs in an hour against the West Indies. But against spin, from around 1992 to 1994, I had few attacking shots I felt comfortable with, so the scoreboard got stuck and the pressure mounted.

Going into that first Test against India in Kolkata, I felt like I was in the form of my life. I played as well as I could – and I really mean that – in the nets beforehand. Trouble is, I was facing Devon Malcolm, Paul Taylor and Chris Lewis on a fast, bouncy net. When the match started it was on a slow turner and I didn't face a single ball of pace in the match. Even the nets we had at Lilleshall before the tour bore no resemblance to the Indian wickets – they turned and bounced really sharply rather than being slow and uneven. Fail to prepare …

Even though I only made 8 from 74 balls in the second innings of that first Test, I was starting to feel more comfortable when I was given out caught behind off Rajesh Chauhan when I hadn't edged the ball. Suddenly, I had started the series with scores of 1 and 8 and I was under pressure, at least in my own head. A similar thing happened in Australia in 1990–91. After that miserable start to the tour, I was 30 not out and playing well on the first day of the Boxing Day Test when I was given out caught behind off Merv even though I didn't hit it. A bad shot and a cheap dismissal in the second innings meant I was back where I started.

I'm not moaning, as there were many times when I benefitted from umpiring decisions or dropped catches. I just find it fascinating how precarious luck and form can be.

I remember, for example, the Lord's Test against Australia in 1989, when I somehow got away with being hit plumb in front by Steve Waugh. I couldn't believe it when the umpire Nigel Plews gave it not out. When I was captain of Hampshire, the one thing I would not accept under any circumstances was dissent to an umpire, or even a player slagging them off when they got back to the dressing room. It just didn't sit well with me. Umpiring is a bloody hard job. Once, one of our batsmen threw his bat across the dressing room after getting a dodgy decision. I asked him, 'How many times did you play and miss in that innings?'

'I don't know, maybe seven or eight.'

'Right, well you made seven or eight mistakes and the umpire has only made one, so put your toys back in the pram and show some respect.'

That India tour in 1992–93 was stressful and miserable for all of us. We were favourites beforehand, and most people thought Phil Tufnell and John Emburey would out-bowl their spinners. Instead, we lost all three Tests heavily on turning pitches. Embers was treated like a net bowler, particularly by Navjot Sidhu, and Tuffers was driven to the brink.

Ever since I brought Philip Patel home to live with us at the age of 10, I have befriended and protected those I felt were being discriminated against, excluded or treated unfairly. I don't know why, but it's in my nature. So when I went on England tours, I tended to room with the eccentrics or the odd men out. I shared with Wayne Larkins, who was a chain-smoker and therefore not everyone's idea of an ideal companion, but my dad was a smoker so I never really minded. Chris Lewis would go to sleep at 8 p.m. and get up at 1 a.m. to go to a nightclub. He didn't drink so it didn't affect his performance – he just got his eight hours' sleep in a different way to the rest of us.

Jack Russell would set everything up in the room and start painting. I used to love watching him, and I've still got a portrait he did of me during a plane journey. I was one of the first people to commission him, as well, when he did a painting of the Salmon Leap on the River Test in Romsey. I still have it at home. I paid him a bloody fortune; I thought I'd get a discount! Watching Jack paint was the good bit about sharing with him. The bad was that there were things everywhere – easels, used teabags[1] and underpants. He didn't trust the hotel staff to wash his underwear. So he'd wash his pants, vests and jockstraps in the bathroom sink, not always as thoroughly as he might,

---

[1] He used the same teabag 30 times when on tour.

and then hang them everywhere – from lights, on top of the TV, over the bath. I tended to prefer a shower when I shared with Jack.

Devon Malcolm was good fun to share with. He was neat, thoughtful and tidy, at least when he was awake. While he was asleep he would wrap himself up in the bedsheets, with the fabric rolled up at the bottom and the top, and he'd stir in the morning looking like a Christmas cracker. He also liked to do hundreds of press-ups just before going to bed, which often kept me awake.

I roomed with Tuffers a few times and always looked out for him on tour. He's a genuinely good bloke, very sensitive despite the cheeky-chappy exterior. His mum died when he was a teenager and that hit him so hard. Tuffers was having a really difficult tour of India. He went as our match-winner but was left out of the first Test because of indifferent form in the warm-up games. It was a ridiculous decision. Before the second Test we played a match against the Rest of India in Visakhapatnam, and Tuffers lost his rag when Richard Blakey failed to stump Sachin Tendulkar. At the end of the over he hoofed his cap away, had a row with the umpire and was later fined £500.

I saw trouble brewing and sat with Tuffers on the coach back to the hotel. I sensed his morale was at an all-time low. He was also having problems with his ex-wife Alison, who he had separated from a few years earlier, and he looked as if he was at the end of his tether.

We were in our room having a chat when Goochie started thumping on the door, clearly in the mood to give Tuffers a serious bollocking. Goochie, in fairness, had no idea just how fragile Tuffers was. Goochie was tough, and in those days nobody really knew much about the concept of mental illness. You were expected to be a man and get through it.

My protective instinct kicked in – I told Tuffers to hide in the toilet and said I'd deal with it.

Goochie kept banging on our door. 'Tuffers, I know you're in there.'

I opened the door and put on my best acting face. 'What are you going on about, Goochie? He's not here, he's gone out for a walk.'

Goochie hissed at me. 'I know he's here's, Judgie.'

'Look, he's not here,' I said, opening the door fully. 'Come in and take a fucking look if you don't believe me.'

The bluff worked and Goochie stomped off down the hallway. Tuffers emerged a few minutes later, so I left him to it and went out for a while. When I returned Tuffers was sitting on the edge of the balcony, looking down. There was no railing and we were about 50 metres above the ground.

I was instantly terrified, so I sat next to him on the balcony. I didn't particularly enjoy having my feet dangling over the edge but I didn't know what else to do. I put my arm around him and we started chatting. 'It's too much, and today has topped it off,' he said. 'Judgie, I've had enough.'

He kept jolting forward, and I was frantically trying to work out what to do if he jumped. If I tried to grab him, I'd probably fall with him and it would look like some kind of suicide pact.

I begged him to have a beer and talk it through for a bit. While keeping my eyes on him, I swung my feet back into the room and called the Reverend Andrew Wingfield-Digby, who was on tour with us as a spiritual adviser. He was a delightful man, totally non-judgemental, and with a serenity that made everything seem okay.

Wingers arrived straight away – maybe he'd seen the signs too – and started to chat to Tuffers while I chipped in occasionally. Tuffers and I were in tears. After two horrible hours in which I feared my mate might take his own life, Tuffers came back into the room. I honestly think Wingers saved his life that night.

Tuffers played the second and third Tests without much success. All our bowlers were powerless, and Phil DeFreitas didn't take a single first-class wicket on the tour. Early on, in a tour match, Chris Lewis said of the young batsman Vinod Kambli, 'I reckon I could get this bloke out with an orange.' In the third Test, as Kambli went past 200, I suggested it might be time to ask the umpires if we could have a go with that orange.

There were some brilliant hundreds in that series, including maiden Test centuries for Graeme Hick and Lewis. I was so chuffed for them both, especially Hicky after all he'd been through. But the best innings was played by their captain Mohammad Azharuddin in the first Test. He was fighting for his job after they had lost in South Africa, and he hit an unbelievable 182 to set the tone for the whole series.

I remember Goochie pleading with Devon to bowl outside off stump. The next ball went scudding through midwicket for four.

'Outside off stump, Devon, for heaven's sake!'

'Captain, that was outside off stump.'

Azha was using his wrists to take everything from outside off and fizz it through midwicket. It was unbelievable batting, one of the best hundreds I've ever seen.

The second Test was a bit of a farce, because half the squad were taking turns to use the toilet. A few of us got sick on the morning of the Test, and the press reported that we all ate some dodgy Chinese prawns the night before. Even Arthur Daley put the boot in during an episode of *Minder*, when he said, 'I mean, look at our cricket team. One man's bowl of prawns is a nation's humiliation.'

Sorry, Arthur, but I didn't touch the prawns. I'm not sure what made me sick. But a few of us had to play even though we were feeling rough, and it wasn't much fun batting when I was sick at both ends. It played havoc with my concentration. I know this sounds crude, but honestly, I was trying to focus against Anil Kumble or Venkatapathy Raju with men round the bat, and all I could think was, 'Whatever you do, Judge, don't fart.'

Even though I was feeling rough I made a good half-century in the second innings – and then, the moment I reached fifty, I tried to consolidate and got out pushing tentatively at Kumble. As at Trent Bridge in 1989, when I made 101 against Australia, I paid the price for going into my shell after reaching a milestone and I was really angry with myself.

That match was the second time I'd been ill on the tour. I've always had to battle to keep my weight under control; I think it's in the genes on Dad's side of the family. When I was at Hampshire, the lads would often stop for a McDonald's on the way home, but I had to abstain because I know I couldn't be drinking lager *and* having a Big Mac and fries. Somewhere in my subconscious I could hear Kippy calling me a 'fat little shit' and flicking butter at me.

There were a few months between the end of the English summer and the start of the India tour, so I decided to work really hard and get down to my fighting weight. I was in great shape and thought I'd reward myself by bringing an extra suitcase full of Marks & Spencer's finest food. I took a load of jars of Branston Pickle as I knew Gatt loved it, and also filled the suitcase with tuna and rice. I boasted about this to the guys, who were pissing themselves when I then went down with a dodgy tummy a couple of days into the tour. I lost about a stone on top of the weight I'd already lost, which meant I was now too skinny!

On top of my stomach troubles, I had a few niggling injuries – a broken toe, a thigh muscle problem and a long-standing shoulder injury, which stemmed from me dislocating it while playing rugby at school, that urgently needed an operation. Every time I threw the ball in from the outfield, it felt like I was being knifed in the shoulder.

There was an air pilots' strike, so we weren't in the safest hands, and there were a couple of flights where a few people were seriously saying their goodbyes. There were constant security concerns, too. These days they have expert advisers like Reg Dickason but there was none of that for us, so the players were a bit jumpy as there was a lot of civil unrest, with over a thousand people killed. The first ODI in Ahmedabad was cancelled because our safety could not be guaranteed. One day, in Lucknow, I was in a hotel room with Neil Fairbrother and Tuffers when three blokes with guns wandered casually into our room. Thankfully, they only wanted an autograph, but it shows how lax security was.

Most of us would have been happy to go home. I was good friends with the *Daily Mail*'s Peter Hayter and did an interview in which I said that if things got any worse we should consider abandoning the tour. A perfectly reasonable comment, I thought, given that I quite fancied staying alive a bit longer, but a lot of people who had never experienced anything like that said I was an ungrateful so-and-so. That really upset and annoyed me.

The third and final Test was another heavy defeat. Poor Kath had flown over just for the match and spent the week in bed with stomach trouble. I top-scored with a good 62 in the second innings, when I played much more positively. As against Pakistan, I think I relaxed because I knew the ordeal was almost over. I then played really well in the last four ODIs[2] to become top scorer on either side in a really entertaining series that ended 3–3. I hit four sixes in a rapid hundred at Gwalior when, yes, we lost. The format made me play much more positively against the spinners, in this case Kumble, Raju and Maninder Singh, and I was far more effective.

We finished the tour with a one-off Test in Sri Lanka, when I opened and batted throughout the first day for 91 not out. I was absolutely shattered that night, and the next day I managed to nudge my score up to 128. The heat and especially the humidity were like nothing I have ever experienced. I was so dehydrated that I literally didn't have a piss for two days. I changed my shirt 13 times during the innings and ran out of dry batting gloves.

A young Muttiah Muralitharan was in their team and they had another offspinner, Jayananda Warnaweera, who also gave it a rip, so it was really hard work. That was my best innings against spin, and possibly my best overall in terms of concentration, fitness and resilience. I didn't play any beautiful square drives or anything like that as there was no pace in the wicket. In fact, I barely played an attacking stroke. But I hung in there, getting outside the line to Murali whenever I could, and got ugly runs.

Sadly, we were beaten again to complete a miserable winter. We had one night out before we went home, in a nightclub at the bottom of the Taj Samudra in Colombo where we were staying. At 3 a.m., I had Peter Hayter by the throat in a lift. And he was the journalist I liked the most! We laughed it off the next day, and neither of us could remember what it was about. It was probably residual frustration from those reports during the India tour. It wasn't his fault – people had taken it out of context – but it had been a long winter.

Who knows? Maybe, at some subconscious level, I was taking out my frustrations about all those journalists who had written that I couldn't play spin.

---

[2] The first two were played before the Tests.

Chapter 16

You've been Warned

On a crisp winter morning in August 2016, I got up as usual at 5.30 a.m. to cycle across Perth to work. I was riding along when my phone bleeped with a text message from my old buddy Mark Nicholas. 'Unlucky, Judgie, your record has gone.'

The record was for the highest ODI score by an Englishman. Alex Hales had smashed 171 against Pakistan, beating my 167 not out against Australia 23 years earlier. I was a bit sad to lose the record but not remotely surprised. Given how much one-day cricket changed in that time, I still can't believe I kept it for so long.

That innings, against Australia at Edgbaston in 1993, is probably the most famous of my career. Towards the end, for maybe an hour or so, everything slowed down and I felt like I could play any attacking shot I wanted.

I was batting at No. 3, my favourite position in one-day cricket. I liked batting No. 4 in Tests but in one-dayers there was usually a bigger gap between innings, 40 minutes rather than 10, so I had more time to prepare. And I had more time in the middle. I was never very good at scoring quickly from the off, but once I got myself in I'd catch up, so No. 3 was the perfect position.

I had to be quite careful at the start of that innings against Australia, because they put us in and the ball was doing a fair bit. I'd only scored 22 runs all summer so I wasn't exactly in form either, and I had to work so hard for the first hour. Craig McDermott, in particular, bowled brilliantly. I know it's a cliché but I really did have to earn the right to play my shots later in the innings.

The wicket got better as the match went on. I reached my hundred from 136 balls and then exploded, hitting 67 off the last 27 balls. Whenever I hit a boundary, the lusty cheers of the crowd made me want to hit the next ball even further. Apparently, when Steve Waugh was asked to bowl, he joked about calling for a helmet. Near the end I played one of the best two shots of my career,[1] hitting a yorker from Paul Reiffel back over his head for six. I ended with 167 not out from 163 balls, with 17 fours and three sixes. The next highest score was Graham Thorpe's 36.

And we still lost the game. They needed 278 from 55 overs, a huge ask in those days, but Mark Waugh and Allan Border saw them home with ease. Although I could see the game slipping away, as a cricket-lover and a student of batting I was fascinated with how they approached the run-chase. They were clinical, composed, unhurried and they chased down a big target without breaking sweat. There wasn't one slog. I was captivated watching them until I suddenly realised, 'Ah shit, we're going to lose.'

The prime minister, John Major, said some very kind things about the innings, comparing me to Gilbert Jessop. It was lovely to play like that in front of Allan Border, one of my heroes, as well. I received the Man of the Match award despite our defeat and asked AB and Goochie to sign the ball, which now sits in the Robin Smith Suite at Hampshire with some of my other memorabilia. I don't have any memorabilia on show at home – unless you count a copy of the computer game *Robin Smith's International Cricket* for the Commodore 64 – but I'm happy that there are some nice items at the Ageas Bowl.

---

[1] The other was the off-drive off Waqar Younis in the gloom at Lord's during the 1991 NatWest Trophy final.

Australia decided not to play Shane Warne in the one-day series, figuring it would be better if we didn't get a look at him before the Test series. Even in the tour game at Worcestershire, when Hicky took him apart and scored 187, Warney was told to just bowl leggies and keep his tricks under wraps.

I'm sure you know what happened next. We started the first Test at Old Trafford well, with Peter Such bowling them out fairly cheaply, and they were in a bit of trouble when Warney came on in the afternoon session on the second day. We'd all been sitting on the balcony, but when he was introduced we decided to go back into the dressing room to look at the TV. We'd heard so much about him that we wanted to have a close look on the monitor. Gatt played the first ball nice and late, as he always did against spin, and it exploded across him to hit off stump.

What the hell was that?!

I was the next man in and, like everyone else, I was mesmerised by the replays. Eventually I got a tap on my shoulder and it was Gatt. He said, 'Mate, they're waiting for you.' I was almost timed out.[2]

I drove Warney for four to get off the mark. In his next over he produced a beauty that drifted one way, turned the other and took the edge on its way to Tubby Taylor at slip. Richie Benaud said it was as good as the Gatting ball, but because I played forward I nicked it. It looks much more spectacular when you're bowled rather than caught at slip.

I was confused as to how to play him. Some said play late, others said play with your bat in front of your pad. I pushed with hard hands in the first innings, so in the second I played as softly as possible. After battling for an hour and a half for 18, I played a soft-handed defensive stroke and watched in horror as the ball spun back onto the stumps. Damned if you do, damned if you don't.

We prepared turning pitches all summer – goodness knows why – and they added the offspinner Tim May to the side from the second Test onwards. He was an underrated bowler, who flighted the ball beautifully and turned it prodigiously. In fact, he turned his offspinner

---

[2] By the way, it's occasionally reported that Gatt only went in at No. 3 because I was stuck on the loo, but that's not true – I was always down to bat at No. 4.

as much anyone I ever faced, and I'd include Murali in that. The difference with Murali, which made him so difficult to face, was that he had so many variations.

May had me stumped at Lord's, the first person to be given out via TV replay in an Ashes Test, and the stuff about me not being able to play spin went into overdrive. England were 2–0 down after two and it was already time for changes. Gatt and Hicky were dropped, though some people called for me to go.

By chance, Hampshire were due to face Australia between the second and third Tests. I released some frustration by smashing a run-a-ball 191, with 32 fours and four sixes. Warney wasn't playing but May was and I took him apart. I brought that confidence into the third Test, when I scored two hyper-aggressive half-centuries. I was 14 away from a century in the first innings when the left-arm quick Brendon Julian took an unbelievable return catch. We had a young team, with four debutants including Thorpey,[3] who made a magnificent century, and would have won the match but for a last-day rearguard from Steve Waugh.

The change of mood didn't last, for me or the team. We were massacred by an innings in the next Test at Headingley, where they scored 653–4 in their only innings, and I went back into my shell. Then at Edgbaston, where I'd pummelled 167 a few months earlier, I scratched around for 21 and 19. In the second innings Warney nailed me LBW with the flipper as I shaped to cut. I was probably outside the line but it didn't change the fact I hadn't picked it. When I got back to the dressing room I stared at the TV for an age, trying to work out what I could have done differently. Batting had become such a trial.

Athers had taken over as captain from Goochie – who'd had enough after a run of eight defeats in nine games and resigned after the fourth Test at Headingley – and was staying at my house when Hampshire played Lancashire in the County Championship. Athers and I had a lovely dinner and shared a couple of bottles of expensive red wine. The next morning, over breakfast, he told me I was going to be dropped for the final Test at the Oval.

---

[3] The others were Mark Lathwell, Mark Ilott and Martin McCague.

It must have been tough for Athers, and a bit awkward, but he told me to my face and I respected that. I said, 'Okay, mate, I'll try to score the runs for Hampshire and get back in. And if I'd known, I'd have given you the cheap wine last night!' It was just my luck that England won at the Oval, a brilliant victory that raised hopes of a brighter future under Athers. Because I missed that game, I hold the record for playing the most Ashes Tests without being on the winning side – 15 games. That's one record Alex Hales or anyone else is welcome to break!

I didn't have a complete shocker in the 1993 Ashes – I averaged 28 in the series – but I was struggling and I had no real complaints about being dropped. There was a bit of relief too, that I could have a little time out and hopefully get my place back for the winter tour to the West Indies. I wasn't in great shape physically or mentally. I'd postponed that shoulder operation, which I needed for that old rugby injury, to play in the Ashes. And at the start of the summer I needed 18 stitches in my forehead after diving into an advertising board while taking a catch against the Combined Universities. I looked like Basil Fawlty with a big bandage round my head and a glazed look in my eye.

Warney got me four times in ten innings that summer. I faced some of the fastest bowlers in history but he was the one bowler who really intimidated me. Give me Sylvester Clarke on a dodgy pitch over Warney any day of the week. Clarke might knock me out; Warney would just get me out. He got in my head and tormented me with demons which, half the time, didn't even exist. He barely said a word but the way he looked at me really unsettled me – it was superior and knowing, as if he'd already decided exactly how and when he was going to put me out of my misery. Warney had this incredible vision and knowledge of the game, which enabled him to set batsmen up all the time. He seemed to always know what shot you were going to play, and he was so accurate that he gave you nothing. There was a drip effect until it all became too much.

That 1993 Ashes was the only time I faced him in international cricket, though he tried to bowl to me in the nets when he later came to Hampshire. It was only then that I fully realised how big a hold he had over me.

As captain I ordered him – I didn't ask him – to bowl in another net, because I wanted to come out of there feeling upbeat about my game. There was no chance of that if I was facing him!

The strange thing, looking back, is that nobody really offered any help or technical advice. Our coach Keith Fletcher was a brilliant player of spin, and after that we had Ray Illingworth, who took 100-odd Test wickets as an offspinner. Yet neither of them said much to me about adapting my technique. In those days, whether it was mental or technical, you were generally left to fend for yourself.

I should have asked for a bit more support in trying to get specialised spin-bowling coaching but I was too proud and too humble to ask, especially once I became stereotyped. In my head, to ask for help would have been to show weakness and prove the press were right. I would have loved to work with another Fletcher, Duncan, who improved England's batting against spin enormously when he became coach in 1999.

If I was advising my younger self, I would probably say to play a little more on the back foot rather than pushing forward with hard hands. I know Mark Nicholas thinks all those sessions on the bowling machine, though valuable, meant that at times I could be a little robotic. I understand what he means, but I would still say my biggest problem against spin by far was mental, not technical.

I was able to finally have the shoulder operation at the end of the 1993 season. It meant I couldn't touch a bat for 12 weeks but it needed to be done. What was supposed to be a one-hour operation took four hours, and the surgeon said he was surprised by the state it was in. There was a lot of arthritis around the joint, and he said that had I left it another two years it could have collapsed completely.

England's next series, at the start of 1994, was away to the invincible West Indies, who still hadn't lost a Test series since 1980. Athers pushed through a very young squad, with the plan to invest in them through thick and thin, just like Australia had done so successfully in the late 1980s. My record against the West Indies meant I was recalled straight away. With Goochie unavailable, I had more caps than anyone in the squad. Most pundits said I was certain to score big runs in the Caribbean. And I did – but only when it was too late.

Chapter 17

What goes on tour ...

WHEN WE WERE TWO young blokes making our way in international cricket, Mike Atherton and I undertook a ritual on the afternoon before every Test. When training was finished, we'd go for a spaghetti carbonara and share a bottle of pinot grigio. We did it once and both scored runs the next day, so it became a superstition for the next few years.

I got on well with Athers and liked him a lot. But, as you'd expect, our relationship changed slightly once he became captain. He could be a bit distant and I always felt a little bit on edge, as if I was playing for my place in every Test match. That was more because of the coaches but I was slightly cautious around Athers. He wasn't always a great communicator, and though he's a nice person he wasn't overtly compassionate. I suppose because he was so mentally tough, so self-sufficient, it might have been hard for him to understand those of us who were more fragile and needed affection – whether it was me, Tuffers, Ramps, Hicky, whoever. There were times when I didn't do myself any favours either, and I'm pretty sure my socialising on the West Indies tour of 1993–94 pissed him off.

We had a long build-up to the internationals, nothing like the modern tours, and a few of us took full advantage off the field. I'd really been looking forward to getting away. I was back in the England team, we were going on my favourite tour, to the West Indies, and it meant I had a few months' respite from the woman who was blackmailing me. (At least I thought it did – as it turned out I had to fly her over to Jamaica.)

I had plenty of beers on the flight over and got on famously with Matthew Maynard, who was touring with England for the first time. We weren't playing in one of the early tour games in Antigua and stayed out a bit later than we should have done one night. In our drunken wisdom, we decided to squirt tomato sauce all over Matty, wrap a couple of towels around him as a makeshift sling and tell the physio, Dave 'Rooster' Roberts, that he'd been seriously injured. We knocked on Rooster's door but he took a while to stir; the noise woke up Athers, who happened to be next door. It's fair to say he didn't find it quite as funny as we did.

I missed the team bus the next morning and they sent Doug Insole, the chairman of the TCCB, to look for me. I'd just woken up and wasn't completely with it so I politely invited him in for a cup of tea. He declined the offer and informed me that I'd have to make my own way to the ground as the team had gone.

Athers wasn't happy and I knew it wasn't good enough, whether I was playing in the game or not. He said, 'Look I'll have to make an example of you and give you a mouthful in front of the team. Don't take it personally but I think you should apologise.' I stood up in front of the team to say sorry and that was it.

I suppose it's not what you expect of your most experienced player. But the truth is I wasn't cut out to be a senior figure, as the role didn't come naturally to me. It affected me not having people like Lamby to lean on. Don't get me wrong, I still had some very good mates in the dressing room: Hicky was a good buddy; Thorpey I really liked. I took a shine to Jack Russell – he was a beauty, apart from his underpants. I liked everyone really, I didn't have any enemies. And I tried my best to create a positive mood, saying to people like Ramps, Hicky and Matty what Lamby would have said to me.

I was seen as a certainty to get 400 runs plus in the five Tests in the West Indies. I managed 320 and finished third in the England averages, but more than half of those came in the last innings of the series. I got 0 and 2 in the first Test in Jamaica, when I was bounced out for one of the few times in my career, and never quite recovered. I made a good 84 in the second Test in Guyana but that was about it until the last Test. I was having a few technical problems as well, with my bat coming down at an angle – I'd forgotten the hot potato – which is probably why I was bowled or LBW more than usual.

We lost the Test series 3–1, though we were 3–0 down after three. The last of those games, in Trinidad, included one of the most devastating spells of fast bowling ever seen. We started the fourth day as strong favourites to win the match with West Indies on 143–5 in their second innings, a lead of 67. We'd played so well and were on a real high as we went to the ground. We didn't win too many Test matches in those days, so when we got to the ground I filled the team bath with champagne and beers in expectation of a good afternoon and evening.

We dropped Shivnarine Chanderpaul twice and he got a vital fifty, which left us needing 194 to win on an uneven pitch. At the close we were 40–8, and I was scrambling round to hide the champagne, after an awesome spell of bowling from Sir Curtly Ambrose. I was the third man out, bowled second ball for nought to leave us 5–3.

He normally bowled around 85–88mph, and you knew that bounce and accuracy were the things to worry about. That day I played the perfect forward defensive stroke – and my off stump went flying. I looked at my position afterwards and thought, 'How did he get through that?' Ambrose never, ever beat me for pace. I don't know what stirred him but he was ferociously quick that day.

We were bowled out for 46 the next morning, a total humiliation, and things got worse before they got better. In the tour match before the next Test, we collapsed from 140–1 to 165 all out and eventually lost to the West Indies Board XI by nine wickets. I opened in the second innings, and in the first innings I'd got out to a young legspinner called Rawl Lewis. As I walked out for the second innings with Ramps, Keith Fletcher told us to get our heads down and fight. I replied cheerily, 'Okay, coach, I'll do my best.'

Out of nothing, he snapped. 'You'll do more than your fucking best, and don't get out again to the legspinner!'

That story is an example of Keith Fletcher's man-management, which just didn't cut it, I'm afraid. I didn't get out to the legspinner, by the way. I was out LBW for nought padding up to Anderson Cummins in the first over!

Somehow, from the depths of Trinidad, we won the following Test in Barbados – the first time West Indies had lost there in 59 years. Alec Stewart, with two magnificent centuries, and Gus Fraser, with eight wickets in the first innings, produced the performances of their lives. A few days earlier, Ray Illingworth was confirmed as England's new chairman of selectors, and in an interview after the game he said Gus, who had bowled his heart out yet again, wasn't fit enough. Great man-management, that.

Unfit Gus bowled another 45 overs in the last Test in Antigua, where Brian Lara hit a world-record 375. For the first two days he played perfectly, he didn't play and miss at all, and at stumps he was on 320. He needed another 46 to break the record held by Sir Garry Sobers.

That night he said, 'Judgie, what are you up to?'

I said, 'Nothing planned but I'm always available, Brian.'

We went to a nightclub and he couldn't stop talking about how nervous he was. I wanted him to get past Sobers – we weren't going to win the game, and I thought he deserved the record. He had an ability and stature that made him worthy of such an achievement. I suppose that might sound strange, but cricket was always more than just a game to me. It was about friendships, too, and appreciating the excellence of others. I was desperate for England to win when I played, but I also loved watching great players at work, especially if I was friendly with them off the field. We all see each other a lot less these days, because life gets in the way, but when we bump into each other it's like we've never been apart. That means a lot to me.

Brian was still very nervous the next morning. He played and missed at a few and I said, 'Just relax, BC.' Eventually he got the runs and it was carnage. The supporters all charged onto the field and it took about ten minutes for them to disperse. They were skidding all over the wicket, doing pirouettes on a length like John Travolta in *Saturday Night Fever*. Athers and I were there trying to shoo them away, knowing we had to bat on it at some stage.

When our turn came, Athers and I added 303 to save the game. He made 135 and I hit 175, the highest score of my Test career. It was an aggressive knock, with 26 fours and three sixes, and I took out some of my frustration at having had such a poor series. I was out twice off Courtney Walsh no-balls early in my innings, another reminder of the importance of luck.

When I got to about 160, Brian walked over to me. 'Judgie, you're not going to break my record are you?'

'Brian, mate, you would have nothing to worry about even if this was a timeless Test.'

In the end I fell a mere 200 runs short of his record. Something strange happened during that innings. A lot of West Indian fans used to bring transistor radios to the ground, and at some point during the innings I became aware that I could hear the commentary while I was batting. It must have been something to do with the acoustics of the ground, as it never happened anywhere else, but I could hear the commentator – I think it might have been Tony Cozier – talking about my innings as I was playing it.

Of course, once I became aware of it I couldn't get it out of my head. It's a basic point of psychology that, when you start to notice something, you notice it more and more.[1] It really affected my focus. I was trying to concentrate as Curtly was running in, and all I could hear was, 'And in comes Ambrose ...' I didn't hear how the commentary finished because I was too busy fending the ball away from my face. I asked Athers if he was picking it up. I think he thought I was mad.

There had been a rest day in the middle of the Test match. I was 68 not out at the time and, for reasons I still don't quite understand, Keith Fletcher decided to call a press conference and criticise me. He said I wasn't focused on cricket, that I needed to 'be aware what

---

[1] Apparently, this is called the Baader-Meinhof phenomenon.

comes first in life', and had 'too many fingers in too many pies', a quote that was regularly recycled over the next few years.

I had two businesses – Masuri, which made cricket helmets, and Chase Sports. But I never let them get in the way of my cricket. It annoyed me because, whatever the truth, mud sticks.

Fletch might say it had the desired effect, as I got 175 the next day, but that was purely a coincidence and in the long term it did a lot of damage to my confidence. I don't want to be wrapped up in cotton wool but equally I don't want people throwing shit at me for no reason when I already have low self-esteem and don't believe I'm good enough.

I felt Fletch was wrong to have such a limited view. If you eat, sleep and breathe nothing but cricket, it will consume you. You need to have other interests in life. Also, I was well aware of what came first in life: supporting my family.

In those days, we were not encouraged to pursue careers outside the game. I know it's very different now with the Professional Cricketers' Association, who do a great job of making people aware of the black hole of retirement. They educate players from academy level upwards about the need to prepare for retirement and have more in their lives than just cricket, and have also introduced a Transition Conference for players nearing retirement. I also think that having outside interests makes us appreciate how lucky we are to play this wonderful game for a living.

I thought the criticism was really unfair. Nobody had a go at Jack Russell for getting his easel out. He would have the odd day off so he could go somewhere and paint, and that was absolutely the right thing.

Looking back, Fletcher was right about one thing: I had lost a bit of focus and I wasn't practising quite as hard as I usually did. But it had little, if anything, to do with my businesses. It was because I was knackered mentally after 15 years without a break from cricket, and because my confidence was as low as it had ever been. I needed less cricket, not more.

There's one other thing about Keith Fletcher's comments. If you're so old school, why wouldn't you have that sort of conversation in private?

Chapter 18
Judge dread

IN ONE OF HIS early magazine columns, back in 1991, David Gower wrote a profile of me in *Wisden Cricket Monthly*. He pointed out how often I used the phrase 'if selected', even though I was at that stage ranked No. 2 in the world. It was a bit of a running joke – typical modest Judgie and all that. It wasn't so funny in the second half of my career, when I went into almost every Test match with England fearing it would be my last.

It soon became apparent that Ray Illingworth, who took over as chairman of selectors during the West Indies tour, was not my biggest fan. He backed up Keith Fletcher's comments about my business activities, even though he'd never been in the dressing room at that point, and I subsequently discovered that I was almost left out for the first Test of the home summer against New Zealand even though I'd scored 175 in my last Test innings.

There was very little communication with the players when Illingworth was in charge. Everything seemed to be done behind your back, often in newspaper interviews. The selection culture of the time, which was two bad games and you're out, meant that most of the team were playing under unbelievable pressure. It would be wrong to run a village team that way, never mind the national side. In a way,

I was one of the lucky ones – I was only dropped three times from the Test team, four if you count the start of the 1989 Ashes series when I was originally left out of the squad. Mark Ramprakash was dropped 11 times and Graeme Hick 10. After his brilliant debut series in 1991, Ramps made 14 appearances in the next six years, during which he was dropped *eight* times. And then people criticise him and Hicky for not fulfilling their potential! How are you supposed to play your best in that situation? I have no doubt whatsoever that, in different circumstances, they could have averaged at least 45 in Test cricket.

The higher the level you play at, the more the game is played in the mind, and in the 1990s we just didn't look after our players in that way. Any acknowledgement of what went on upstairs, never mind any attempt to improve it, meant you were seen as weak. Occasionally, we had a sports psychologist who came in and talked to us for an hour while putting a few things up on the noticeboard. It was a token gesture, and not nearly enough – you need to employ somebody full-time, to drift around, sit next to a player and get to know what they are like. Are they nervous? Do they like to talk before they go out to bat? Do they like their own space? Everybody is an individual. You have to understand somebody before you can start helping them, so you've got to observe them over time and win their respect.

A good sports psychologist can make you feel invincible, and I knew having somebody full-time would really help me and some of the other insecure characters. It would probably help the tougher nuts like Athers and Alec Stewart as well. If it worked for world-class golfers, or American teams, then I thought it was good enough for us.

I enthusiastically broached the idea to Fletch. I gave him the full sales pitch: how people say at least 50 per cent of the game is in the mind, yet only about 2 per cent of our preparation focuses on the mental side.

'Anyone who needs a fucking psychiatrist,' he said, 'shouldn't be fucking playing for England.'

I felt a bit sorry for Fletch that he didn't even know the difference between a psychologist and a psychiatrist. But I also thought it was incredibly narrow-minded. Stiff upper lip, soldier on, don't show weakness, all that old-school bollocks.

It didn't make sense to me that there was such hostility towards the idea. Mike Brearley is rightly revered as the greatest captain England ever had, and his main strength was in psychology and man-management – and that was 15 years earlier. Beefy will tell you that he played his best cricket by far under Brearley's captaincy. I tell you what, if I had him as my skipper, I would have been a different player.

We had loads of support staff, dieticians and things like that. Surely having somebody to help you bridge the gap between first-class and Test cricket is far more important than somebody telling you how many calories there are in a bloody chicken salad?

I felt Fletch was average in all aspects of the game. He was supposed to be a coach, but he was a poor coach for me because he didn't help at all. Illingworth was the same. I might be wrong but I can't think of a single England player who improved because of their coaching.

If they weren't coaches, they should have been managers. In that case you have to manage people – to make sure they are pumped up and walk out feeling magnificent about themselves; that they are inspired by a manager who is willing them to do well. For a lot of us, not just me, the opposite was true. I honestly felt they were looking for reasons to drop me. The team has always been important to me, that sense of the greater good, but it's hard to be inspired by that if you think your coaches don't want you around. Look at what happened when José Mourinho was replaced by Ole Gunnar Solskjær at Manchester United. The carrot will nearly always be more effective than the stick.

I did an interview with *The Wisden Cricketer* in 2010 when I said Illingworth and Fletcher were 'the most appalling man-managers, the most appalling coaches and the most appalling people that I've met'. That wasn't fair and I apologise to them for that. I was in a dark place in my life and I lashed out. I don't know them well enough to comment on their characters, and people whose judgement I trust speak highly of Fletch, in particular. I just thought they were poor coaches.

I was flying high under Micky Stewart, averaging over 50 in Test cricket when he left the job. He was ahead of his time, and then we started to go backwards with Fletcher. When Illingworth took over, we reversed at speed to the 1960s. We needed somebody a bit younger with new ideas and an understanding of the modern game – and, more importantly, of the modern player. You shouldn't treat players in the 1990s like you did thirty years earlier because time had moved on. Masculinity had moved on. Illingworth was in his mid-sixties and it was very hard for him to understand the mentality of a 25-year-old. One of the first things Illingworth did was to sack the team chaplain, the Reverend Andrew Wingfield-Digby. 'If players want a shoulder to cry on,' he explained, 'they are not the people to stuff the Aussies on the Ashes tour.'

I had a bad fear of failure at the best of times, so when I was playing for my place it was almost overwhelming. I dreaded batting like never before. I distinctly remember one innings, against New Zealand in the second Test at Lord's in 1994, when I was so nervous that I physically couldn't concentrate.

Even though I'd scored 175 and 78 in my last two Test innings, I felt like I was on trial. That 78, in the first Test of the summer, was very frustrating because I was run out after being sent back by Steve Rhodes. The replays suggested it was too close to call but the third umpire Merv Kitchen gave it out. I could and should have got a big hundred there. It completed an annoying match when I dislocated a finger trying to catch their captain Ken Rutherford.

By now my problems had nothing to do with spin bowling. New Zealand had a left-armer called Matthew Hart but it was the seamers who got me out. I played one really poor pull shot off Dion Nash at Lord's, when I misread the length and the ball got big on me, and in the third Test at Old Trafford I dragged a square cut onto the stumps. Even my signature shot was letting me down.

The frustrating and confusing thing is that I was in great form for Hampshire, but I couldn't transfer it to international level. England won the New Zealand series 1–0, and Illy said in the press that I was a definite pick for the second series of the summer. It was a really big one for me – England's first against South Africa since their readmission into international cricket. They had an all-pace attack, which was in my favour.

On the weekend before the first Test at Lord's, Lamby was hosting a belated fortieth birthday party at his house in Scaldwell. I didn't think I'd be able to go as we were playing the third day of a four-day Championship match against Gloucestershire. But Shaun Udal, bless him, wrapped the game up by lunch on the Saturday, which meant that, although we had a Sunday League game the next day, I had a chance to go to Lamby's. I spoke to Mark Nicholas, my Hampshire captain, who said, 'Judgie, I'm not going to stop you going but just make sure you look after yourself and you're in good shape for tomorrow's game. We need you at your best.'

'Captain, my leader, no problem.'

I drove the 130 miles up to Scaldwell and got there nice and early. There were so many people at the party, including Earl Spencer, the younger brother of Princess Diana, not to mention some legends of South African cricket like Garth Le Roux, Peter Kirsten and Mike Procter. Kevin Curran, the father of Tom, Sam and Ben and Lamby's teammate at Northants, was also in attendance.

Lamby had a magnificent marquee and the whole evening was wonderful. I had one drink, and then another drink, and the next thing I knew it was midnight and we were having a huge South Africa v England scrum in Lamby's kitchen. At that stage I called it a night, or at least I tried to do so. Procky and Peter Kirsten kept telling me it was a once-in-a-lifetime party and I succumbed to peer pressure. I eventually got to bed at 6 a.m., woke up at around 11 and had to race back down to Portsmouth. One of the umpires in the game, I think it was David Constant, said I overtook him at speed on the way down there. He knew this because I had my name emblazoned all over my sponsored car.

I arrived on time and tried to brazen it out with Mark. I was wearing my Bolle sunglasses, though he saw straight through that tactic.

'Judgie, would you like to take your glasses off for me?'

One look at my sunken eyes told him all he needed to know.

'Judgie, I asked you to look after yourself. You have not been to bed. Now, I want you to get a chair and sit under those bloody showers for the next hour. I don't want you to come out for the warm-up. Oh and by the way, the pitch is a greentop and they've got Courtney Walsh. If we lose the toss and they put us in, you're opening the batting. Good luck, Judgie.'

It was the same day I found out I'd been dropped by England for the South Africa series. That was a shattering blow, as much as anything because of what Illingworth had said a couple of weeks earlier. He later claimed he was misquoted. It was a bittersweet day because one of my best mates, Shaun Udal – known to us all as Shaggy because of his resemblance to the Scooby-Doo character when he was younger – was called up to the Test squad for the first time. I was so, so happy for him.[1]

In the end, we won the toss and put Gloucestershire in. I fielded with a degree of sluggishness but then top-scored and we won the game by five wickets. As I drove home I thought, 'Judgie, you've done it again!'

In a way, that weekend sums up my whole career. I burned the candle furiously at both ends, I experienced the high of a match-winning innings and the low of losing my England place. I had a great time with some of my best friends in cricket and revelled in Shaggy being called up by England. My career was often this slightly confusing mixtures of highs and lows.

A couple of weeks later, on 28 July 1994, my beautiful daughter Margaux was born. After the frustration of not being allowed to fly home for Harrison's birth, there was no way I was going to miss Margaux coming into the world. We were playing Northants at Southampton and, though I took part in the game, I had dispensation to leave whenever I wanted. Kath was in labour for 32 hours, so I was shuttling back and forth from the ground. As it turned

---

[1] As it turned out he was left out of the final XI and had to wait another 11 years to make his debut, when England toured Pakistan and India in 2005–06. He played a big part in England's famous win at Mumbai, when he took 4–14 in the second innings.

out, Margaux was born during the night. I didn't just witness the birth, I helped bring her into the world. It was absolutely magical. If you're a parent you'll know what I mean when I say there's nothing that can ever compare to the feeling of seeing your child being born.

The joy of fatherhood helped me get over losing my England place. On the first day of that South African series, I hammered 162 in a low-scoring match against Worcestershire to send a message to the selectors. But deep down I knew it was futile. If I wasn't picked against South Africa's all-pace attack then I had no chance of going on the upcoming Ashes tour due to the presence of Shane Warne. In Illingworth's book, *One-Man Committee*, he listed the batsmen who were on the shortlist for the last three batting places on that tour: Mike Gatting, Craig White, John Crawley, Mark Ramprakash, Nasser Hussain, Neil Fairbrother, Darren Bicknell and Alan Wells. That means that in a year I'd gone from being a senior player to not even among the best 13 batsmen in the country. Although Warney intimidated me, I would have loved to have had another chance to play against him and learn. You can't improve watching on TV.

I didn't know what burnout was at the time but I realise now that I was suffering from it. I'd played cricket constantly, every summer and every winter, since 1981 – that's 27 consecutive seasons. I was tired, unhappy and relatively unfocused. My shoulder needed a second operation and my mind needed a break. I had a few months off and then, in late January, went to Adelaide and Perth as part of the first Judge Tours excursion. It's a good job I did have my fingers in some other pies or I would have been on the dole until the start of the county season.

I needed every penny I could get after being stung badly by an accountant called Andrew Day. He was a bloody shark and I was so naïve. I arranged a meeting with him a couple of months before the West Indies tour of 1993–94 and we spoke about the money that was owing to the Inland Revenue. He said it would be due while I was away so I wrote a cheque for £45,000. I made it out to his company trust account, thinking he would then forward this on to the Inland Revenue.

A few months later I found out that they hadn't received the money and that I was legally responsible for the debt. I tried to track him down and eventually I got his home address. When I drove round there I saw a lovely BMW 635 outside and thought, 'You bastard, I'm the one who's paid for that.'

It turned out a few of us had paid for it. He had also been living it up at Harrods, Harvey Nichols, Selfridges and various posh hotels in America. I'm a very loyal, trustworthy bloke, and I always try to see the good in people. I'd certainly never steal a penny from anyone. You feel terribly let down when something like that happens.

He made himself bankrupt so there was no money for anyone, and I later found out there were many other creditors. We all had a meeting, which was awful and depressing. A lot of people were pensioners, and he'd stolen all their savings. I stopped feeling sorry for myself straight away. At least I was still playing professional cricket and had the chance to recover some of it. He was eventually convicted of swindling £240,000 from four clients and jailed for three years. I never saw him again. I'm glad I didn't as I probably would have given him a smack and ended up in jail myself.

I missed the England tour of Australia and was also left out of the England A tour of India the same winter. In a newspaper interview, Illingworth said the Indian spinners would have 'destroyed' me.

Come on, Illy! You just don't say things like that. I know there are times I should have been mentally stronger, but you cannot tell me that's good man-management. It wasn't just me either. He criticised half the team in the press. And if I was so bad against spin, how was I supposed to improve without exposure to quality spin in different conditions?

Even though I needed a break, I didn't make myself unavailable for that India A tour. There's an argument I would have benefitted from going, and had I been asked, knowing me, I'd have struggled to say no. But I have no doubt it was best for me to spend six months away from cricket. I was able to have my shoulder operation, refresh my mind and get down to the same weight as when I was a teenager.

I was also, for the first time since 1992, finally free from the black-mail. Those were also the worst two and a half years of my England career, but I don't want to use that as an excuse. I always felt I was reasonably good at compartmentalising different parts of my life. The blackmail was Robin Smith's problem. It didn't affect the Judge when he was batting, at least not on the surface.

I started the 1995 season feeling fresher than I had for years. I was told by David Graveney, who was new to the selection panel, that there were a few players in front of me but that I should keep going and try to score big runs. It wasn't what I wanted to hear but I appreciated the fact there was some communication. I planned to score the mountain of runs that would get me back in the England team. It turned out I barely needed a molehill.

Chapter 19

Fifty shades of black and blue

THANK GOODNESS FOR THE West Indies. If England had been playing anyone else in the summer of 1995, I doubt I would have been recalled. But my reputation against fast bowling was enough for me to get back in the team at the start of the series. Over the next two months I batted 17 hours on lively pitches against bowlers trying to knock my head off, and ended up in hospital. It was bloody wonderful to be back.

The first Test, however, was a bit of a disaster. I was asked to open so that Alec Stewart, who was keeping wicket, could bat lower down the order. It threw me a bit as I wasn't comfortable in that position, but I certainly wasn't going to turn it down. I scored 16 and 6, batted very nervously and we were trounced by nine wickets. After one Test back in the team – one single Test – I was back, as one journalist described it, 'on death row'. The general consensus was that, if I failed in the second Test at Lord's, I would dropped for good.

On the day before the match I had a long net against the seamers and then asked the bowling coach Peter Lever to underarm balls at my head from eight yards while everyone else practised against half-volleys. If it was going to be my last Test, I wasn't going to die wondering.

There was still confusion over my role. Ray Illingworth was in sole charge now, with Keith Fletcher sacked after a 3–1 defeat in the Ashes. Illy was the coach, manager, chairman of selectors, the lot. Eventually he decided that if we batted first, Alec would open and I'd bat No. 5, and if we bowled they'd make a judgement based on how long we'd been in the field.

We batted first and I was in just after lunch, at 74–3, and fighting a thousand demons. Sir Richie Richardson dropped me on 14, a stroke of luck I needed, but after that I played really well in partnership with Thorpey. When he reached fifty, everyone stood up on the balcony to applaud, with Illingworth right at the front. When I got to my half-century a few minutes later, he was nowhere to be seen. Dad noticed it on the TV. For all I know Illy may have been in the toilet, but it felt like a bit too much of a coincidence. By the end it was pretty blatant he didn't want me in his team.

I wish I'd been more like Lamby. He wouldn't have given a single shit whether Illingworth was on the balcony or not. He's a beautiful man but he's not sensitive and shy like me and had such natural belief in himself.

The match turned out to be a bit of a classic. I top-scored with 61 in a total of 283, then they got a lead of 41 despite a brilliant five-for from Gus Fraser, and in our second innings we eked out every run we could. I batted over six hours to top-score for the second time in the match before being pinned LBW by Sir Curtly Ambrose for 90. I was gutted to miss out on a century but I knew I'd played my best Test innings since the hundred in Sri Lanka two and a half years earlier.

We set them 296 to win and stormed to victory by 72 runs on a memorable Monday, with Dominic Cork taking seven of the last eight wickets to fall. He made useful runs in both innings and then took 7–43 to win the match. He was very emotional at the end. He even came up and offered me his Man of the Match award, saying, 'You deserve this, Judgie.'

I was more than happy for Corky to have it. I felt great. England had won a brilliant match and I'd got runs – the two didn't always go together in my career – and I knew that, after a miserable couple of years, I was pretty much back to my best. I couldn't wait for the rest of the series.

The mood in the team was just as upbeat. When the next Test started at Edgbaston, we really fancied our chances of backing it up with another victory or a least a solid draw. That optimism lasted exactly one ball. Ambrose's first delivery exploded over the head of Mike Atherton and the wicketkeeper Junior Murray for four byes. To be honest, Ambrose's bouncer was never that threatening, because you could duck it comfortably, but the trajectory meant it looked awesome. Especially when it was the first ball of the match.

At that moment, half the dressing room started frantically rummaging around for extra protective equipment – chest guards, inside thigh guards, titanium boxes, anything. Everyone went pale. I tried to play the part of the positive senior player – I started rubbing my hands and said, 'Guys, here we go! This'll be fun!' Inside I was thinking, 'We're buggered.'

On a personal level, I couldn't wait to get out there and test myself on an unpredictable wicket. We were beaten up by an innings in just over two days; it was the shortest Test in England since 1912. I top-scored in both innings with 46 and 41 but we were blown away for 147 and 89. In nearly twenty-five years as a professional cricketer, batting was never tougher than that. I'm not sure it was ever more enjoyable, either. Athers wrote in his autobiography that it was the bravest batting he saw in his career. Coming from him, somebody who knew so much about courage, that meant a lot.

The bounce on that pitch wasn't up and down, it was up and up. A lot of the players were bruised and injured, and Alec, Jason Gallian and Richard Illingworth all had fingers broken. We were so under the pump that Corky came in at No. 5, not even as a nightwatchman. I took the precaution of wearing a grille for the first time in my career, though I wasn't hit in the face. That was one of the few places they didn't get me. I was hit maybe 20 times, all round the body, and after the game I was fifty shades of black and blue. In the press, Fred Trueman said, 'Robin Smith won't be sleeping on his left side for a while.'

At times, especially in the second innings, I thought they got carried away and bowled poorly. When Courtney Walsh comes round the wicket, you know he doesn't want to get you out – he wants to hit you. He did nail me on the elbow in the second innings, mind you, and I knew plenty about it. But generally I didn't mind ducking and diving all day. I loved swaying back and feeling the ball whoosh past my nose.

After that battering, you'd think we all deserved a bit of respite. There were no central contracts back then, so most of us played in the Sunday League for our counties on what would have been day four of the Test. Nobody complained, we knew no different and loved playing the game. After fighting for every run at Edgbaston I cashed in with a spectacular 115 against Yorkshire. Yes, we lost.

Before that, on the Friday night of the Test, some bloke was so disgruntled with England's performance that he tried to start a fight with me in the toilets at TGI Fridays. I was there with Corky, Darren Gough and a few of the other players. He'd been drunkenly eyeballing us and followed me to the gents, looking for trouble. He was a big bugger who started shouting about how we had no fighting spirit. 'You England blokes are weak as piss.' As I'd top-scored in the first innings, was not out in the second and had a body that was like a colour chart, I thought it was a bit harsh. He then pulled out his front teeth, literally, and started rambling about doing martial arts for ten years. Part of me really wanted to show him some fighting spirit there and then, but I figured we were going to get enough negative head-lines as it was. We decided to leave before it got any worse.

After Edgbaston it was on to Old Trafford for a memorable fourth Test. We took a huge first-innings lead but Brian Lara wiped out most of it on his own. When he was in the mood, the bowlers were utterly powerless. Then Cork, who had burst onto the Test scene, got a hat-trick in the first over of the fourth morning. In the end we needed 94 to win, and were wobbling at 45–3 when I came in. As I left the dressing room, I looked at two helmets – one with a grille, one with just the ear protectors and a chinstrap. I picked up the second one and walked out.

I'd been in for a quarter of an hour when Bishop bowled a beau-tiful short ball. I lost sight of it for a split second and instinctively broke my golden rule – never turn your head away from the ball.

This time it took the shoulder of the bat and deflected onto my face. I heard a crunch and it was … sore.

I don't remember much after that. I was a bit dazed and my face was numb. Dave Roberts, our physio, came on and I told him I wanted to carry on, even though my face was already starting to swell. Apparently I said, 'I'll be fine, Rooster, give me a minute! Where's my bat, we're cruising.'

I was in another world and I reluctantly went back to the dressing room. An ambulance was waiting outside and the paramedics came up to give me gas and oxygen. I vaguely remember being put on a stretcher and carried downstairs. As that was happening, we lost another wicket and I told them I wasn't going anywhere until the game was over so that I could go out to bat if needed. They gave me more gas, after which I was high as a kite, and they bundled me in the ambulance. I needn't have worried: from 48–4 (effectively 48–5 with me on my way to hospital), Jack Russell played a brilliant little innings to see us home.

I wasn't in any pain by that stage as the gas and then the painkillers were working nicely. I drifted into a peaceful sleep at the hospital and woke up the next day, when the doctors told me I would need extensive work on my cheekbone as I had suffered two depressed fractures. We decided I'd go back to Southampton before having the operation, so that I could recover at home. Bishop came to see me at the hospital with a get well card signed by all the West Indies players. I revelled in that culture of playing hard on the field and staying friends off it, and the West Indies were always my favourite opponents. As we saw when they blew England away in 2019, Test cricket is so much more enjoyable and exciting when there is a strong, flamboyant West Indies side.

The specialist cut a hole above my left ear so that he could operate, and another in the upper left side of my mouth so that he could insert a steel plate. Even now I can't feel that side of my face properly. He said I was half a centimetre from losing the eyesight in my left eye, which would have finished my career there and then.

But I did lose something – my fearlessness. In my career I had never been concerned about getting hit in the face. Never. That's one of the reasons I was a decent player of fast bowling, because I had no fear of pain or getting hit. If I watched the ball, with my reflexes, it couldn't happen. It was impossible.

When Courtney Walsh hit me in 1990, I was young and carefree and I soon forgot about it. This time, it was on my mind constantly, and it was the first time I'd ever had negative thoughts about being hit. It was like my superpower had stopped working.

In early October, when I had recovered from the operation, I had a net at Southampton against the bowling machine, facing nothing but short stuff. I really struggled. The next day I went back, turned the speed dial even higher and forced myself back on the horse for an hour and a half. It felt much better, though I still wasn't completely right. I was supposed to be the Judge, the hero who fought the fastest bowlers in the world. So when I started to doubt myself, I was confused, worried and increasingly desperate. I was willing to try anything.

I'd never been hypnotised before, unless you count facing Shane Warne, but I was keen to give it a go. Medha Laud, a wonderful lady who worked as the ECB's International Teams Administrator and looked after absolutely everything, got the contact details of Paul McKenna, one of the world's most famous hypnotists, and arranged an appointment at his office in London. He said he would need three sessions and that after that I'd be fine.

Medha organised some footage of me playing fast bowling – just ball after ball of me swaying out the way of short deliveries. Paul sat me down in front of a TV screen and then put me in a trance. Within ten seconds I was in a hypnotic state. I wasn't asleep, I was still aware of the TV and of Paul's voice, but I was oblivious to everything else.

He was talking to my subconscious mind, and as I watched the video he was putting all these positive thoughts back in there. Then he said, 'I'm going to bring you back now – 10, 9, 8, 7, 6, you'll be starting to regain consciousness, I'm now talking to your conscious mind, 5, 4, 3, 2, you'll be coming back now, 1.'

He clicked his fingers and I was back. He asked me how long I thought I'd been under for, and I said about 10 or 15 minutes. Turned out it was an hour and a half.

I didn't feel anything immediately, but as the hours passed and a couple of days moved on I realised I was thinking less and less about short-pitched bowling directed at my face. I went back to see him a couple more times and was pretty much back to how I was before. All I needed to do now was test myself in a match situation.

England drew the last two Tests to complete an admirable 2–2 draw against the West Indies. I missed both games with my facial injuries, and as luck would have it they were by far the two best batting pitches of the summer – one of them at my favourite ground, Trent Bridge. There had been one century in the first four Tests of the series. There were five in the last two – and four more players were out in the nineties. I missed out on a few runs there.

I was still very happy. The operation was a success and I'd had a really good series against the West Indies. For the first time in years I felt my place was secure, and I had a huge series to look forward to. It was time to go back to South Africa.

Chapter 20

Homecoming

FROM THE MOMENT SOUTH AFRICA were readmitted to international sport, it was my ambition to play a Test match against them. I missed out in 1994, when I was dropped on the eve of the series, but I went on tour in 1995–96 knowing that, at the age of 32, I would almost certainly get my chance.

The day before the first match of the series, I was out in the middle at Centurion Park inspecting the pitch with my close friend and mentor Mark Nicholas, who was covering the match for Sky TV. And I was in tears.

It had nothing to do with the emotion of playing against the country of my birth, even though that was a huge thing for me. I'd simply had enough of feeling unwanted and undermined by people who were supposed to be on my side. Even though I'd had a bloody good series against the West Indies, and taken some career-threatening punishment, I again felt like I had no support from the management.

In the build-up to the first Test, Hicky was bowling to me in the nets with John Edrich, our batting coach, and the head coach Ray Illingworth in the vicinity. I bat-padded the fifth ball through where short leg would have been, and Edrich turned to Illingworth. 'Mate,' he said, 'if that was you bowling, you would have got him out three balls earlier.'

I didn't hear it but Hicky did and told me later. That's my bloody batting coach! And I already knew what Illingworth thought of me after his previous comments. I couldn't believe I had so little support, and it became too much for me when I was chatting to Mark the day before the Test. He told me to pull myself together and focus on batting for England. What else could I do?

Earlier that year, Edrich had advised me that I should not play the square cut – my signature shot – until I had at least a hundred on the board. I was tempted to point out the tiny flaw in his logic, that I wouldn't get to a hundred in the first place if I put away my best shot, but I just nodded my head.

I suppose it's unusual that somebody who wasn't scared of 95mph bowling could be so easily reduced to tears. I've always worn my heart on my sleeve, ever since I was a child and I wrote those notes to put on Mom's pillow. I can't change who I am – a very emotional person who has always been susceptible to a bit of schmaltz. It confuses me, too. How can I be so strong and so soft at the same time?

I sometimes wonder whether my premature physical growth stunted my emotional development. I was so much bigger and stronger than my peers as a teenager, which is one of the reasons I was very good at a number of sports. That meant I became used to a successful, sport-focused life, and never really had to deal with setbacks or raw emotions in those vital formative years. It's almost like I skipped adolescence.

Whatever the reason, I went into the first Test in South Africa in a pretty fragile mood. I'd started the tour a bit apprehensively; I hadn't batted for three months since being put in hospital by Ian Bishop, and I was getting used to batting with a grille on my helmet. It's a bigger change than you might think – when you've spent your whole life batting with a clear view, suddenly you feel like your vision is being impaired. I took off one of the bars because it was very claustrophobic and I felt like I couldn't get my chin and my shoulder close enough together, which was very important for some of my cross-bat shots.

South Africa had Allan Donald and Shaun Pollock, who bowled an excellent bouncer that could be hard to avoid. I came in just before the close on the first day of that first Test after a terrific partnership between Athers and Hicky, who smashed them everywhere to make 141.

My first scoring shot the next morning was a cut for six off Pollock. He didn't think much of that and came back at me with a beautiful bouncer. I got back into line and then it started to get big on me. Shit! I had nowhere to go and instinctively turned my head, and the ball hit me on the side of the helmet where I had added the grille. Pollock looked at me and said, 'Plenty more of those, mate.'

What happened to respecting a fellow Northlands Old Boy, eh, Shaun?! Actually, it was lovely for Northlands High to have both of us out there in in the middle, and we both donated a shirt from that series – I think they're hanging in the Old Boys' pub in Northwood.

The South Africans were well aware of what had happened with Bishop and their pace attack had a clear strategy. It was good for me to face that delivery so early in the innings. It hit me and I thought, 'Yep, that's fine.' Donald peppered me from the other end and I felt comfortable. Soon after I hit him for three fours in four balls, and I got to 43 before being bowled by a jaffa from Brian McMillan. After that I felt confident enough to take the grille off and I went back to batting without any facial protection. If I was starting my career now I would definitely wear a grille, but I was so used to not wearing one that it became almost impossible to change.

The South Africa series was frustrating, because for long periods we gave as good as we got against a really good team and we were close to a famous series victory. The first four matches were drawn, two of them rain-affected, before we were thrashed in the last Test at Cape Town. I had a decent series, with lots of scores between 30 and 70 – not the dizzy heights of my early years but still useful runs on lively pitches against an excellent seam attack. The one thing I didn't do was get a big score, though twice I was well set and gave my wicket away trying to farm the strike because I was batting with Nos. 10 and 11.

Athers saved the second Test in Johannesburg with that legendary 185 not out, when he batted almost two days. It was a draw that felt like a victory and we celebrated in an aptly named bar called Vertigo.

Beefy invited Athers for a Cane and Coke challenge, in response to Athers suggesting that the great drinkers were past their best once they turn 40. Beefy had hit that milestone a few days earlier, so he laid down the terms of their session. You can imagine what that entailed, and how it ended up.

A few of us were still going strong at the airport the next morning as we prepared to fly to Cape Town. Goughy has since said that he saw a look of disdain in Illingworth's eye that day and thought I was in trouble. In his autobiography, Goughy wrote that, 'Illy could not see beyond Judgie the Party Animal who enjoyed himself too much.'

By 1995, the era of Botham, Lamb, Gower, Emburey, Gooch and the rest was over and I was the last man standing at the bar. I accept that I occasionally got it wrong, that I should have had one or two more early nights. I don't endorse it, but life is there to live and we all get carried away from time to time and have the extra beer or glass of wine. But I very, very rarely had too many during a Test match – and one of the few times I did, at Trent Bridge in 1989, I played the best attacking innings of my Test career. It's a complicated subject, I know, but I will never believe that all players should behave in exactly the same way. You should do what works for you.

There were a couple of other times when I annoyed Illy on that tour. I had a mantra, 'Be strong', which I would say while giving teammates a little punch on the arm. The other players started doing it and it became a team thing. 'Come on, it's a tough away tour, we've got to be strong.' We were on a plane one day and I was walking down the aisle. As I went past Illy I gave him a playful punch and said, 'Illy, we've gotta be strong!' He looked at me like I'd just called him a Lancastrian. Maybe I'm naïve but I don't see that as offensive or nasty.

One strange thing is that, when he was a commentator on the BBC, Illingworth was always really kind about me. Dad told me this because he used to always watch the highlights. Illy gave me Man of the Match at the Oval in 1991, for example, when it could easily have gone to Tuffers or Syd Lawrence. I must have done something drastically wrong after that. He was never nasty to me – I just got the distinct impression he didn't want me in his team.

He also wasn't happy when I encouraged the wives, partners and children of the players to come to South Africa. My benefit year was coming up and I wanted to arrange a dinner at the Grosvenor House Hotel in London before we flew to the World Cup. I asked the players if they would each sit on a corporate table, and in return I'd pay for their wives and partners to come to South Africa. Money was a bit tight for us in those days, especially some of the younger players, so they were chuffed with the idea. Illy wasn't. Having families on tour wasn't the done thing; apparently they were an unwelcome distraction. My argument was that it would reduce stress and make players happy – and therefore improve performances in the middle. And actually, any distractions were snuffed out because everyone would be in the hotel with their families rather than staying out late. I thought that was what they wanted.

Lamby and I also brought a benefit and testimonial tour to Cape Town for the final Test as part of Judge Tours. He was managing it day to day – I didn't want to have my fingers in too many pies – and they all stayed at the Vineyard Hotel, which was next door to the ground. My family was there too. Our physio Wayne Morton tried to get his family into the Cape Sun, where the team were staying, but it was fully booked.

They couldn't stay with him as his room was partly a physio room, so I said he could have mine and I'd stay with Kath and the family at the Vineyard. I would drive back to the England hotel, and every day I was first for breakfast and last out of the team room at night before driving back to the Vineyard. I thought it was a nice gesture, but apparently that didn't go down well at all. These are fairly minor things, I realise that, but when you add them together they create a powerful sense of being unwanted. You might even call them unwelcome distractions.

I'm told my tour report was not particularly good. I'd love to read it. I tried to get hold of it for this book to no avail.

Funnily enough, even though my tour report was not great, Illingworth wrote some nice things about me in *One-Man Committee*.

Robin Smith did a good job on tour. He started off out of nick, but we always wanted him to play in the series. I was disappointed that he didn't turn a couple of his good innings into major ones, but he helped to hold things together at Centurion Park, the Wanderers and Newlands, and his 34 at Durban steadied the innings. He still lunges too much, too early, and is now a limited fielder, but he's got plenty of guts and that quality makes up for a lot.

That 34 in the third Test was a disappointment. It was in my hometown of Durban and Mom and Dad were there on their fortieth wedding anniversary. It was a rain-affected, low-scoring match, with nobody getting 50. The match was washed out soon after I was dismissed so I wouldn't have had time to make a hundred anyway, though I didn't know that at the time. I was playing nicely until I edged a good ball from Craig Matthews to second slip.

I was booed and called a traitor quite a lot during the tour. It would have been nice if people had understood my decision to play for England but I wasn't welcomed as I'd hoped. It's pretty upsetting when you walk out in the places you learned your cricket and you are booed.

I know that Kevin Pietersen got it far worse than I did when he returned in 2004–05. I spoke to him about it, but he's so resilient, a bit like Lamby, and he was inspired to ram it down their throats with three monstrous hundreds. For me, it was just a bit upsetting.

Going back to South Africa was a huge deal for me, and there were a few demands on my time. The highlight, without question, was meeting Nelson Mandela during a tour match in Soweto at the start of the tour. I'd read his autobiography and had such admiration for him, so I thought I'd be cheeky and ask if he might write something for my benefit brochure. He was so sharp. As you probably know, he was imprisoned on Robben Island from 1964 to 1982. Without skipping a beat, he said, 'Robin, I spent 18 years in prison on your island. Why would I want to write something for your brochure?'[1]

---

[1] He was only joking and did agree to write something, but it turned out it was too late to meet the production deadline for the brochure.

It was the first time I'd been back to South Africa in over a decade, and I caught up with so many old friends. I saw David, who worked at our house when I was a boy, and my second mother, Florence. Both stayed with the family long after I left South Africa. David also worked for Dad's company as a sales rep, driving around Zululand selling various leather goods. I went to Dad's office on Smith Street and caught up with all the people I knew who had worked there, and then went for dinner with them in the Indian community in Chatsworth. Dad had bought houses for four of his Indian employees – he reasoned that they'd helped him develop the business so he helped them settle into a nice home. They're now about 15 times wealthier than he is!

That was the last time I saw David and Flo. The England team were staying at Elangeni Hotel in Durban, so I asked our tour manager John Barclay whether I could invite a special guest to sit on our table at dinner. Flo was so chuffed and had a huge smile on her face throughout.

By that stage she had retired to her home in Zululand. Dad had prepared a pension for her, which was paid out every week, but in 1998 he received a call from the Post Office to say it was no longer being collected. That was the last contact we had from her and, though we could never confirm it, we're pretty sure she passed away. She'd been such a huge part of my life and it hit me really hard. I'll never forget all the things she did and all the love she showed for her little Nunu.

I batted No. 4 in that match in Durban, having started the series at No. 6. Then it was back to No. 6 for the fourth Test and up to No. 3 for the third, when we played an extra bowler to try to force a win. Given that run-scoring had been our problem, not taking wickets, it was a surprising decision.

Somebody had to move up to No. 3. Thorpey and Hicky didn't want to bat there. Nor did I, but I'd do anything for the team. I should have been firmer and more selfish. 'I'm the senior player here, I'm comfortable where I am. Find another No. 3. Find another opener.' I never really learned the word 'no'. If it's going to make someone else happy, I'll go along with it.

I do sometimes wonder whether I could have been more open to batting at No. 3. On the face of it, it was my perfect position – I could come in against the new ball and either counter-attack or defend, depending on the match situation. It would also mean I usually had my eye in when the spinners came on, rather than starting my innings against them. And I wouldn't have had as much time to think and worry on the balcony. But for all that, I really hated feeling rushed and I liked to have that extra bit of time. In first-class cricket, No. 4 just felt right.

Even though I didn't want to bat at No, 3, I got stuck in and top-scored with 66 in the first innings. The next day, John Etheridge of the *Sun* wrote that I'd finally resolved England's nine-year search for a decent No. 3.

'What a relief. Our greatest problem has been solved. Now we only have to worry about the ten other blokes!'

We collapsed and I was left with the tail, so I tried to farm the strike and was bowled by Paul Adams. We were all out for 153, a well under-par score. They had a never-ending batting line-up – Jacques Kallis was at No. 7, Pollock at No. 9 – but our bowlers did fantastically to reduce them to 171–9 before a crazy last-wicket partnership of 73 between Dave Richardson and Paul Adams effectively cost us the series.

In the second innings I was given out caught behind off Adams, even though I missed the ball by a mile. The umpire, Dave Orchard, later apologised to me. We lost by 10 wickets and Illy blamed it all on Dev in the dressing room. Dev didn't bowl well during their last-wicket partnership but to blame him solely for the defeat was ridiculous. There was a blazing row, and a number of players were pissed off because Illy had arranged an additional one-day match without consulting us. Devon was about the only one who kept his cool, and eventually Illingworth stomped off. After a couple of minutes, I broke the silence by saying, 'The sooner we get rid of that prick, the better!' Everyone started laughing and it released some of the tension.

Illingworth had the last laugh, though. A couple of days later, he was quoted as saying that only six players were guaranteed starters in the first Test of the following summer: Mike Atherton, Graham

Thorpe, Graeme Hick, Jack Russell, Dominic Cork and Peter Martin. That irritated me because I had played really well since getting back in the team against the West Indies, but I knew if I got runs at the start of the season I would be fine.

We went straight from the Tests into a one-day series, which we lost 6–1, and then on to the World Cup. I had a groin injury at the start of the tournament so missed the first few games. As in 1992 with Martin Crowe, I had a bet with a mate as to who would score the most runs. This time it was Gary Kirsten of South Africa. In his first game, against the United Arab Emirates, he smashed a World Cup record score of 188!

I was finally fit for our fourth group game against South Africa, and England opened with Smith – but it was Neil Smith, the Warwick-shire offspinner and pinch-hitter. I was fit to play, yet I was told that the official line was that I was unavailable. I still have no idea why. Our physio Wayne Morton walked out of a meeting in a huff, saying, 'I'm telling you, he's fit.' Robin Jackman and Derek Pringle, two former players turned journalists, both asked me why I wasn't playing and I had to tell them the official line.

Neil Smith was out of his depth against Pollock and Fanie de Villiers and I was picked for the next game against Pakistan. They threw me in to open against Wasim and Waqar in front of 40,000 aggressive fans in Karachi. I top-scored with a fluent 75, though we were well beaten. We were useless in that tournament and played one-day cricket from the 1960s.[2] The only sides we beat were the UAE and the Netherlands. That was enough to qualify for the quar-ter-finals, where we were massacred by the eventual winners Sri Lanka. Sanath Jayasuriya hit 82 from 44 balls, which was unheard of in those days, and they chased down a target of 236 with nearly 10 overs to spare.

I'd opened the batting again and was going well on 25 when I was run out. It was a dodgy decision – I watched the replay in the dressing room and the commentators all agreed I was safely home.

---

[2] While the rest of the world had moved on, we had a very safe, orthodox style of play.

It was possibly the only time in my career that I was really angry with an umpiring decision. I was playing well, I knew I wasn't out, and I was desperate to get England to another World Cup final – and hopefully play in it this time.

I went upstairs to give the third umpire a piece of my mind. Before I got there, Bob Willis and Beefy warned me off. 'Judgie, if you go in there with your mood,' said Bob, 'you'll never play for England again.'

I knew Illingworth would love an excuse to drop me and what they said made sense, so I didn't go in there. I should have done – I never played for England again anyway.

Chapter 21

The former England batsman

IT'S STRANGE HOW MEMORY works. The premature end of my international career is one of the most important events of my life, in many ways the catalyst for all the problems I had after retirement , yet I can't remember how I found out about it. I might have had a call from Mike Atherton, the captain, I might have read about it on Teletext. I have no idea.

What I do remember is a creeping sense of unease at the start of the 1996 summer. A number of newspaper articles said matter-of-factly that Illy planned to get rid of four senior players for the Test series against India: me, Alec Stewart, Gus Fraser and Devon Malcolm. These things snowball so quickly. Before I knew what was going on, it was widely accepted that I was going to be dropped again – so much so that when I *was* left out at the start of June, it was barely mentioned in the newspaper reports.

Illy was still chairman of selectors, though he had stepped down as coach to be replaced by Lancashire's David Lloyd. Bumble was my kind of coach, somebody who made you feel a million dollars, and I'm really disappointed I never had the opportunity to play under him. He would have been perfect for me.

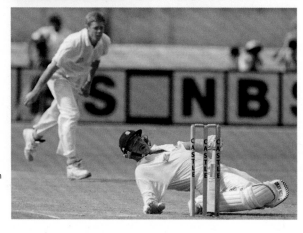

Top: Ian Bishop inspects my wounds after breaking my cheekbone in 1995. I almost lost the sight in my left eye

Middle: One of the best days of my life: meeting the great Nelson Mandela in Soweto during England's tour of South Africa

Bottom: Avoiding a short ball from Shaun Pollock on my return to Durban in 1995. I loved feeling the whoosh of air as a bouncer flew past my nose

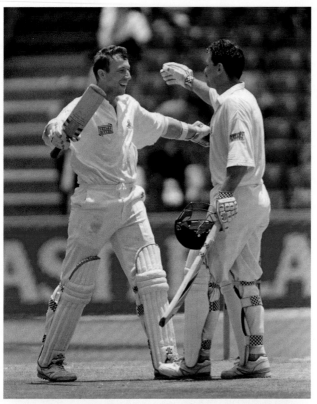

Top: Congratulating
Athers on reaching a
hundred during his
immense, match-saving
innings at Johannesburg
in 1995

Bottom: Meeting the
great Archbishop
Desmond Tutu during
the South African tour

Top: Getting ready to do some backbreaking work on the site of Hampshire's new ground, the Rose Bowl, with my teammates Will Kendall, Giles White and Shaun Udal

Middle: Sir Viv Richards was and will always be my hero, so to become a friend of his was – I don't use the word lightly – an honour

Bottom: With Viv and Malcolm's wife Connie at the Malcolm Marshall Memorial Match in 2000, a celebration of a great man, taken far too soon

Top left: Limping off after the final innings of my Hampshire career, more than 20 years of hard work written all over my face

Top right: Playing beach cricket with Martin Crowe, a beautiful man who I miss dearly

Middle: An important team selection meeting with Warney at Hampshire

Bottom: Holding the Ryder Cup with my dear friend Rod Bransgrove

Top: Two of the proudest days of my life were seeing Harrison and Margaux graduate

Middle: My two children have grown up beautifully. They are my best buddies in the world

Bottom: Harrison is a very talented painter who specialises in abstract art

Top left: With my partner Karin after my last-ever cricket match, playing for my local club in Perth

Top right: A birthday kiss from Karin at Sopranos restaurant, where we went on our first date

Bottom left: Paul Terry and I have been through a lot together, and now we coach at the same private school

Bottom right: Kippy shows off his fishing catch during a trip to the Melville Island. It's a stunning place, run entirely by indigenous communities, and we had the privilege of coming onto the island to experience indigenous life

Top: I get so much joy from coaching young batsmen like Shreyas

Bottom: A special Crimewatch reconstruction of Dennis Lillee stealing my bike.
If anyone has seen this man, please call the authorities

Top: Whatever happens in our lives, the Smith family will always get together for Christmas

Bottom: I was very apprehensive about returning to Hampshire for the Captains' Dinner in 2018, but it was so worth it

I cracked a finger against Warwickshire at the start of the season and missed the one-day series against India, though I'm sure I'd have been left out anyway. I was fine with that – I was 32 and it was the start of a new four-year cycle before the next World Cup. But I knew I was still one of the best Test batsmen in the country. I tried to plead my case in a couple of newspaper articles but I could sense which way the wind was blowing.

That finger injury denied me the chance to get big runs at the start of the season, and when the squad for the first Test was announced, the four senior players were left out as predicted. I later found out that Illy had tipped off some journalists, off the record during the South Africa tour, that he wanted rid of the four of us. He fell out with Dev, Alec was having a poor trot and he never liked Gus for some reason.

The other three all got back in at a later date – Alec in the second Test of 1996 because of a finger injury to Nick Knight, and Dev and Gus when Illy was no longer chairman of selectors. Alec, who is six months older than me, took his chance and stayed in the team for another seven years. I'm not sure I could have played Test cricket for that much longer but I had at least two or three more years in me.

After we were dropped together, Alec played another 80 Tests and made over 5,000 runs. I played 0 and made 0. I don't begrudge Alec a single thing, he's one of the good guys, but it's hard not to wonder what might have been.

I felt like I had so much to offer. I was coming into my prime. I was 32, I realised I was good enough and had become mentally stronger. I was still sound technically and had become a better, more confident player against spin. I was not quite the dominant punisher I had been at twenty-five but I was even more resilient and sold my wicket more dearly than ever. I think I had become a very reliable middle-order fighter.

In his autobiography, Athers, who was captain at the time, wrote about the decision:

It could be argued that a man with such a fine Test record should have played more than he did, but difficult decisions have to be made and they are made in good faith and for the right reasons. In 1996 Smith was thirty-two years old, and his average had dropped from the low 50s to the low 40s and we decided to move on. Who can say whether it was the right thing to do? But I was keen to follow the example of other Test-playing countries that seemed to realise, before it was too late, when a player was past his best. In England we rarely did.

I'm sure it's not a decision Athers would have taken lightly. But I would challenge the perception that I was in decline. My Test career is usually split into two halves – under Micky Stewart, I averaged 50.86 and under Fletcher and Illingworth, I averaged 35.35. It was by no means as good but that was still the same as most people's career average. Lamby and Mike Gatting averaged 36 in their Test career, and they are legends of English cricket. Hicky averaged 31, yet he played more Tests than me. Don't get me wrong – they were all brilliant players, but I sometimes wondered whether I was judged to a higher standard than many other batsmen. Maybe I started too well for my own good, which meant people expected more from me. I don't know.

I'd argue that there were actually three phases of my England career: 1989–92 under Micky, then the first couple of years under Fletcher and Illingworth, and finally the spell after I was recalled in 1995.

I had a terrible spell in 1993 and 1994. I was dropped twice and rightly so. But I was playing so much better after I came back against the West Indies in 1995. I averaged 44 in that series, which includes two innings when I batted out of position as an opener, and 36 in South Africa. If I had played for my average twice, at Johannesburg and Cape Town, I'd have averaged 50 in South Africa. I was never one to do that but if I knew then what I know now, I'd have got a nice not out both times. I was also on the wrong end of a very bad umpiring decision in what turned out to be my last Test innings.

The argument against me is that I didn't get a century in either series, and I accept that criticism. But there were a lot of low-scoring games, and in those nine matches there were only two hundreds by England players – one by Athers and one by Hicky. I might also have made a hundred had I not been left with the tail twice in South

Africa. And a lot of people said my 46 and 41 on that dodgy pitch at Edgbaston were worth hundreds.

I think I'd done more than enough to keep my place. In those nine Tests I played after being recalled in 1995 I averaged more than any England batsman, and only Athers scored more runs. The average wasn't that high, 39.92, but that's because the matches were played on some lively pitches. I top-scored in six of my last 13 Test innings and made the highest score on either side in my final match. I'm not sure it's right to drop someone who is your top scorer almost half the time.

Maybe it had nothing to do with run-scoring. There are two sides to every story and there's every chance they had an issue with my extra-curricular activities. If they felt that way, fair enough – cricket was changing rapidly off the field. But surely they should have marked my card first. If you work for a company you don't just get the sack – you get a warning and are told to sharpen up.

I just wish somebody had said, 'Mate, you are so close to being dropped from this team, not because of the way you're playing but because you're drinking too much and setting a bad example. Rein it in a bit. You're not playing with Botham and Lamb any more, times have changed.' If they had said that, I would have done.

But the fact is that I had the constitution to party hard without it affecting my batting. And if I was such a powerful influence, why was nobody running back to the hotel from the ground with me on overseas tours? Why was I still the first in the nets every morning at Hampshire?

I had been spoilt by playing on the big stage for so long and enjoying the butterflies and that incredible adrenalin surge. When that was taken away, it was awful. If I'd been replaced by five Ricky Pontings I would have put my hand up and said fair enough. The two players who came into the top six were Nasser Hussain and Ronnie Irani. Nasser was a very good player and established himself at No. 3, but when I look at it objectively I think I was probably a better batsman.

I'm not proud to say that, for a while after I was dropped, I didn't want England to do well, and I certainly didn't want the people picked ahead of me to get runs. I suppose it's just human nature but I didn't like myself for thinking that way. I was such a prick, so self-centred. It was nothing personal, I just didn't want the selectors to be validated in their decision to leave me out. It's funny – one of the people I hoped wouldn't do well, John Crawley, became a great mate when he joined Hampshire a few years later.

I soon got over that phase, but I didn't get over missing out on international cricket. The fact I was never given an explanation made it so much harder. Part of me thinks I should have been stronger, but that's who I am. I'm sensitive, I'm fragile and I adored playing for England. How can it not break your heart to lose it? That's my career. That's my life.

I wasn't the first and I won't be the last player who has been dropped by England and finds it hard to go back to the daily grind of county cricket. I gave my all for Hampshire, but it's not easy to find that relentless drive and focus to bash out hundred after hundred and demand a recall. I did make a point by hammering 141 against Derbyshire while England were playing the first Test of the 1996 summer against India. But while I still did well – from 1996 to 1999 I averaged 43 in first-class cricket – it wasn't as eye-catching as some others. People like Hicky and Ramps were brilliant at reeling off century after century.

I don't always agree that scoring loads of runs at county level means you have the credentials to be a Test-match player. In his book, *A Beautiful Game*, Mark Nicholas said he was thought I was Hampshire's greatest-ever cricketer. That was incredibly humbling, and the reason he gave was my big-match temperament. It takes a special kind of street fighter to score runs under extreme pressure. I was usually better coming in at 20–2 than 200–2 because I relished that challenge. It's probably no coincidence that when I made my career-best score, 209 against Essex in 1987, I walked to the crease with Hampshire 5–3.

There is such an enormous difference between Test matches and county cricket, and you need to be careful not to read too much into the domestic averages. We saw that with people like Marcus Trescothick and Michael Vaughan, who had modest records when they were picked for England by Duncan Fletcher. Look at David Gower, the definition of a genius. He didn't even average 40 in county cricket but his Test average was the highest of that England generation. He needed the big stage to stimulate him. There are a hundred people who can play the cover drive or the square cut, but only a few can do it at Test level.

Please don't think I'm disrespecting first-class cricket, not just in England but around the world. My brother is a classic example of the value of concentration and being able to convert starts into big scores. He was obsessive about his stats and greedy for every run.

Over the next couple of years, I spoke to three of the four selectors when they came down to Southampton to watch Hampshire play. Each time I asked why I wasn't in the England team, and each time they said, 'Well, look. There's four of us, and if it was up to me you'd be in.' I'm not the best at maths but even I could work out at least one of them was talking rubbish.

I should have been more forthright and confrontational, not just then but throughout my career. I should have made Goochie feel uncomfortable when I was left out of the World Cup final in 1992. I should have insisted I bat at No. 4. I know that later, when I was captain of Hampshire, I was always more inclined to stick with those who challenged my decisions.

If I'd known I'd played my last Test then I might have rocked the boat, but I always felt I could get back into the side so I didn't want to do anything that might jeopardise my chances. And confrontation is just not in my nature. My England hopes faded away for the next couple of years, and it was quietly heart-breaking to read the occasional mention of me as 'the former England batsman'. I thought I might go to the West Indies in 1997–98 because of my record against fast bowling. When I wasn't picked, I knew deep down it was over.

I ended up going on that tour anyway, with Judge Tours, and took my bat so that I could play a bit of beach cricket – and just in case somebody broke a finger and they needed an urgent replacement. That didn't happen, so instead of facing the West Indies' fast bowlers I bumped into someone who had given me an even bigger working-over: George Carman QC.

In 1996, I had to go into the witness box during a libel case between Beefy and Imran Khan. Imran had written an article in a magazine which Beefy believed made him out to be a cheat, uneducated and a racist. Beefy sued him and had about 20 England players subpoenaed, including me.

I was to be questioned about whether I'd ever seen Beefy cheat by tampering with the ball, which I hadn't. Imran's QC, George Carman, started to cross-examine me. I was bloody terrified and couldn't stop sweating. He was using long words I'd never heard before. I'd been told by Beefy's lawyers that if I didn't understand something I should ask Carman to repeat it. 'He'll try to baffle you with bullshit,' they said. I asked him to repeat one question, and his response was priceless. He put his foot up on the pew, tutted and looked at the jury as if to say, 'This is what I'm dealing with.' Then he said, 'How much more simply can I put it …'

It made me feel so small. He was deliberately intimidating me, and did so for the best part of an hour. At lunch, Beefy said, 'Mate, can't talk to you.' I thought I'd pissed him off! I realised later he couldn't talk because I was still in the witness box. I couldn't bloody talk to anyone! I sat in a park for half an hour, collected my thoughts and tried to get myself ready for another barrage. I did another half hour, when I felt incredibly uncomfortable, and that was it. All the England cricketers who went up said the same as I did: that we'd never seen Beefy cheat or tamper with the ball. We all thought he'd win the case hands down. We were astonished that he lost.

I despised George Carman but afterwards I sat down and thought, 'He's just doing his job, that's why he's the best.' I saw him during that West Indies tour almost two years later – he loved his cricket and was in Trinidad, staying at the same hotel as me. He was in the bar and came up to shake my hand and said hello. We had a beer and eventually I got him a couple of spare tickets for mates he had coming over.

Being cross-examined is so weird – even if you're telling the truth, you start doubting yourself because the lawyers are so good that you have to be careful they don't put words in your mouth. It was fascinating how he worked. I didn't think that at the time, mind you.

I'm not always at my best when out of my comfort zone. In 1996–97, I went off on Judge Tours to watch England in New Zealand and was asked to do a bit of commentating for Sky Sports during the

Tests. It was going smoothly and I was starting to feel comfortable. Then Daniel Vettori came on to bowl, and Beefy said to me, 'What do you think of this young spinner?' He was only 18 but you could tell he was a serious talent. I said, 'Yeah, Beefy, I do really like the look of this young Frankie Dettori.'

Oh, bloody hell.

Beefy looked at me, moved the mic away from his mouth and burst out laughing. John Gayleard, the Sky producer, came over in my earpiece and barked, 'Have we got a fucking jockey bowling all of a sudden?' I was hoping that Beefy would try and help me out by talking and pretending it didn't happen, but he didn't say a word. He was laughing so hard he almost fell off his chair. All the commentators in the back were pissing themselves and I was left trying to pick up the pieces, stuttering and muttering away. I was unbelievably embarrassed and didn't know what to say. I didn't do much more commentating after that.

Chapter 22
Captain, leader, worrier

I'M A FOLLOWER NOT a leader. I was never particularly comfortable in the role of senior player in the England team, so I certainly didn't think I was captaincy material. But when Hampshire asked me to do the job in 1998 after John Stephenson resigned, I was never going to turn the opportunity down. I'd been at the club for nearly 20 years and I loved everything about the place. I had no wish to leave and had turned down a massive pay rise to go to Northants as captain when Lamby retired.

One of my first games as captain was against Dorset in the NatWest Trophy. All the Minor Counties looked forward to the first round of that competition because it was their yearly opportunity to do some giant-killing. Dorset were captained by Jon Hardy, one of my best friends, who had played for Hampshire and Somerset and was my partner in the Chase and Masuri businesses.

We hadn't played at Dean Park in Bournemouth for six years. It's a beautiful, picturesque ground and it was sold out for the occasion. We had an overseas fast bowler, Nixon McLean from the West Indies, and when I went out for the toss Jon suggested we go easy on his team. 'Judgie, mate, why don't you guys bat first? If we get put in, Nixon will destroy us. We'll be bowled out for 75 and the game will be over by lunch. We've got 5,000 people here and we want to entertain them all day.'

It looked like a typical outground[1] wicket, with a nice tinge of green. It was overcast as well, so conditions were clearly good for bowling and I was uneasy with the idea. It was unthinkable for any of the big teams to lose to one of the Minor Counties. If I was just a player, I'd have been less concerned, but as captain I felt responsible for everything. They had a very good legspinner called Vyvian Pike, who had played for Gloucestershire, so I said we'd bat first provided that, when I came into bat, Jon didn't put the leggie on. He shook on it, we faked the toss and told everyone Dorset had won it and put Hampshire into bat.

A few minutes later we were 0–3. Nought for bloody three! I was at the crease, wondering what the hell was going on. I got a few runs and then Jon really took the piss: he brought the leggie on! I said, 'Jon, we're 10–3 here, I'll get slaughtered if we lose. You're being an absolute prick.'

He just sniggered, 'Judgie, you'll be fine.'

Yeah nice one, thanks, mate. Fortunately, I got 144 and we won easily, but it wasn't looking good for a while.

That little story is an illustration of how stressful captaincy could be, especially for someone like me. We didn't have a great team in those years. Most of the legends of the 1980s and early 1990s had gone and, though we had some terrific overseas players like Shane Warne and Matthew Hayden, we weren't really challenging for trophies. I worried a lot – about results, about dropping people, about letting players go at the end of their contracts, about the impact on their families. I worried about everything.

I suppose that's the downside of being a soft, caring person. I concern myself a lot about the smallest things, and that can't help my mental state. I sometimes forget about what's good for me because I'm too busy worrying about others.

Even though it didn't come naturally, I tried to lead from the front and take responsibility for the welfare of Hampshire, and to create

---

[1] The smaller grounds which are used occasionally.

a unique team spirit driven by solidarity. The 1999 season was the last before the County Championship was split into two divisions, so we needed to finish in the top nine to ensure we'd be playing Division One cricket in 2000. The pressure of the last game, away to Derbyshire, was unreal. It was rain-affected, so I went to see their captain Dominic Cork to discuss a declaration. A draw was the same as a defeat for us and so I offered them a very gettable 285 in four sessions if, in return, they would promise to go for the runs even if they were nine down.

It was a fantastic game and we won by two runs. As it turned out, Derbyshire sneaked into Division One as well because of their first-innings bonus points. But Warwickshire missed out, and they were furious. I had John Carr, the ECB director of cricket operations, on the phone to tell me there had been a complaint and they were going to interview the umpires.

I asked him, 'What have we done wrong?'

'You've contrived a result.'

'John, do whatever you want, I don't care. Would this have been brought up had it been the second game of the season?'

I was absolutely livid. Declarations like that had been going on for twenty-five years in county cricket. In the end, the ECB exonerated both me and Corky.

I really wasn't in the mood for their silly bullshit. At that stage a huge shadow hung over everyone at Hampshire – we all knew that our coach Malcolm Marshall was dying of cancer. He was a very proud man, who always held his head high, and he kept it to himself for a long time. None of us really knew why he was losing weight so dramatically. Eventually, halfway through the season, we found out, because it was obvious he needed to stand down.

Macko was the best fast bowler I ever saw. By the time I faced him he was fractionally past his peak, which is why I say Ian Bishop was the best I faced, but I saw Malcolm at his absolute best for Hampshire in the mid-1980s. I might be biased because I also thought he was an absolutely wonderful man – gentle, kind, sincere, thoughtful. But as a bowler he had everything. He moved the ball both ways in the air and off the seam, he had a skiddy bouncer that was almost impossible to avoid – he hit more batsmen than any bowler in world cricket – and he was so smart. He could work out a batsman's strengths and weaknesses in three or four balls, and he had the ability to do something about it. I've never seen a fast bowler better at setting a batsman up. He used to tell us in advance how he was going to get someone out. Remember how, in Barbados, he even told me how he was going to get me out?

At Hampshire he took 826 wickets in first-class cricket at an average of 18.64. He used to joke that if I wasn't at gully he'd have averaged 16.

Malcolm had been with his girlfriend Connie for almost 20 years. He always promised they'd get married one day, and she said, 'Yeah, I'll believe it when I see a ring.' He knew he only had a few months to live, so in September 1999 he and Connie were married at Chilworth Manor in Southampton. Malcolm was so frail and so sick. It was devastating to watch him get weaker and weaker. It's particularly hard when you've seen him as the most dangerous bowler in the world. You think someone like that is invincible.

On 4 November 1999, Malcolm died aged 41. He weighed less than four stone when he passed away. The Reverend Sir Wes Hall, who was arguably the first great West Indian fast bowler, was by his side. The funeral was in Barbados, and Connie called me to say that Malcolm had asked in his will whether I could be one of the pallbearers. It was such an honour to help lay him to rest with the likes of Tim Tremlett, Sir Vivian Richards, Joel Garner, Sir Gordon Greenidge, his best friend Desmond Haynes and other West Indian teammates.

After that we went to a big sporting hall where Mark Nicholas gave the eulogy. He was about the only person who didn't break down, although I know he struggled to control himself in front of the congregation. It was just stunning. I was sitting a few seats away from Viv and he was in floods of tears, as everyone was. I'm not sure I've ever been more emotional than I was in those minutes.

After the eulogy, a few of us were invited by Sylvester Clarke, that demon fast bowler, to go to his local, a little rum shack. There were about eight of us there and I was touched to be invited into the inner circle. We sat outside and went through a few bottles of Cockspur

Rum, which Malcolm loved. Sylvester went to that rum shack every day. Two weeks later, he was sitting in the same spot when he had a heart attack and died at the age of 44.

The next time I went to Barbados, I had an important task to perform. One of Malcolm's favourite drinks was J&B whisky. When it got cold at Hampshire he'd call for a nip from the 12th man to warm him up; we were sponsored by them so there were always a load of miniature bottles in the dressing room. Near the end of his life, he made me promise that, whenever I went to Barbados with the family, I would go to his grave, say a prayer, and pour a miniature bottle of J&B on his tombstone.

'Judgie, please do this for me, china, and think of me.'

This I did, Macko, though I'm sorry to tell you I may have had to drink some of it!

The following summer, Viv and I captained the two teams in a special charity match to raise funds for Connie and Mali, Malcolm's wife and son. It was organised by Rod Bransgrove and David English, the larger-than-life character who has raised millions for charity since founding the Bunbury Cricket Club in 1987. David's work sometimes goes unnoticed and he deserves more credit for being the good Samaritan of cricket. His energy is incredible. If he could bottle it, he'd make millions – but then he'd probably give it all to charity anyway.

Chapter 23
The Rose Bowl

MY FIVE SEASONS AS captain of Hampshire coincided with the move from Northlands Road to a state-of-the-art new ground, the Rose Bowl. It should have been a joyful time, but the transition was so difficult that the club almost went bust.

The move was 14 years in the making. It was first discussed in 1987 when Mark Nicholas, then captain, raised the subject with the club's vice chairman Bill Hughes in an Italian restaurant in Leeds. Mark pointed out the limitations of Northlands Road, charming though it was, and suggested Hampshire should look at finding a bigger ground. Bill, who was also a surveyor, was so excited that he stayed up all night sketching what the new ground might look like.

Mark set up and chaired a voluntary committee, which continued to explore the possibility over the next few years. In the 1990s, the club found an area of land just off the M27 and negotiated two leases – one for the stadium and one for the wider site. Mark and I were the first people to place a shovel into the ground and symbolically begin the building of the Rose Bowl. In 1997, Hampshire received a £7.2 million grant from Sport England to develop an international cricket stadium and arranged the sale of Northlands Road.

There were some lovely, enthusiastic people on the Hampshire committee, and everyone had the best intentions, but I'm not sure they had the expertise or manpower to manage a project of this size. The club started to run into financial problems in the late 1990s – development costs overran badly and a number of initiatives to raise capital didn't work.

It became clear the club was technically insolvent and in serious trouble. The stadium was unfinished and building had stopped. That's where Rod Bransgrove, a tireless entrepreneur and Hampshire's white knight, came in.

I'd known Rod for a few years, having been introduced to him by Paul Terry, and we got on famously. He made his fortune through the pharmaceutical industry and was the person who came up with the female hormone replacement programme. I'll never forget when we were staying together in the Crowne Plaza Hotel in Perth during one of the Judge Tours, and I accompanied Rod to collect a fax from reception.

'Well, fuck me,' he said, his eyes like saucers. 'I've just had the first viable offer for the pharmaceutical business. Order the champagne, Judgie!'

I'd known him for three or four years and thought he was a sales rep for a pharmaceutical company; he was so modest that he never mentioned that he owned the company with his partner, Jan Mohammad.

When he explained that he was a bit more than a sales rep, I asked him who the offer was from and when he would sell. 'Judgie, I didn't say I was going to *accept* the offer.'

Rod knew this was just the start and that he could use it to get a much bigger offer – which is exactly what happened.

He was so much fun to be around. The best nights out are often unplanned, and one of my favourites came in New Zealand with Rod and Mark Nicholas. We were in Wellington – Rod and I with Judge Tours, Mark doing some broadcasting work – and popped out for a quick pub lunch. We were still there 12 hours later, having shared 12 bottles of Church Road chardonnay, six beers and a few shots of whisky.

As we were stumbling back to our hotel that night, Mark – the esteemed, statesmanlike broadcaster Mark Nicholas – decided to sit down in a precinct and do some busking. With an air guitar. He ran through a load of Bruce Springsteen songs while Rod and I, pretending not to know who he was, lobbed coins at him and told passers-by that they should listen to this amazing singer.

During the long afternoon we had come up with an idea about the development of the Rose Bowl which we all agreed was a stroke of genius. We were all very serious about it. 'Guys, this is totally confidential. What we have talked about, make sure it doesn't go outside these walls.'

It didn't. The next morning, none of us had a clue what our brilliant idea had been.

A few years later, with Hampshire on the brink financially, I sat down with Rod in Judge's Wine Bar in Romsey. We had him to thank for that place as well; he had bought the freehold of a beautiful old building and funded its restoration. I asked him if he'd be interested in buying something else with his millions: Hampshire Cricket Club. I gave him the full sales pitch, and probably told him how desperate we were.

'How much do you reckon it'll cost me, Judge?'

'Pocket money to you, Rodders, a few million at half the price.'

I sounded like a bloody fish seller in Billingsgate when I was trying to sell a multi-million-pound cricket club. But Rod liked the idea, and I knew that once he was committed, there would be no turning back. It's no exaggeration to say he saved the club from oblivion.

Rod put many millions into the club. But it would be insulting to talk purely in terms of money, because in the last 20 years he has given so much time, commitment, passion and expertise when he could have pulled the plug at any stage and had a much easier life. Rod gave up some of his other businesses so he could spend more time focusing on Hampshire. He would never have been able to get so involved without the support of his lovely wife Mandy, who also really bought into the idea.

I always loved and respected Rod, but the efforts he made to take on Hampshire brought our friendship to a whole new level.

Rod eventually took over Hampshire on the condition that the club became a proper limited company with a board of directors. He also replaced Brian Ford as chairman. It took some heroic work, particularly by the chief executive Tony Baker, to ensure everything was done in time and we could start the 2001 season at our new ground, the Rose Bowl.[1]

There were loads of unsung heroes who helped secure the move to the Rose Bowl. Hampshire should also be eternally grateful to Patrick Trant, the building contractor who continued to excavate the ground at a hugely discounted price when the money ran out. I really warmed to Patrick, a charismatic Irishman with a raw charm and an allergy to bullshit.

The logistics were really complex and we had to make a few compromises. For the first year, administration staff worked in Porta-kabins and the team got changed in temporary marquees. In a strange way, that helped our team spirit – we all look back fondly to the days of makeshift changing rooms and portable showers.

Rod had such great enthusiasm for the project throughout. As much as anything, I think he did it to honour his late father, who was a huge Surrey fan. Rod wasn't good enough to play for a county but he thought that, if his dad was looking down, he'd be really proud of what he was trying to achieve.

Rod changed the whole ethos of the club and made us think about everything on a grander scale. He was very keen on raising the profile by getting in big-name overseas players, so we went for the biggest of the lot – Shane Warne. Rod asked how well I knew Warney and whether I could give him a ring. He was about to join Lancashire but he changed his mind and came to us.

We also signed Alan Mullally, the England seamer, from Leicestershire. Even with those two, we had a tough season in 2000 and were relegated to Division Two. As captain, our struggles really got to me. Warney used to hang around after play and we'd sit in the bath, having a beer and talking about how we could improve the team. He felt we were too soft and too casual in the nets.

---

[1] The ground was originally called the Rose Bowl but has been sponsored by Ageas since 2012.

We were dismissed for less than 100 on four occasions that year. It was embarrassing and I felt responsible. It didn't help that I was having probably the worst season of my career with the bat. When I was captain the stress, worry and fear of failure were multiplied.

We did well in the NatWest trophy, and breezed into the semi-finals before losing a tight game to Warwickshire. We were without Warney, who had to go back to Australia to play in an indoor match against South Africa. Shaun Udal's last ball of that match was hit for four; it was the first boundary he'd gone for in the whole competition. Shaggy was such a great one-day bowler who batted and fielded well and should have played 100 ODIs for England rather than 11.

Warney was part of our little Australian group around that time. We also had Matthew Hayden in 1997, Simon Katich in 2003 and Michael Clarke in 2004. Haydos was a charming bloke, who I met every morning by the bowling machines. We were always the only two players there, with Dad feeding the machine to me, and Haydos's wife Kellie loading up the other machine. He was a deep thinker about the game, always analysing his technique.

I introduced him to visualisation, which I know he used a lot later in his career. You'd see him out there in the middle for 30 minutes before the start of each day, going through his innings in his head. Maybe that's why he was able to smack the fast bowlers back over their heads in the first over!

It was great that the Aussies, including Warney and Haydos, came to play at the Rose Bowl as part of the Ashes tour in 2001. It was a huge occasion in our first year at our new ground. Their captain Steve Waugh didn't know much about the wicket and asked me what the best bet was if he won the toss.

'Bat, mate. We always bat first here.'

I'm usually a terrible liar but I managed to keep a straight face that time. It always did plenty in the first session and we had no enthusiasm for facing Brett Lee, Jason Gillespie, Damien Fleming and Ashley Noffke on that pitch. Instead, Alan Mullally and a young debutant called James Schofield whipped them out for 97 before lunch.

I think Waugh saw the funny side, although there was a bit of payback when I came into bat. Their quick bowlers absolutely peppered me, and they had Warney as well. I cracked my rib and took some serious punishment but batted almost six hours for 113. It felt so good, a last hurrah against international opposition – and in front of my home crowd, too.

It was a great game, which we eventually won by two wickets in a manic run-chase. There were only nine balls to spare when we got the winning runs, and a crowd of about 2,000 went mad.

I can always say I scored a hundred against Shane Warne. But I should also say he gave me a bit of help! I think he wanted me to get the hundred and, while he didn't exactly bowl long hops and full tosses, he would tell me in advance when he was going to bowl a flipper or a googly. I suppose that might be viewed differently in the modern era but it was just a bit of fun.

Most of my runs were scored off the quicks and the offspinner Colin Miller so it wasn't exactly a freebie. I was sweating like a bugger as their quicks bombed me. Brett Lee in particular found this very funny, until he was told I was wearing one of his chest guards, which had been lifted from his kitbag by Warney.

At the close of play, Steve Waugh came up and said, 'Judie, that's the best knock we've seen by an Englishman all tour – even if Warney did help you a bit!' I was the first person to score a century against Australia that summer, and there was an even a little bit of talk in the press about an England recall, though I didn't get my hopes up.

I received an even nicer gift the same summer when Southampton University awarded me an honorary Master of Arts degree as a thank you for some of the community and charity work I did in the area. I used to go to the university and talk to the students on a regular basis. I enjoyed that as it was fairly informal, but giving a speech in front of 1,000 students, all gowned up, was another matter. I was so nervous and, as I said during my acceptance speech, I'd have been much more comfortable walking out in front of 90,000 Aussies at the MCG. Public speaking always made me nervous. I've been best man five times and also had to stand up in front of big crowds when I received a couple more honorary degrees – a Doctor of Letters from Portsmouth and a Master of Arts from Nottingham.

Those highs aside, it was another stressful summer, and the pressure of being captain occasionally made me do funny things. I was never a big sledger, but that year we were under so much pressure as we chased promotion. One of our last games was against Warwickshire. We took some early wickets and then a teenager called Ian Bell came in and started playing very nicely. He got to about 20, really looking the part, so I thought, 'We've got to try to unsettle him.'

I gave him everything I could. Every. Thing. I. Bloody. Could. He caught an absolute mouthful, a bit of Border's medicine. He was just so resilient, though – it went in one ear and out the other, and he kept batting beautifully. He got a brilliant 98 and I thought, 'This bloke can really play.'

We were in the dressing room afterwards when one of the guys said, 'Judgie, come and have a look at this.' They'd been reading the *Cricketers' Who's Who* to find out more about Bell, as we were all so impressed with him. They were going through his profile and pointed me towards one line in particular.

Cricketers Most Admired: Robin Smith

I was mortified. I'd done to Ian Bell what Lamby did to me all those years ago. My old mate Gladstone Small, who was part of the backroom staff, introduced me to Belly in the bar that night, and I was full of apologies. 'Mate,' I said, 'you played so well. Please don't take any of that stuff personally. I don't usually sledge but we're under the pump. But I thought you were absolutely outstanding and if you play like that – with that temperament and technique – you will play for England for many years.'

Anyone who got runs at the Rose Bowl was worth keeping an eye on. For the first few years we had a shocking wicket. It was a disaster to bat on, with sideways movement and inconsistent bounce. There was nothing we could do – we had an outstanding groundsman in Nigel Gray, who was doing the best he could, but at any new ground the turf takes time to settle. The more traffic there is over a wicket, the more consistent it becomes.

As a batsman, a dodgy pitch like that has a dual impact. You don't get any runs at home, which drags your confidence down so much that you then don't cash in when you play on better wickets away from home. It was a really difficult period for Hampshire cricket, but I'm glad I was there to help and try to massage the players' egos when things weren't going well, because there was a lot of unrest about the fact we were playing on such bad pitches.

We had a young Michael Clarke as our overseas player in 2004. I'd retired by then but was still around the club in an ambassadorial role. One day he came to me and was quite emotional. He was desperate to impress, to get in the Australian Test side, and he'd been looking at all the averages of the other Australian batsmen in county cricket. Michael was barely averaging 35, while Andrew Symonds was averaging 73 at Kent, David Hussey and Brad Hodge were averaging 60-odd at Notts and Leicestershire – and Martin Love averaged 394 in a couple of games for Northants.

I tried to explain that, at that stage of his career, a year on a dodgy wicket was the best thing that could happen to him. He'd grown up on flat wickets in Sydney, so this would help him learn how to fight for his runs.

It's good for a young player, but when you're in your late thirties you don't need wickets like that. My form was really poor for a couple of years, apart from that hundred against Australia. But by then scoring runs was not as important. My motivation had changed – I was working closely with the club and Rod and I wanted the transition to the Rose Bowl to be successful. I threw myself into that side of the job and it probably affected my batting.

I had to make the best of a bad situation – never more so than we played India in 2002. They were at the Rose Bowl for a tour match a few days before the first Test against England, and the pitch was misbehaving even more than usual. Balls were taking off from a length, it was downright dangerous. At tea on the second day, Rod came into the dressing room looking worried, and dragged me outside for a chat. He was a paler shade of white, and I honestly thought someone had died. It turned out India wanted to call the match off as they were worried about one of their superstars breaking a finger. We knew if that happened, the negative publicity would be a savage blow to Hampshire's hopes of hosting international cricket, and a financial catastrophe. We might never have recovered.

He said, 'China, would it be possible for you to use your indisputable charm to encourage the Indian team to play on? We need to salvage the game at all costs.' He must have been in shock because I think that's the only time he's ever spoken to me without using one expletive or another.

I went into their dressing room and pleaded with them to complete the game, explaining what the consequences would be if the game was called off. Most of them looked at me with an expression that said, 'Judge, do you think we care?' I was desperate, so I told them if they played on we would bowl at half pace and pitch everything up to ensure none of their batsmen got injured, and when it was our turn they could bowl as they pleased. They started talking in Hindi, so I had no idea what the answer might be until I saw a few heads nodding, including Sachin Tendulkar's. Thank goodness for that!

Our dressing room wasn't especially happy about the revised playing regulations. In fact, I couldn't believe the reaction, which was far worse than I'd anticipated. I tried to explain that we had just saved the bloody club but a few of them started complaining about their averages and what impact it might have on whether they got a new contract. They kept on moaning until, for the only time in five seasons as captain, I lost it and raised my voice. 'I'll make sure that any statistics from this match are not considered when we discuss next season. Stop bitching about your contracts – because I'll give you a tip, and here's a bit of insider trading for you, if this is game is abandoned there might be no bloody contracts for any of us!'

They reluctantly agreed and we deliberately bowled everything on a full length outside off stump in India's second innings. I stood at mid-off, waving my hands in apparent frustration at our bowlers. I'd walk up to them as they went back to their mark, pretending to be annoyed while quietly saying, 'Keep going, love your work.'

We took a bit of a battering in the fourth innings, and after the game I saw our wicketkeeper Adie Aymes in the shower, his body black and blue.

It was all proved worthwhile a year later when, on 10 July 2003, the Rose Bowl hosted international cricket for the first time – an ODI between South Africa and Zimbabwe. I'm amazed it hasn't hosted more Test cricket. There have been only three Tests, the most recent a brilliant match against India in 2018. It's now known as the Ageas Bowl and, while I know I'm biased, I think it's a wonderful, stylish ground, one of the best in the country. I don't know whether the ECB simply haven't recognised Rod's good intentions or whether there is something else at play.

Even so, the move has been an undoubted triumph. After a few years in the doldrums, Hampshire re-established themselves as one of the leading teams in the country. In the last 15 years, the club has won six major trophies and a number of home-grown players have played for England, including James Vince, Chris Tremlett and Mason Crane. I'm far removed from it all now, but I'll always love Hampshire and I'm glad to have played a part in helping the transition from Northlands Road to the wonderful Ageas Bowl.

Chapter 24

The end

I STEPPED DOWN AS captain in 2003 so that Warney could take over. He was then banned for a year for taking a diuretic, so John Crawley became captain instead. I'd made my decision and didn't fancy another year of fretting and worrying. I also wanted to enjoy my batting again.

We had a new coach – Paul Terry, who had taken over from the South African Jimmy Cook. That was great news for me as he was one of my oldest friends, and I was instrumental in him getting the job. I went into the season thinking it would probably be my last. My contract was due to expire and I was approaching my fortieth birthday, which felt like a perfect time to move on to something else.

There was a lot of sadness before the season, with two tragic deaths in March. Charles Knott, who had been club chairman when I joined in 1981, died at the age of 88. Two weeks later Major Ronald Ferguson, the father of the Duchess of York, who had become a great friend of ours, passed away. I was honoured to be asked to give the eulogy at his funeral, though I did so with the heaviest heart.

I had a strong start to the county season, with a lot of fluent attacking innings. The highlight, on a personal level, was an 83 not out and the Man of the Match award when Hampshire played Scotland in Edinburgh. With Mom being born in Edinburgh, I had extra motivation to do well. I felt I was playing as well as at any point since I last played Test cricket in 1996 – and, just as importantly, was enjoying it more than I had in ages. Warney was due to return in 2004 and I loved playing with him, so I started to reconsider my retirement. Goochie played county cricket until he was 44 and Lamby and Gatt played on after their 41st birthdays, so there were some encouraging precedents.

At the start of July, we played Northamptonshire away from home in the County Championship. During the match, Paul asked if he could have a quick chat, so we sat in the old grandstand with the usual county cricket die-hards. I assumed that, as his oldest friend at the club, he wanted to talk about a problem with one of the players.

'Judgie, we've decided we're not going to offer you a contract next year. We'll give you the opportunity to retire and say it was your decision, but this will be your last season here. Judgie, I'm sorry.'

I had suspicions it might happen – you'd have to be pretty naïve not to when you're pushing 40 – but that didn't make it any easier. I had a queasy feeling in my stomach straight away. I felt like I'd been told about a sudden death – *my* sudden death, because so much of my identity was wrapped up in cricket and being the Judge. I think that, on some subconscious level, I instantly understood the long-term impact this would have on my life.

Of all the places for it to happen, too – at Northants, the county who offered me a huge pay rise to join them when Allan Lamb retired. I rejected that because of my loyalty to and love for Hampshire. I had always assumed it would be reciprocated.

I was in a daze for the next few minutes, just as I had been 11 years earlier when Graham Gooch told me I wasn't playing in the World Cup final. I didn't say much, I never really do in situations like that.

I didn't want to retire. I was playing well and still practising hard. Dad was still diligently feeding the bowling machine every morning and reckoned my hand–eye coordination was pretty much as good as it had been when I was twenty-five. As with England, it seems Hampshire may have wanted to change the old drinking culture. There was talk of splitting up the USA – that's Udal, Smith and Aymes. I accept that times change, but I still think it's vital to maintain the old culture of talking about the game with your teammates, your opponents, the umpires – and the people who pay your wages.

When we played at home and I was captain, I felt it was imperative that the players stay behind for a bit and speak to the members and the corporate sponsors. I always felt the players left the ground too early. Some of them were down the fire escape and off to the marina on the pull before I'd taken my boots off. There were days, especially when we were struggling, when I felt like saying, 'Get your fancy clothes off, sit down in the corner and think about that crap you produced today, and why we lost. Going straight down to the marina on the pull? Fuck that! Playing for Hampshire obviously doesn't mean much to you.'

I brought in a rule that nobody left the ground for an hour after the day's play. It wasn't a drinking culture, and I didn't care whether they had whisky or Ribena. I just wanted them to have a shower, talk about the cricket and – especially when we'd had a bad day – to walk past the sponsors and the members and speak to them rather than sneaking off down the fire escape.

A couple of the wives called me to complain. I twigged that their husbands had said I'd ordered them to stay at the ground until 9 p.m., 10 p.m. or whenever, not just for one hour, when in reality they were off down the marina. I knew what they were up to because I'd done it myself. You can't con a conman!

The funny thing is that, when Warney came back as captain in 2004, one of the first things he did was initiate a victory song. The second verse starts:

'Now we do what Judgie did and now we have some beers,

'Now we celebrate as Hampshire has throughout the years.'

I suppose in the end the game had moved on from the days of working hard and playing even harder. But I was still scoring runs and felt I had at least one more year in me. It's not missing another year that hurt as much as the rejection, both by Hampshire and England. Was I really that bad a person?

Don't get me wrong, I'm sure retirement – and finishing my international career – would have hit me between the eyes even if I had picked my own ending, but the circumstances definitely made it worse. Although I had theories as to why, the fact I was never given an explanation killed me. It was like the unsolved mystery of my own professional death.

There was no fairy-tale ending. A couple of days after Paul's bombshell I was batting with Simon Katich in a Sunday League match on the same ground in Northampton. I was playing seriously well and on about 30 when he called me through for a single and I pulled my hamstring. We called on Derek Kenway to be a runner. He was run out in the next over.

I was out for six weeks and then returned against Durham at the end of August. I top-scored in the second innings, though we lost by an innings, and a few days later we went to play Somerset at Taunton. In the first innings I strained my hamstring again so had to retire hurt when I'd made seven. I sensed this might be it so decided I was coming back the next day on one leg if needs be. I hooked Steffan Jones for six and finished on 56 not out. As I walked off, I knew I'd batted for Hampshire for the last time. It was a lovely way to go.

My relationship with Paul, who had been a great friend for over 20 years, inevitably suffered, and things were very awkward between us for a while. It must have been incredibly hard for him as well, both to make the decision and then to tell me face to face, and I know his only thought would have been to do what he felt was best for Hampshire. He's always been a fantastic bloke and our friendship recovered over time. I see him a lot now. We both live in Perth and coach together at one of the more prestigious private schools.

Most players say you wake up one day and know it's time to retire, but I'm not sure that would have ever happened to me. It probably needed someone to make the decision because I loved the game too much. I loved the camaraderie, the friendships, the atmosphere, the adrenalin, the butterflies and playing with my mates. It was all I'd ever known, all I'd ever wanted.

Just like other professional sportspeople who are released, I scrambled for my dignity by announcing I'd made the choice to retire. I behaved as if I owned my fate. I didn't, at least not where Hampshire was concerned. I could have continued my career elsewhere for a couple of years, but I had no interest in playing for a county other than Hampshire.

The injury meant I didn't get to say farewell at the Rose Bowl. Instead I announced my retirement in a low-key press conference at the end of the season. 'I have come to this decision after long and careful consideration.' I said in a prepared statement, 'but my body tells me it's time to go.'

When I announced my retirement, there were some lovely tributes in the media, particularly from people I had played against. 'There have been many players who have suggested they would rather face 90mph throat balls than gentle leg-breaks,' wrote Angus Fraser in the *Independent*, 'but Smith is the only one I truly believe.'

Mark Nicholas, my Hampshire captain and mentor, wrote that I had been 'the most universally popular cricketer in the world game', and Simon Hughes's piece in the *Telegraph* had the flattering headline, 'There will never be another batsman like Robin'. I didn't see these articles at the time but it was nice reading them in Dad's scrapbooks.

There's a Q&A in my benefit brochure, seven years before retirement, which is quite revealing.

Worst day in life
'Not had one yet – but probably the day I retire from cricket.'

For twenty-five years there had been no real difference between cricket and life. They were so intertwined that they depended on each other and became one. Cricket dictated when I got up, when I went to bed, who I slept with, what I ate and where I went. It influenced my finances, my social engagements and my charity work. Cricket was more than just a game, it was my life. And it was over.

Chapter 25
Fractured identity

LIFE BEGINS AT 40, but not always in a good way. I announced my retirement from professional cricket on the last day of my thirties and, though I had a few business ventures, I had no real idea what I was going to do with the rest of my life.

The implications of retirement didn't hit me at first. I kept myself extremely busy in the winter of 2003–04, which meant I didn't have time to stop and reflect. In a way nothing had changed, it was just the off season. I had various businesses to work on – Masuri helmets, Chase Sports, Judge Tours and Cotton Graphics, an embroidery company that I set up towards the end of my cricket career.[1]

I regularly drove up north for sales meetings with retailers, either on my own or with my business partner Jon Hardy, and started to combine that with after-dinner speaking in the same area. Those speeches could be really nerve-racking but I wanted to keep myself as busy as possible and I never liked turning down invitations. I would usually have dinner, do my bit and then start the long drive home. When I was on the road I usually got in at around 4.30 a.m.

I also had a few months left of my testimonial year so there were various functions to attend, many of them coupled with local charities.

---

[1] This grew out of Chase Sports when we decided to diversify.

One of the best items we auctioned was a big frame containing three shirts signed by great sportsmen who wore No. 23: Warney, David Beckham and Michael Jordan.

It only really sunk in that my cricket career was over when Hampshire's pre-season training started in the spring of 2004. I always looked forward to catching up with the guys and chatting about what we'd all done over the winter. That first day back was one of the best of the whole year and it felt strange not to be part of it. I knew life would go on without me, but it was still a hard thing to accept.

The most difficult thing was visiting the dressing room. When I was captain, I always invited ex-players to come in, talk to the young players and pass on their knowledge, and I couldn't understand why they were so reluctant to do so. I always wondered whether I'd pissed them off! When I retired, it all made sense. Being in the dressing room brought back so many magnificent memories but it was painful to revisit them. I wasn't made to feel uncomfortable – quite the opposite – but I knew I didn't belong there any more. I felt like an intruder in my own home.

I missed the mateship, banter and solidarity so much. I missed the shared goals and sense of belonging. I missed Dimi Mascarenhas's radiant smile, Shaun Udal's dry wit and the 'my way or the bloody highway' attitude of Alan Mullally and Adie Aymes. There had always been such strong personalities in the Hampshire dressing room and we were each other's support network.

It wasn't just my old teammates who I missed. My retirement meant I saw less of my parents, too. Dad had fed the bowling machine every morning for me. It was a routine that kept us close and I missed the camaraderie of our morning practice, which evoked a more innocent time in my life back in Durban. In 2004, with my cricket career finished, Mom and Dad relocated to Perth to be near Kippy and his family and to enjoy a warmer climate in their retirement.

Although I had no wish to join another county, I did accept one invitation to dust off my Gray-Nicolls gear. Patrick Trant, the man behind the excavation of the Rose Bowl, asked if I would play for his work team, Trants, in the Southampton Evening Cricket League.

The matches were played at a recreation ground that was known by cricketers as Dog Shit Park, a name that should be self-explanatory.

Patrick described this 'opportunity' as if it would be some kind of transcendent experience. He relayed my career milestones in reverse – England was the first rung of the ladder, then Hampshire and now I had received the ultimate accolade, a chance to bat for the brotherhood of Trants at Dog Shit Park. Patrick was so funny, a typical gregarious Irishman, and he always had us in stitches.

The wickets were appalling but I was successful most of the time. I used to time my shots to miss the passing cars or avoid the exposed windows all around. I didn't want any disgruntled old ladies marching over like Mrs Iris Clarke had at Northlands Road all those years earlier. A few young bowlers tried to make a name for themselves by giving me abuse. I didn't always see the funny side of that, at least not at the time. I didn't mind being sledged by players who were as good as or better than me, but when I went down several leagues I didn't expect to cop a heap of shit from blokes who weren't fit to feed my bowling machine!

Though I loved playing for Patrick's team, the rush was obviously nothing like playing for Hampshire. There were no butterflies in my stomach any more, and I was desperate to experience the adrenalin and nervousness of batting in big games again. One thing I really missed was the uncertainty of each day, and the unpredictability of cricket. The routine was the same but the details of each day and each innings were different. Now it felt like every day was a repeat of the last.

Hampshire offered me an ambassadorial role, which I was very happy to accept. As with Judge Tours, it seemed the best way to prolong the cricket lifestyle, if not actually the cricket, and I could do it in conjunction with overseeing the businesses. Whenever Hampshire played at home, I hosted a hospitality suite. I would get to the ground around 10 a.m., watch the players train and chat to them. Then I would get suited and booted and go to one of the suites, where I would host the corporate sponsors for the day. My job was to make sure everyone got value for money and left the ground happy – whether that meant chatting about what was happening in the middle, getting something signed for their young son or daughter by one of the players, or reminiscing about life at our old ground in Northlands Road.

Most of my work was in the Robin Smith Suite, which was officially opened in 2004 by the Duke of Edinburgh. Every time I'd met him in the past he'd mixed me up with Allan Lamb, which was always a bit embarrassing, so I was glad that wouldn't be a problem on the day he was opening the Robin Smith Suite. Hampshire were playing so we sat down to watch the cricket and started chatting.

'Lamby, tell me, what's it like to face those West Indies bowlers.'

I politely corrected him and he couldn't have been more apologetic. A couple of minutes later he had another question for me.

'So, Lamby, who was the best bowler you ever faced?'

I gave up after that. I should have started introducing him as the Duke of Glasgow!

He was a charming gentleman and so much fun. He's a seriously good bloke, and it was a real honour to sit next to him for a few hours. He was quite knowledgeable about the game, too, if not about my name.

I had many fun times in the Robin Smith Suite, but I started to realise that accepting Hampshire's generous offer wasn't such a good idea. It slowly killed me watching the club, especially as I felt I was still good enough to be playing. It all felt a bit humiliating.

Hampshire really struggled for runs in 2004, and results were poor. Every day, as I walked round the ground, somebody would make a good-natured suggestion that I should come out of retirement. 'Judgie, Hampshire needs you!'

'Yeah, and I bloody need Hampshire too.'

I didn't say that, of course. It hadn't got out that I'd been forced to retire in 2003, so I spouted the usual crap about knowing when it's the right time, and how we had to give the young kids a chance in the first team.

I could see the disappointment on people's faces, as if that was a weak excuse, so then I started to feel an irrational guilt about letting them down by retiring. That's typical of me, I suppose, to feel guilty about the impact of a decision I hadn't even made!

Although almost a year had passed, I couldn't escape the feeling of betrayal, the sense that people I knew and loved – the coach Paul Terry, the director of cricket Tim Tremlett and who knows who else – had been plotting my retirement behind my back. The thought of those clandestine discussions destroyed me. I just wish it all had been a bit more transparent.

I've discussed this a million times with Kippy in the last decade or so, as I know he will give me a straight answer rather than the one I might want to hear. He has helped me see it from Hampshire's point of view, why Paul may have felt they needed to move on despite our friendship and my status at the club. He also pointed out that, if I was really desperate to keep playing, I could have gone somewhere else. That was a non-starter – I was desperate to keep playing, but only for Hampshire – but I take his point.

Kippy also made an interesting point about the cut-throat nature of business and, increasingly, professional sport. When he took over as chief executive of the WACA in Perth in 1992, a really huge job in Australian sport, he had to answer to 12,000 members and was tasked with many major areas of responsibility. The first was running a multipurpose stadium which hosted major sport for 90 days a year. He also had to reduce $20m of debt at 21 per cent interest and revitalise a state team that, after 20 years of enormous success, had become old, unsuccessful, militant and difficult. Within two months, Kippy had sacked 32 full-time staff, which was about 50 per cent of the workforce. It was purely his decision, backed by the board, and he went through with it. Kippy worked with reduced staff levels for the next two years, during which time he cleared $10 million of the company debt.

Kippy is a tough bugger and he was comfortable making those brutal decisions. He was also part of the decision-making group that nicked Adam Gilchrist from New South Wales in controversial circumstances. Kippy reminded me that Paul Terry worked under him for many years at the WACA and got used to that culture of uncompromising, unsentimental decision-making.

Kippy is one of my pillars of strength and I wish he'd been in England at the time. His hardarse attitude and general pragmatism would, I believe, have stopped me losing my way. I am sure I would have dealt with the situation differently and not started to spiral out of control.

I made a mistake by not surrounding myself with people who might have been a bit more objective and given me a blunt answer – whether it was about my businesses or my grievance over being dropped by England and Hampshire. Kippy would have done that but he was living in Perth, and most of the people I knew told me what I wanted to hear. I don't blame them for that, but it probably didn't help me.

In hindsight, I should have taken a clean break from Hampshire for a few years. I could have thrown myself into my businesses and found a renewed sense of purpose that way. After a few years, when I was comfortable that there really was more to life than cricket, I could have returned to Hampshire and enjoyed it.

I didn't want to be at the Rose Bowl but I didn't know where else to go. It was the easy option, because I was apprehensive about the outside world. It's hard enough to reinvent yourself at 25, never mind 40. Once you get to 40 you get a bit frenetic and desperate because you feel like you have less time to change things. You have to answer the most basic questions – Who am I? What am I going to do with my life? – but without the fearlessness and resilience of youth to fall back on.

We lived in a village near the New Forest called Nomansland, which suddenly felt pretty apt. I was in limbo between my cricket career and the rest of my life, and my identity became fractured. I still wanted to be the Judge, but now I was Robin Arnold Smith. The Judge was a fearless warrior; Robin Arnold Smith was a frantic worrier. I had suppressed Robin Arnold Smith for so long – all my adult life – that I didn't really know how to assume that side of my personality.

I internalised my pain and put on my mask of masculinity, making sure that all people saw was the sociable, good-time Judge. Cricket-lovers around the world, especially in England, saw me as strong, brave and fearless, always with a beer in hand and a smile on my face. Even after retirement, when I was hosting corporate boxes, I felt I had to live up to my cricket persona. That's the story of my life. I never really made choices for myself, and it's in my nature to be respectful and do what I'm told or what's expected of me. I wasn't living a lie so much as being economical with the truth by only presenting one side of my personality.

Retirement took a greater toll on me than I realised at the time. It's only now that I look back and see I was a bit of a zombie, devoid of energy or enthusiasm, which was totally unlike me. I had my cheek-bone fractured by Ian Bishop in 1995, which led to surgery through the side of my head. But, trust me, fractured identity is a hundred times harder to deal with. It was the beginning of the most difficult period of my life by far.

I was grieving the death of the Judge, which created a powerful feeling of loss and negativity. I had an exclusive athletic identity and couldn't see or accept that cricket was only part of my life. I know I'm not the only one to suffer like this. Every sportsman or woman falls when their career is over. The only differences are how far we fall and how quickly we get up. I've read so many heart-breaking stories of former sports stars searching for meaning in the second half of their lives. Cricket seems to be the most extreme of all, because it consumes even more of our lives than other sports, and that comrade-ship is something you miss terribly.

In recent years, the Professional Cricketers' Association has done some wonderful work, helping people to bridge the gap between their playing career and the rest of their life. In our era, it was frowned upon to think about tomorrow. But it's so important to realise that professional sport doesn't last for ever and to be prepared for that. Don't take your career for granted. Enjoy it, respect the game, continue to work hard. But take time to stop and smell the roses occasionally. And whatever you do, make sure you keep half an eye on the future. I did prepare for the future in practical terms, but I wasn't prepared psychologically for being an ex-cricketer.

I started to suffer anxiety attacks for the first time in my life. One of the worst things about anxiety is how randomly it can strike. You don't need to have done anything wrong, you might think you're in a pretty good place, but then it comes out of nowhere and your heart starts beating at 100 miles an hour. It feels like your body is telling you, 'You might think you're okay, china, but you're not.'

During my career, I rarely had trouble sleeping. I'd put my head on the pillow, drift off almost instantly and wake up seven or eight hours later. In 2004, I started stirring in the middle of the night. I always woke with a start, with my heart racing and my breathing erratic, and it often took me an age to get back to sleep.

If I close my eyes, I can still see the LED light on the alarm clock by our bed, flashing 2:45 back at me. I always seemed to wake up around that time. It really freaked me out and I didn't know what to do, so I stared at the red numbers and used them as a portal to retreat into the past.

I entered the rabbit hole of nostalgia and ended up looking at the neon sign of Joe Bananas club in Wan Chai, Hong Kong. From there it was a short hop on my train of thought to the Hong Kong Sixes in 1994. Though I was out of the England Test team at the time, I'd been picked for the annual six-a-side tournament. We won the final against Australia, whose team included Matthew Hayden, Damien Martyn and Merv Hughes. I was playing as a wicketkeeper because my shoulder was too bad for me to throw, but I somehow picked up the Man of the Tournament award.

There were some great lads in our team, including Gladstone Small and Matthew Maynard, and we celebrated our win with gusto. That night I stood at the urinal in Joe Bananas, thinking it was going to be a bloody good party. I wasn't quite finished when I felt a thump on my shoulder. I swung around, expecting trouble, only to be faced with the moustachioed sumo I had just faced on the pitch.

I assumed Merv was going to grunt an eight-letter word beginning with A at me. Instead he caught me off guard with a cheery greeting. 'It's about time we had a drink, mate, whaddaya think? D'ya fancy a beer?' We'd had a beer at the Oval in 1989 but I'd never spent any serious time with him. We had a few that night and for the next couple of days we were inseparable. I laughed out loud at the memory, looked at the clock now flashing 3:15 at me, rolled over and went to sleep.

Those overnight panic attacks became a regular occurrence. There's no escape from your thoughts in the early hours. You can't go down the pub or do something with the children.

Where are you now, Judge? Who are you now, Judge? What will you do now, Judge?

My heart raced and I was drenched in sweat.

I'm nothing and I'm nowhere.

Kath was oblivious to this and slept contentedly, her rhythmic breathing a soundtrack to my internal angst. I thought about how meekly I accepted Hampshire's decision to get rid of me. Why didn't I challenge them? Why didn't I speak up? I treated them with the respect for authority that was drummed into me as a child in South Africa, and to hell with the impact on my own dignity and purpose.

I'm sure you've been through something similar. Everyone has spells in their life when stress turns into insomnia. Time goes at different speeds in the dead of night – sometimes very fast, sometimes painfully slow. I was desperate to get back to sleep. I tried counting sheep but that didn't work because every time I did my train of thought took me from sheep to lambs to Lamby to all the shit we'd done together!

2:45. 2:46. 2:47. 3:41.

I tried counting my pulse instead but that just freaked me out, especially if I was having an anxiety attack and it was going too quickly. You know instinctively what your pulse should be, and how long each beat takes – about the same as the reaction time I had when I was facing Ian Bishop, funnily enough. It freaks you out when it should be going 'Pump … pump … pump' and instead it's going, 'Pumppumppump'.

I thought about my brother's words, repeated throughout my life. 'You're a soft cock, Robin. Toughen up. You've got to practise the power of the mind.' But the only way I could do that, and escape negative thoughts, was to hide in my safe place: the past. I shook my head and smiled as I remembered the story of getting a deserved smack at Coco de Mer nightclub when I tried to chat up the wrong woman. My anxiety started to subside as I sniggered at the stupidity of my 18-year-old self. But all the memories that lifted me were a band-aid for a bullet wound. The past was fine but what about the present and the future?

It wasn't just the rush of cricket that I missed. It was *everything*. I lived life at 100mph, cramming as much as I could into every single day, and that busy routine kept me going. Life was full to the brim. Now, despite my various jobs, I still had plenty of gaps in my schedule. I started to dread those periods, because dead time meant time to think about what I had lost. I felt constantly uneasy, like I no longer had any goals in life.

I continued to search for something to stimulate me. We knocked down our house and applied for planning permission to build two properties on the same piece of land. I decided to manage the project myself rather than get a building company involved. In the meantime, we moved to a charming but run-down old house in the same village, with a view to doing it up.

I loved planning the two houses but I made the mistake of getting emotionally involved. You can't do that, especially if you aren't going to be living in the houses yourself. I overdeveloped the plot with specifications that were too high – effectively they were £1 million specifications for a £500,000 home. With a downturn in the housing market happening around the same time, I lost about £200,000 by the time the houses were sold. At least I had a go, I suppose, but if I had my time again I wouldn't play with so much money in an area where I had no experience.

Kath was increasingly agitated by the impact retirement had on me, and bitter at those who had imposed it. She wanted to help but didn't know how. It wasn't her fault. She couldn't understand what I was going through; I didn't know myself.

I certainly didn't want my mood to affect my children, who meant more to me than anything in the world. Their happiness was worth a hell of a lot more than my own. Watching my children grow up so beautifully, with such sensitive, effervescent personalities, was the thing that gave me the most joy in that time – and, looking back, greater enjoyment than any Test hundred I ever scored.

I loved listening to Harrison play the piano. I still do. It's something he started at the age of 13 just after I retired. He used to spend four hours a day practising at weekends, and it was worth it: fifteen years later he's a very accomplished player of classical music, especially Chopin.

I was always so grateful that we were able to give our children a good upbringing. We sent them to Chafyn Grove, one of the more prestigious junior schools in the area, and then Harrison went to Bryanston. I used to go to sports days at Chafyn Grove, where they had parents' races as well. Sting's daughter was in Harrison's class so he was often there. The less said about my performance in the egg-and-spoon race, the better.

When he was 12, Harrison was leading the 100m, but he slowed down towards the end and was pipped at the line. Although he did it in a subtle way, I could tell it was deliberate, so I asked him afterwards what was going on.

'Dad, I feel like he wanted to win more than me. It was going to make him so happy.'

I was so proud of him.

One of my abiding memories of Margaux as a child is how much she loved visiting Barbados. We must have been there 15 times on family holidays. We had a wonderful friend, Angus Edghill, who Kippy and I met when we went there in 1984. He was a property developer who loved his cricket, and he gave us free accommodation at one of his magnificent hotels along the Saint Lawrence Gap. Every day she would ask me to take her to the beach so that we could sit under a palm tree and wait for the pineapple man, who would walk up and down the beach cutting up pineapples and selling them. Even at that age, she had the travelling bug.

Although the children were growing up so nicely, my marriage to Kath was ebbing away. I didn't know how to save it and that created a lot of difficult feelings because I didn't want to give up on it or hurt Kath. I felt terribly guilty that I couldn't give Kath what she wanted and deserved. I appeased her for a while by going to marriage counselling, where I was told to light candles around a bath filled with rose petals and drink a fine bottle of red wine.

Really? I paid £200 for this?

My family life had been so idyllic when I was younger and I couldn't understand why my own marriage was failing. I didn't really think about divorce. That was something that happened to other people. I grew up in a country where 'real men' never, ever divorced their wives – that was deeply ingrained in South African culture. But I knew the marriage wasn't working, so I felt trapped.

The businesses were also not developing as I hoped. They were good products, and are all still going strong today, but at the time we had problems. I tried to plough on and in doing so I ignored the truth. I couldn't accept failure because at that stage I'd been successful in almost everything I'd done. I would sweep everything under the carpet, where it was hidden but not forgotten, until one day everything got so overwhelming that I fell over the carpet. I didn't confront the problems at home, I didn't ask why I was dropped by England, I just let everything fester.

This was the beginning of a debilitating situational depression, or adjustment disorder. I have never suffered from clinical depression, and my heart goes out to those who do. Mine was related to my change of circumstances and my struggle to cope with both what had happened and why.

I didn't go to a doctor. It wasn't a macho thing; I wasn't too proud to seek help. It was just that at the time I didn't realise I was depressed, and I'm not even sure I had a GP.

I found that alcohol was the best over-the-counter medicine I could get. I would take my beautiful dog Violet for long walks in the New Forest and stop off at our local pub, which was only 100 yards from our house, on the way back. I had lots of friends there and the company, along with a couple of pints of lager, lifted my mood. Alcohol was the one thing that gave me a bit of a spark, a glint in my eye.

The pub was a focal point in our life – the children also liked going there to play pool, and Kath often came down as well. Maybe it was just an excuse for me to have another pint. I know Kath thinks my drinking got worse after I was dropped by England but it was purely a social thing. If it was a bigger problem, I would have used my after-dinner speaking as an excuse to get hammered, but I stayed sober and drove home from Middlesbrough, Lancashire or wherever in the early hours.

Things started to get worse as the housing project progressed, because I could see the losses coming well in advance. It was all very stressful, and my way of dealing with it was to go to the pub and have a few pints. I wasn't getting pissed and staggering home but I was having five or six pints most nights.

Even a decent drink didn't stop me waking in the small hours to play a different episode of Judgie's Happy Memories. I could almost feel the friendship and hear the banter of Mark Nicholas, Malcolm Marshall, Kippy, Alan Wilkins and Jon Hardy, to name a few, when they came to hang out at our house in South Africa. I recalled us messing around in Durban's Diamond Circle nightclub, and practising during the day on the pitch Dad had created at our home. In the sweltering Durban heat, Flo would appear with magnificent tuna salads and an endless supply of cold Castle lagers.

After a while I stopped searching for those memories in the middle of the night because I realised that, while it was comforting in the short term, it wasn't healthy to focus so much on the past. I had to do something, I just didn't know what. I needed to move forward with life rather than look backwards every night. After discussing it for a few months Kath and I decided it was time to try and start again somewhere else, to rejuvenate our marriage and give our children a happier life.

There was one obvious destination: Perth.

As in so much else, I was inspired by Kippy's success. After his spell as chief executive at the WACA, he bought a small company, with just two employees, and made it into the largest embroidery business in Western Australia. The business opportunities were particularly appealing to me – I could focus on the Masuri helmet franchise and try to make that the No. 1 in Australia.

Kippy and Julie were very happy in Perth, and I'd had a great time there in the 1980s. Mom and Dad were also there, so it was a bit of a no-brainer to reunite the whole Smith family. But that would mean leaving behind Kath's family. Although it was a mutual decision, I tormented myself with the idea that I had separated Kath from her family, and that I was letting her down again. She felt it was the right decision, especially for the children, and at no stage did she resist, even though it meant moving away from her mum, dad, brother and sister. We wanted to give our children a new and happy life in Australia.

Though we were all really excited and optimistic about making a fresh start, we left with a heavy heart. I'll always love Hampshire, the place and the cricket club. I'd gone over for a three-week trial and stayed for 26 years. But I knew that it was time to go.

Chapter 26

Fresh start

THE MOVE TO PERTH gave me the sense of purpose I craved. I had a long list of goals: to get my marriage back on track, help the children forge new lives, establish a successful business and enjoy getting up every morning to go for a walk by the beach in a beautiful sunny climate.

When we arrived, we rented in the prominent suburb of Dalkeith and bought a plot of land in Wembley Downs so that we could have a house built to our specifications. This time it was fine for me to get emotionally involved in the build. We spent ages planning it and it was so much fun, especially talking to Harrison and Margaux about what they wanted in each room. While that was happening, we rented in the same suburb and enrolled the children into the finest schools in Perth.

I set up Masuri Australia, effectively a franchise of the parent company back home in which I still had shares. I was a one-man company and even did an accountancy course so that I could take care of that side of things. I sold the other businesses to some old Hampshire friends – Jon Hardy bought me out at Chase Sports and Shaun Udal took over Cotton Graphics.

During our first year in Perth I started to realise that, for all my good intentions, the new life was just the old life in a warmer climate. I tried to ignore it but I couldn't. I desperately wanted to make Kath happy but I knew it wasn't working, and the Masuri business wasn't giving me a spark. I wasn't lonely, as I had a mezzanine office at Chris's embroidery factory, but it was repetitive and didn't give me the buzz or the sense of purpose that I needed.

Is this it now? Is this the rest of my life?

There was nobody I could talk to, or at least nobody I felt I could talk to, which was ridiculous because Kippy was 20 yards away at work. I'd made friends in Perth but I didn't want to unload on them, and I didn't want to talk to Mom, Dad or Kippy because of the guilt I felt at letting them down.

I became depressed again, though I didn't recognise it as such at the time. I'd only ever really drunk lager during my playing days but afterwards I started to move on to vodka. It was partly because I thought people wouldn't be able to smell it on my breath – turns out they can – but mainly because I was worried about my weight now that I wasn't training every day. Vodka also gave me an instant hit of calmness that I didn't really get with a swig of lager. There was a steady increase in how much I drank. In 2004 I would enjoy a refreshing vodka, lime and soda. A couple of years later I was having a double vodka, lime and soda. Then it became triples and eventually I was having neat vodka.

What's that Pink Floyd song, 'Comfortably Numb'? I've never taken drugs, and I know that's what the song is supposed to be about, but it also sums up how I felt about vodka. It gave me a warmth and a hazy comfort that I couldn't get with anything else. I loved the feeling of that first drop, how my mind and muscles started to relax. I loved the instant self-confidence and the feeling that everything was going to be okay.

As the stress of life got greater and greater, vodka kept me going. I felt very guilty because I was now drinking in secret, alone and sometimes in the morning. When I was younger I needed alcohol to function socially. Now I needed it to function.

We moved into our beautiful new home in Wembley Downs in January 2010 – another fresh start, my last fresh start. Over the next few months, Kath and I reluctantly accepted our marriage was over. Our children had kept us together, but now they were 19 and 15 and we worried that staying together was doing more harm than good. After 22 years of marriage we decided to separate.

Barry Richards, the legend who encouraged me to go to Perth in the first place in the 1980s, was looking to invest in a property in the area. He knew about my situation and suggested I look for an apartment that I thought was good value, then he would buy it and I'd rent off him. I found a place in Scarborough, a small two-bedroom apartment, and moved in soon after. It meant moving out of our dream home after only six months.

Real men don't leave their wives, Judgie. Real men look after their families for ever.

As I settled into Barry's apartment, I thought back to my first meetings with him as a young bloke in Durban, especially when I appeared in his coaching book. The hopes and dreams of that small boy, to play cricket at the highest possible level, had been realised, so why was life so bloody hard?

I threw myself myself into work, which was the one area of my life that was successful. Masuri was in the process of becoming the most popular brand of helmets in Australia, and most weekdays I worked from 6 a.m. till 8 p.m. in the office. There was so much to do. I was the marketing manager, secretary, accountant, CEO, the lot. I even assembled the helmets. Each one took a while, and it wasn't the kind of mass production that you could do mindlessly. You had to really concentrate because there were so many different details for each helmet.

There were loads of little stresses that added up to a whole lot of stress – chasing money that was owed, sorting everything out when some of the helmets that arrived were the wrong shade. And because the helmets were so popular, the demand, and the demands on me, became greater and greater. I should have said no or sought help, but I have always had a simple answer to adversity: work even harder.

I became a victim of my own success. I needed to pay for stock being manufactured in Jullundur in India nine months in advance of us being able to distribute it, which meant I was badly undercapitalised. And then the big retailers, the ones I felt I had to be with if I wanted to get a share of the market, were able to beat me down on price. That made everything worse. It doesn't matter whether you have the best or most popular brand on the market – if you don't have the necessary cash flow you're in trouble. I ploughed on, trying to ignore the upcoming problems, hoping they would go away. I couldn't cope, but I was too proud and too stubborn to seek help or advice.

I've always been a contradiction of pride and humility and I think both were a factor in me not seeking help, whether it was from Kippy, a GP or anyone else. My way of dealing with things was to bottle them up and then hit the bottle.

We had to sell our dream home to clear the debt I'd accrued through the business. As my mental state worsened, I became more isolated. I usually loved company and had always been the life and soul of the party. Now I was alone in a small apartment that didn't even belong to me. I didn't respond when friends sent texts or emails asking how I was because I felt ashamed and irrelevant. I know I hadn't been forgotten but that's how I felt at the time.

It wasn't the loss of material things like my properties, cars and money that pained me the most, although it is hard when you are used to a certain quality of life to see it taken away. The thing that really unnerved me was the loss of my physical and mental fortitude. After decades of building myself up to be an almost invincible athlete, I felt weak and vulnerable.

I was also aware there were people in the world with far bigger problems than mine, which in turn made me feel guilty, inadequate and even more vulnerable. I felt like an ungrateful prick.

I was so wrapped up in my own problems. I wasn't capable of rational thought, either, and I couldn't see a future. I'd lost the one thing nobody should have to live without: hope.

Grayson Heath, my mentor and batting coach, has a theory that the more talented sportsmen struggle in later life because the game comes so naturally to them that they never really need to consider cause and effect and analyse *why* they are successful. Those who have to work harder to make it, like Kippy, learn things they can then transfer to other walks of life. Cricket was my comfort zone, and

I had little idea how to function outside of it. One example is that I'd hardly ever cooked before. Throughout my life I followed what others suggested – Dad, Kath, my teammates. Now I had to make all these decisions for myself, large and small. When you're in a rut, the smallest decisions – like what to eat – can seem so intimidating. So I didn't bother, I just drank.

As the stress increased, I started to bring my medicine to Kippy's business where I was working. Most days I drank at least a bottle of vodka in my office. I was never properly drunk, I just topped up, a quick swig straight from the bottle to keep me going. I was still able to function as normal and operate some intricate (and dangerous) embroidery machinery. You don't want to be going near those when you're drunk.

There were a few times when Kippy sent me home because he knew I'd been drinking, and I'm sure there were others when people were talking about me. Kippy had always run a focused, disciplined business, and I know my drinking brought huge embarrassment to him and Julie. He may also have been worried that I would be charged with drink-driving while in one of his vans, which would have been disastrous for the business. He could, probably should, have sacked me many times.

I'd become a slave to alcohol. I knew it was wrong, terribly wrong, and I knew it had to stop, but I didn't know how to stop it. When you're in such a rut you do what you need to survive. I would be at breaking point, then I'd have a little swig from the bottle and I could get by for another half hour. And unlike all the people in my life, vodka never judged me.

I believed I was invincible with a slug of vodka; it steadied my shakes and calmed my accelerating anxiety. There are no words, certainly not in my vocabulary, that can adequately convey the sheer terror of a panic attack: the palpitations, the tightness in your chest as you scramble around trying to breathe properly. At their worst, you think you're going to die.

I would return late at night from work, have a nightcap so that I could put my head on the pillow to sleep and get five or six hours' respite from my life.

But I'd wake up the next day with the same problems and go through it all again. At that stage I was about 17 stone, the heaviest

I've ever been. I got myself a mountain bike and did the 80-kilometre round trip to work every day. With that and not eating, the weight dropped off me.

I didn't neglect the children, but they and the rest of my family were upset as they realised I was drinking far too much. I was never an aggressive drunk but I looked bedraggled and, though they never said as much, I could see in their eyes that they were losing respect for me. Now, that ... that created the most horrendous guilt.

In February 2011, the cricket World Cup started in India. I barely even noticed. On Friday 25 February, I was due to pick Margaux up from school because Kath was in England. Although I'd had a bit of vodka in the office, I knew I was fine to drive – I might have been slightly over the legal limit but my faculties were all working and I looked sober in the mirror.

When I picked Margaux up, she jumped in the car as normal. I drove off and, as we took the first roundabout, I clipped the edge of it with the front right wheel.

'Dad, stop the car!'

'What do you mean, Margs?'

'Stop the car! I know you've been drinking. Please! Dad! Stop the car!'

I pulled over and, without saying a word, she jumped out and ran back towards the school. It broke my heart. It absolutely broke my heart. I sat for a while, my head on my hand on the steering wheel, and wept. I wanted to get home and put my head on the pillow. I was a couple of miles from Barry's apartment and decided to drive back.

It'll be okay. Just get home, have a bottle to get through the day and tomorrow you'll start again. Tomorrow, you'll make this right.

You can probably guess what happened next. I was pulled over by the police and asked to use a breathalyser. It was 4 p.m. and I was four and a half times over the limit. The police thought the breathalyser wasn't working properly because I was able to stand up and speak normally. They couldn't understand why, with such a high reading, I wasn't slurring my words or falling over.

What the hell was I thinking? Probably that I was the invisible man, and that nobody noticed when I'd had a drink. My constitution was so great that I assumed I could drink as much as I liked without it affecting my interactions with others. I'd lost the clarity of sobriety without realising I'd done so, and I thought I would still be a perfectly proficient driver. I still can't quite believe I did something like that.

The police asked me to do the breathalyser test again. It came up even higher. They asked if I'd been drinking and I told them that I had, and how depressed I was. They took me to Wembley Police station and the car was impounded. It wasn't even my car – I didn't have one, because I knew on some level I was a drink-driving risk, but I'd borrowed Kath's so that I could take Margaux to and from school while she was in England.

The police wouldn't allow me to go home. They were worried about my mental state and insisted I had some support. I didn't want to call Kippy as I was so ashamed at letting him down; nor could I handle the ferocious bollocking I knew he would give me. Instead they dropped me off at the house of Leo Crohan, a great friend who I played cricket with for Western Suburbs, and he looked after me. Leo knew a bit about breathalyser readings because of a conference he'd been at a few years earlier, and when the police told him I had a blood alcohol level in excess of 0.4 he politely corrected them and said they meant 0.04.

No, they meant 0.4. Leo later told me that usually 0.2 means you are incapable, 0.3 unconscious, 0.4 in a coma and 0.5 dead. The whole thing is a bit of a blur but Leo says I was pretty lucid that night, despite the alcohol levels, and painfully full of remorse. He was so good with me. He helped keep things as light-hearted as he could in the circumstances – he told me I'd almost certainly broken another Perth cricket record, this time for the highest blood alcohol reading. He also tried to make me realise how much the cricketers at Western Suburbs loved me. We chatted about our children, and how important it was to stay healthy for them. He wanted me to stay at his home but I insisted that I catch a taxi back to my place, and I called him when I was home safely.

After my drink-driving shame, Margaux and Harrison stopped seeing me. I don't blame them, especially Margaux. A father is supposed to love and protect his daughter, and I jeopardised her welfare in a moment of desperate judgement. It's a decision that will always haunt me.

I was ashamed, disgusted and scared. I loathed the person I'd become; I loathed Robin Arnold Smith. Over the next few weeks, my conscience started to eat me up. I reflected on all the bad decisions I'd made – the financial ruin, the heartache I caused with my deceitful behaviour and misplaced trust in others, dragging the children and Kath to Perth away from their friends and family, the unresolved sadness of being binned by England and Hampshire. I couldn't cope. I had no idea how to cope. I wanted to start again but I couldn't see that far ahead.

The most devastating thing was losing the respect of my family, especially my children. That destroyed what was left of my self-esteem. I looked in the mirror every morning as I brushed my teeth and saw a worthless, derelict fuckwit. The Judge had succeeded in almost everything he did. Robin Arnold Smith was a world-class failure.

I had the same conversation with myself hundreds of times.

'Come on, Judgie, finish this last bottle and let's start a new beginning tomorrow. You can do this. Think of all the good things in life.'

'What good things? Come on, what good things?'

My mind was so blurred and confused. I was howling inside. I wanted to stop my own suffering but, more than that, I wanted to stop my children's suffering. I could see only one way to do that. One night, as I sat on the sofa at Barry's, I came to a decision. I was going to end my life.

Chapter 27
Rock bottom

I KEPT COMING BACK to the same conclusion – I had failed my family, especially Harrison and Margaux, and it was time to stop being such a burden on them. One evening I sat on the beach in Scarborough, thinking about all the games of beach cricket on the same sand with Martin Crowe, Allan Border and the rest. I looked over my right shoulder to the Rendezvous Hotel, the tallest building on the Perth coastline and three minutes' walk from Barry's apartment.

Mate, that's your spot.

I had it all planned. I wouldn't say goodbye to anyone. I'd call in sick to work and then book a room at the Rendezvous Hotel. I would close the curtains, sit on the sofa and remember the good times. I'd smoke a few cigarettes, have two bottles of vodka and a load of sleeping pills. Then, when I started to feel comfortably numb, I would walk onto the balcony, clamber over the railings, close my eyes and let all the pain go.

It's not easy recalling this. It's still so vivid, and I never want to go back to that place again. I thought about how I would end my life so often, multiple times every day. I realise now that I'd lost the ability to think rationally, but at the time it was crystal clear in my head. I was just waiting for the moment to feel right, to have the necessary courage to do it. I knew that one day – it might be tomorrow, it might be next month – I would wake up and know instinctively that I was about to get out of bed for the last time.

My internal monologue always came to the same conclusion.

'Do it, Judge. Everyone will be better off without you.'

'No, it'll scar too many people. Don't do it, Judgie. You'll get there.'

'Oh, really? How? How are you gonna get there? How are you gonna change anything?'

'You're right. I'm not sure I can change.'

I knew my life was unsustainable. I was drinking far too much, yet drink was the only thing that gave me any relief. I had no idea how I'd got into such a mess, never mind how to get out of it. I felt like I was trapped in the body of a stranger, living his empty existence in a surreal alternative reality. Even the past, once my happy place, only added to my torment, because I had no idea what had become of that person.

I continued to work long hours at the office. I may have given up on life, but the work ethic ingrained in me from such a young age was still going strong.

One night in April or May 2011 (as you can imagine, I'm not that keen on remembering the exact date) I was in Barry's apartment, curled up on the sofa waiting for another day to end, when Harrison came round to see me. It was obvious that I was in a desperate state. He told me he loved me, that I would be okay and that, although he was upset and confused by everything that had happened, he would support me and try to help me get back on track.

Those words saved my life. I know that sounds dramatic but it's true. It wasn't just what Harrison said but the sincerity and love with which he said it. It made me realise I hadn't quite been cast aside, and that, contrary to my irrational thought processes, suicide would have a devastating impact on him and Margaux as well. From that moment, taking my own life wasn't really an option. But I have such intense love for my children that, had they totally disowned me, I have no doubt how my story would have ended.

Over the next few weeks, Harrison was incredibly supportive and came to see me regularly. There was no instant cure, though – I had the same problems as before, but now I didn't have the solution of suicide.

I knew I had to change something and knew it wasn't healthy for me to live on my own. Kippy suggested I move into his place for a few months, and he and his wife Julie were a great support. I've known Julie since 1983 and she is the most wonderful, understanding woman, qualities she has passed on to their beautiful children Cameron and Hayley.

They put me in their lovely guest apartment which has an en-suite bathroom and is about two yards from their private pool. There was only one rule: if I touched a drop of alcohol, I was out.

Despite his generosity, Kippy couldn't really understand why I was struggling mentally, or why I turned to drink. He'd say, 'Mate, the amount of times I had my downs in my business. If I resorted to drinking vodka, where would the business be now? I get through the bad periods by reading *The Power of Positive Thinking*.'

I went to the rehabilitation centre at Holyoakes to start a 12-week programme for people with alcohol or drug addiction. There was a 90-minute group session each week. In truth, I found that difficult – the individual stories were so sad that they pierced me, and I found the level of human suffering hard to cope with. I know this sounds awful, but being there made me so depressed that I was more likely to drink, not less – especially as I heard from some men who had been there before that they still struggled.

Those groups work wonders for so many people, so I'm certainly not going to criticise them; they just didn't work for me. I needed to hear more positive stories of people who struggled and found the strength to reinvent themselves and put their lives back together.

I was able to go out socially without drinking and kept myself busy and content by working 60 hours a week. Kippy looked after the Masuri franchise[1] and gave me a new job as a manager at his embroidery business. My job was to look after a number of accounts, overseeing production and ensuring that everything was up to standard. One of the reasons he gave me the opportunity, apart from wanting to look after his little brother, was that I had experience in the trade. I had started to develop my own business, Perth Uniform

---

[1] Eventually we gave it back to the parent company in England as Kippy believed it was distracting him from his core business.

and Embroidery, and bought a $130,000 machine from Japan, so I was able to bring that, as well as my short list of customers.

I was sad to give up the Masuri Australia franchise. Though it had been desperately difficult at times, I can take some credit for sales quadrupling over a three-year period. Masuri is now the biggest helmet manufacturer in Australia and around the world, so I did a few things right.

Kippy continued to expand his empire. Not satisfied with his embroidery company, he founded a dye-sublimation business in 2014.[2]

Why he would want to spend over $1 million creating a business he knew nothing about at the age of 55 was beyond me and the family. It lost about $40,000 per month for the best part of 18 months and he was as low as I had ever seen him. He had enough money to retire many times over, and that's exactly what we suggested he should do. But he couldn't even consider accepting failure. A few years later, the company is a huge success, one of the most technologically advanced dye-sublimation factories and manufacturers in Australia. He is a magnificent advert for the power of positive thinking, and a lesson to everyone that you can achieve what you want in life if you have the right mentality and work ethic. I'm so proud of him.

I had my office at Kippy's factory and he gave me a lift into work every morning. At first it was really tough. One night, when Kippy was driving us back from work, I spent the whole ten-mile journey in tears, saying the same thing. 'How did I get myself into this state?'

Kippy told me he had seen the trainwreck coming because I hadn't listened to his advice, and that when people don't listen to the right advice they usually end up in trouble. He had tried every other approach with me and none of them had worked, so I can understand why he was so savagely honest.

I can't really thank Kippy and Julie enough for the support they have given me throughout my life, but particularly in those first few years after I moved to Perth. I owe him so much. He's often my

---

[2] Dye sublimation is basically the process of applying heat-sensitive dye onto fabric, which allows you to create sportswear. If you want you can check out the company website, where he has a special guest explaining clearly how the process works: dyenamicsublimation.com.au.

biggest critic but he's always been my biggest fan. All those close to what was going on – Mom, Dad, Paul Terry, the staff at the office – would say that without that support from Kippy and Julie I would not have got through those first few years in Perth.

I had the greatest care imaginable when I stayed with them. Julie cooked a beautiful dinner every day and also made me sandwiches for work – something she didn't even do for Kippy – because she wanted to make sure I was eating properly. I was in a secure, comfortable family environment.

For the first time in my life I saw a GP about my mental health and was prescribed anti-depressants. I was also put on Seropax, a very strong anti-anxiety medication that helped stabilise my mood. I was worried about my upcoming drink–driving trial, though, and was still having an occasional drink behind Kippy's back, which made me feel very guilty. But I cut the amount I was drinking by around 80 per cent and didn't touch a drop while at work.

The captain of my local cricket club, Seamus Rafferty, was a lawyer and he offered to represent me at the trial. I didn't know this at the time, because he didn't want to worry me any more than necessary, but he told Kippy that, because I was so far over the limit, there was a big chance I'd end up behind bars

In court, Seamus explained the depression I was experiencing and said I was essentially a good bloke having a bad time. The magistrate showed plenty of compassion and let me off lightly with a $7,000 fine and a four-year driving ban. It was a huge relief.

I stayed at Kippy's for around nine months, after which we decided it was time to try living on my own again, so I rented a small two-bedroom apartment in south Perth. It was a very lonely existence and I could feel myself falling back into old habits – not as bad as before, but still not healthy. The only company I had was my gorgeous dog Violet, a pedigree blue roan cocker spaniel, who sat on the sofa with me and listened to my bullshit without judging me.

This time I didn't ignore the warning signs. I realised I needed the support of family, so I moved back in with Mom and Dad. It made sense as it also meant I could take more care of them. They were in their early eighties and becoming more fragile, Mom in particular, so this allowed me to cook their meals, do some cleaning and look after them. I slept on the sofa bed and tried to live a modest, low-key life.

I was drinking too much again, though, usually vodka or white wine from a water bottle while sitting by the pool at their apartment. Paul Terry, my old friend from Hampshire, was working on the Masuri franchise and saw me every day. He was worried about me and spoke to Kippy, and they decided to contact the Professional Cricketers' Association in England. I will be forever grateful for the amazing support of Jason Ratcliffe and everyone at the PCA. They arranged 15 sessions, at considerable cost, with a therapist in Perth. I was maybe 80 per cent honest with the therapist – the extent of my drinking remained a guilty secret – but that still felt like progress.

One afternoon in January 2013, as I sweated profusely in the fierce summer heat, I noticed a lady sitting by the pool, watching her young daughter swim. I dived in, swam up to her and attempted to break the ice with a truly abysmal chat-up line.

'Your daughter swims like a little dolphin.'

Silence.

About a minute later she spoke. 'Do you live here too? I've just moved here from Christmas Island.'

'Me too.'

I'd made it sound like I had also moved from Christmas Island, which would have been quite a coincidence. I was fumbling my words and because I was so uncomfortable socially, I really wanted a quick drop of vodka to steady myself, but I continued rambling about how I had just moved into this apartment block.

She didn't seem to be that interested, though she was very nice and polite. And at least she spoke to me.

'Do you like cricket?' I said, scrambling for some kind of common ground.

'Oh, no. I've never really watched cricket. I left Australia at nineteen and I've been mostly living in South-east Asia for the last twenty-seven years. It's not that big over there.'

'You must know some names in cricket?'

She looked like she was trying to recall something important. Then her face lit up.

'Oh yes! I remember someone.'

I waited with bated breath.

'Shane Warne!'

Oh, for heaven's sake.

Warney. Why didn't that surprise me? She seemed more pleased with her answer than I was. She hadn't a clue who I was.

'Why did you ask?' she said. 'Are you a cricket fan yourself?'

'I don't really have the time to watch it these days, but I used to play a bit when I lived in England.'

As she and her daughter Ruby packed up their things that day, she casually asked me, 'So, where's home?'

Not, 'Where do you live?', but, 'Where's home?'

I didn't know what to say. *Durban? Hampshire? Perth? The pub?*

I said nothing, but she looked at me in a way that suggested she already had a good idea of the answer.

Over the next few months I saw her occasionally by the pool and we got on well. After the initial blow to my ego, I started to find it comforting that she had no idea who I was. I really enjoyed her company – she was sparky, polite, inquisitive, intelligent and compassionate. She had an accent from nowhere and I started to find out about her fascinating life story.

Karin Lwin was born in London to a French mother and English father, with additional ancestry from Switzerland, Wales, Spain and Asia. Her family moved to Australia when she was six, and every year they would spend a few weeks in Asia. Karin developed a love of Asian culture. She was a single mother with a son and two daughters who she had brought up for 15 years on her own living across South-east Asia, including Singapore, Indonesia, the Philippines and Thailand. Her children were part-Chinese, part-Burmese, and she had moved from Christmas Island[3] to Australia because her two eldest, Maia and Alexander, had been awarded scholarships at Perth Modern High School.

---

[3] Christmas Island is an Australian territory in the Indian Ocean, with a population of around 2,000.

She had just finished a masters' degree of her own at Monash University, and was starting another to teach English. I soon realised that, like me, she was struggling to adapt to life in Perth, and was not quite sure where home was; hence the question when we first met. We were both experiencing a geographical dislocation.

I could see Karin was different. She was always dressed so elegantly, in silk Cheongsam Chinese dresses, and she had the kind of spiritual outlook on life that I had never really encountered before. There was a gentle, humble wisdom in everything she said.

Mom liked Karin as well and used to spend time with us by the pool. When you're as good a dancer as she was, the best in South Africa, it's not something you want to give up, even when you're in your eighties. One day she was doing a couple of pirouettes by the pool when she slipped on the mossy bricks and hurt her hip. She insisted it was just a bruise and refused to go to hospital, despite us telling her we wanted to call an ambulance. The pain got worse and after a few days she reluctantly conceded that it was probably broken. It turned out her hip was completely shattered and she had been carrying on as if it was just a bruise. I told you she was tough.

She was in hospital for three weeks, clearly in extreme pain, and it was too much for me. I adore Mom and I simply couldn't handle seeing her in that state. For a few days, I went spectacularly off the rails. I was mixing alcohol and Seropax, my anti-anxiety medication, which apparently is an extremely stupid idea that causes a debilitating mental fatigue. This was when Dad chucked me out and Kippy sacked me. They wanted me to go to the Salvation Army, reasoning that I needed to hit rock bottom if I was going to ever get my life back on track. Kippy told Karin, Mark Nicholas and others to stay away from me for their own good. I couldn't blame him for that. Kath was also furious with me.

It was then that Karin offered me a bed on her sofa for the night and encouraged me to start afresh. She later told me that, though ordinarily she would never, ever invite someone into her home under those circumstances, she was worried about what I might do and had decided from our chats that, in her words, I was a good man with a bad problem. She also felt I had given up, that I was hopeless in the purest sense of the word. She knew I was drinking all that time, when I thought I was being discreet, but she never said anything or criticised me.

I went to see Mom the next day and stayed with her for a few hours before going back to the pool. That was when I called Dad and he told me not to come home. I didn't have a drink that day despite the kind of comedown I wouldn't wish on anyone, and despite the knowledge that I was only a few hours into the kind of cold turkey that usually lasts the best part of a week. Karin said that, when she arrived at the pool, I was staring vaguely towards the city lights, holding on to the top of the fence as if I was worried about falling off a ledge.

In Perth, it gets dark around 6 p.m. in the winter. We sat by the pool chatting for a while, and then something happened. I broke down and started to tell Karin how I got into such a mess. I told her about everything. The guilt, shame, regret, depression, heartbreak, infidelity and drinking; Illingworth, Fletcher and Hampshire; how I had been one of the world's best players but now I had no identity. Karin hardly said a word, she just sat and listened and told me it would be okay. I was in so much pain that I felt like my head and my heart were going to burst.

It started to rain – not heavily, just enough for it to be an inconvenience. I didn't care. I felt like I'd waited my whole life for this kind of therapy.

I had always tried to internalise my pain. It's what I did, what I thought real men did.

With Karin I felt an instinctive connection, a trust and a comfort that allowed me to open up properly for the first time in years, maybe my whole life. The more I told her, the more I wanted to tell her. It was the first time I had mentioned that I used to play cricket. She had no idea about my past; I was just Robin from the ground floor. I've often wondered why, after suppressing everything for so long, I opened up to Karin at that moment. I think there were two things: the dam needed to burst, and more importantly I felt a connection with her. She had such compassion, such empathy, and for the first time in a long while I felt I was with somebody who wanted to help me rather than judge me.

We chatted for hours that night, until we both realised it was late and I had nowhere to stay. Karin said I could stay on her sofa bed if I needed but encouraged me to check if Dad had left the garden door of the apartment open. I fully expected it to be locked, but when I pulled the catch it started to move. I broke down again and walked back to tell Karin. 'The door's open. I can go home.'

Karin saved my life that night.

I apologised to Dad the next morning, told him how much I had been struggling and how I felt I'd been given a lifeline. I moved back in again and cycled to see Mom every day until she came out of hospital a couple of weeks later. I also apologised to Kippy, who gave me back my job but made it clear I really was on my last chance.

I wasn't angry with Kippy and Dad for cutting me off. I know they loved me and they were simply trying to find a way, however severe, to help me get my life back on track. They thought that going to the Salvation Army would be the shock therapy I needed if I was ever going to get back on my feet. I also know it's hard for them to understand me sometimes, because they are both so resilient and driven, and they don't have the same addictive personality I have.

Kippy, in particular, thought I had stopped functioning and was desperate to try anything. He is tough but there's so much more to him than that. He's a very loving brother who I know cares deeply about me. When he called me an embarrassment to the family, it was at the end of an incredibly difficult four-year period when he and Julie had put up with so much and kept giving me another chance no matter how many times I messed up. He later told me they were so stressed and worried that they were taking Valium every night for three years – something they have never needed before or since. Julie says they were the worst years of her life. It's not easy to hear that, never mind write it, but that's how much of a burden I had become.

I always wondered why Kippy had a photo of me in his office, when there were no other pictures of anyone – not even Julie or his children. I asked him before writing this chapter, and he told me it was to constantly remind him of how I used to be, and to give him the motivation to help me become that person again. I was pretty emotional when he told me that.

There was never going to be a quick fix, but that night by the pool gave me a new determination and purpose. Hour by hour, day by day, I slowly started to get my life back on track. I managed to reduce my drinking, though I didn't stop it completely, and looked forward each day to chatting with Karin by the pool.

Karin noticed I was sneaking off for some Dutch courage every now and then, making various excuses about checking on Mom, or forgetting to put something in the fridge. I thought I was being discreet. Karin had a simple way of checking.

'Have you been drinking, Robin?'

'Karin, I promise you, I haven't.'

'Show me your hands.'

I would hold my hands out, fingers pressed together, and they would be perfectly still. Then Karin would ask me to spread my fingers and they'd start to shake.

Because I can drink a fair amount without falling over, I always think nobody can see when I've had a drink. Kippy and Karin have told me there are subtle visual and verbal signs that you pick up once you get to know me. My mouth goes a bit stiff and I pronounce everything more carefully, because I'm concentrating so hard on communicating normally, and I also occasionally repeat myself.

I asked Karin out for a drink a couple of times and she politely declined. She was very matter-of-fact. 'Robin, I could have a friend who drinks but I couldn't have a boyfriend who's a drunk,' she said. 'But I will never desert you as a friend.'

I had a simple choice. I focused on each day, trying to do things right and repair the relationships I had ruined while also developing my relationship with Karin. Each good day was another bit of positive reinforcement.

Karin constantly encouraged me and boosted my self-esteem by telling me what a decent person I was, that she noticed how much I doted on Mom around the pool, how lovingly I spoke about my children and how well-mannered I was. Karin was tough enough to take whatever life threw at her, but she was also soft and sweet and she had believed in me when I was a broken man. I had reached a point where I didn't think my life was redeemable. She kept telling me it was a temporary phase.

Over the next few months I scaled back my drinking almost completely, and Karin encouraged me further by saying she'd never touch alcohol in my company. She hardly drank anyway, so over the next few months we became Perth's foremost coffee experts. We often spent whole days together at weekends, chatting about everything and nothing.

My family all wondered what Karin and I talked about as on the surface we were so different. Yet we never seemed to run out of things to say. We discussed everything – social justice, politics, historical conflicts, the countries that one of us had been and the other hadn't. I'd always been curious about people and about life, even back to the days of touring with Derek Pringle, and Karin reignited that part of my personality. I'd travelled the world as a cricketer but she was truly worldly.

I was fascinated about her life – how she had just come from working with refugees, how she lived across South-east Asia for most of the last 27 years. She told me about working as a pit boss in the casino industry in places as diverse as the Czech Republic and South Africa, and had some brilliant stories – like the time she was on a casino boat that was attacked by pirates. It was another world and I was fascinated. The more I knew about her, the more I wanted to know. I found I wasn't just listening to her, I was hearing her as well. The more we talked about our different lives, the more we realised we had the same human qualities and core values.

I also continued to feel totally comfortable talking to her about the problems I'd had and my fragile mental state. For the first time in my life, I was being 100 per cent honest. Karin was kind, not judgemental; she never raised her voice, swore or belittled me for my failings. When I had finally told her that I had played for England, she knew that fame would have come with it. Her family had been involved in celebrity circles in the past, so she understood the temptations of fame. But I learned very quickly that she would only really be impressed by good human qualities.

I desperately wanted to be with her all the time. I felt like a teenager. After a few months in which Karin was very cautious about being anything more than friends, I asked if she'd like to go for dinner at the Sopranos restaurant up the road to celebrate the end of her exams. Our relationship slowly went to the next level and we have been together since. If there's a hero of my story, it's her. She has been such a great influence on me. She likes to hear stories about the Judge, and she calls me Judgie now, like everyone else, but it's Robin Arnold Smith who she fell in love with, who she believes in. And she knows me better than I know myself.

It was only when I fell in love with Karin that I realised I had never been in love before. At the age of 49, I became aware of the difference between loving someone and being in love with them.

Karin wasn't looking for a relationship when we met; nor was I. I've never really believed in serendipity but there's something going on that tells me we were meant to be together. We both lived in south Perth in the mid-1980s, we were in the same apartment block and went to the same bar, yet we never bumped into each other. She also lived in Durban, near where I grew up, for a short time in the early 1990s. I wasn't there at the time but it's still quite a coincidence.

But here's the thing – had we met earlier, I doubt we would have been friends, never mind anything more. Karin has always been uneasy with people who were or are famous and says she would probably have run a mile if she knew I'd been a cricketer. The fact she didn't meant she had no preconceptions or expectations. She knew and judged me for who I was, not who I had been. In turn, it gave me confidence that somebody was interested in me rather than my alter ego of the Judge. I was also able to talk to her without worrying that what I said might somehow get spread around the cricket community. She was a safe haven from my cricket life, and from the fear of letting down all the people who remembered me in my pomp.

My life became more and more stable after I started to date Karin. The last but most important step was to earn back the respect of Margaux. It was a really long process, which took two or three years.

I am so grateful to Karin and Kath, who both helped persuade Margaux to give me a second chance at a time when she understandably wanted little to do with me. Kath had been angry with me when I was at my lowest point, but when she realised I was making a serious effort to get my life back on track, she encouraged Harrison and particularly Margaux to see more of me. They are now my two best buddies in the world, the most beautiful children I could have hoped for and a constant inspiration to me. They helped me recover, because I could say to myself, 'Judgie, you really messed some things up, but you must have done something right to help bring up children as beautiful as Harrison and Margaux.'

Despite all my problems, my children have flourished and they now understand, respect and love me unconditionally. That means more to me than anything in the world.

I went on holiday to Bali with Karin and her family in 2015, and while we were there I decided it would be a great place to rekindle the father–daughter relationship. When I returned, I told Margaux I was going to take her on holiday to Bali, just the two of us. She was sceptical because I had let her down in the past and was concerned enough to ask Karin, 'Do you really think he'll take me?'

'Yes, of course he will, Margaux. Your father is a good man. He was born a good man, and he's walking away from a bad problem.'

I promised Margaux I would take her to Bali – and I bloody failed. But this time it wasn't my fault. Mount Raung erupted and we were rerouted via Darwin. Thankfully, we were able to go a week later.

Karin gave us loads of tips about places to visit, and it was the first time Margaux and I managed to bond as closely as we had when she was younger. The environment was new, exotic and beautiful, and the experience we had together, as father and daughter, was fiercely emotional and vitally important to me. I will always regret the terrible crash I had for around four years, but I earned her respect back by doing the right thing every day.

I got back to Perth and bought an apartment on the third floor of our building so that Harry and Margaux could stay there and save on rent while I slept on the sofa downstairs at Mom and Dad's. I'm forever grateful to Kippy and Julie, who guaranteed the finances so that I could buy the apartment. I loved having my children close to me because I had missed having a family. But I still didn't really have an answer to Karin's question, 'Where's home?'

I was now making regular steps forward, though that doesn't mean there weren't occasional steps back. It takes years of trying to do things right, and it's almost inevitable you'll fall along the way. There was the odd occasion when I couldn't cope with life and the negative thoughts ran riot again. One time I decided I was fine and stopped taking my anti-depressants without consulting the doctor. I didn't realise that you're supposed to slowly reduce the dosage; if you don't you can suffer dreadful withdrawal symptoms. I learned that the hard way.

I have not been a regular drinker since that day by the pool in 2013, but I have had occasional relapses. When they happen, they're horrible – for me, for everyone. Karin says it's like an atomic bomb. They usually last a few days, and the comedowns are the most awful experience. If you've been drinking hard, it takes a long time to recover. You have the shakes, you feel so anxious, guilty and depressed, and you have to endure that for days while the alcohol drains out of your system. And all the time you know that one swig would douse the gremlins and make it all go away, just for a while.

I've been fine 98 per cent of the time, and I'm determined to get the last two per cent right. I'm also getting better at spotting the signs and stopping myself before I fall off the rails.

I still get anxious when I'm out of my comfort zone. In 2015, I was asked to fly to Islamabad to do some punditry on the Pakistan v England series. It was the first time I'd done anything like that in a long while and I was so nervous. I had a few drinks on the flight to Abu Dhabi, where I met up with the former Australian batsman Dean Jones, who was also on the commentary team, for a connecting flight to Islamabad. We had a chat during the flight and then got to our hotel around lunchtime the day before the Test. I had a long sleep but when Deano knocked on my door the next morning I was struggling. I'd mixed alcohol with Seropax, my anti-anxiety medication, and had a really bad reaction. I told Deano I was feeling rough and that I wasn't going to make it, but that I'd be fine for the second day.

I slept throughout the day and was fine for the rest of the Test. I really enjoyed the commentary in the studio with Javed Miandad, Saqlain Mushtaq and Deano, and I still have a lovely letter from the director to say how well I had done and that I was welcome back any time. Deano was an excellent analyst and a skilful broadcaster who brought me into all the conversations.

During the Test I received concerned phone calls from Mark Nicholas and Rod Bransgrove, who said they'd heard on the grapevine that I'd gone on a bender and missed the first three days of the coverage. That was completely untrue. It brought me an avalanche of stress and anxiety at a time when I was already bloody fragile. Worst of all, they almost cost me my relationship with Karin. She heard via Kippy that I had apparently gone off the rails; she was so upset and decided that we should go back to being just friends until Mark spoke to her and said, 'Please don't walk away from him.' I was so disappointed. It almost led to Karin deserting me, and who knows what impact that might have had on my mental health. I was disappointed that I'd had a drink on the flight over, but that level of anxiety can be overwhelming. I knew it was just a small blip, and that my life was moving in the right direction. Karin continued to encourage me to jump out of my comfort zone, and so I started to look into some options aside from punditry. At the age of 52, it was time to reinvent myself.

Chapter 28
Reinvention

I'D BEEN DESPERATE TO forge a new identity since I retired, but didn't know how to go about it. I had so much admiration for people like Tuffers and Freddie Flintoff, who successfully turned their hands to lots of different things when their cricket careers were over. Yet I always felt that was beyond me. It was only when two important people in my life started to preach the power of reinvention that I found the confidence and inspiration I needed.

Karin and Martin Crowe were clear about the importance and the spiritual fulfilment of reinvention. Crowey emailed me about it all the time, and one thing he said really stayed with me:

'My friend, we are given these challenges to move on from old unhelpful ways. We are given a chance to regenerate, and for crick-eters like us, that is a must as the game takes us too far away from our true reality.'

During my career I tended to say 'yes' to everything, but after retire-ment, when I felt fragile, depressed and ashamed, my default answer became 'no'. Karin changed that. She constantly encouraged me to step out of my comfort zone, rather than take the easy option, and made me realise that if nothing changes, then nothing will ever change.

She was a constant source of positive reinforcement, reminding me that I could use skills I already had to do something new.

Kippy also helped, more than he'll ever know, with a throwaway comment in the office one afternoon. 'Judgie,' he said, 'why don't you try a bit of coaching?' His theory was that it would break up the monotony of the day job and give me something to really get my teeth into, especially as I had always been fascinated by technique and the mechanics of batting.

I loved the idea, but the thought of actually doing it made me uneasy. I was still recovering and rebuilding my self-confidence. Karin persuaded me to put my name down at Meulemans, a specialist cricket retailer in Perth, and Kippy had some business cards made for me. I gave it a try, word of mouth was good, and the whole thing started to snowball. I've been a specialist batting coach for four years now. I do around 16–18 hours a week on top of my responsibilities at my brother's business. Kippy is great – he allows me to be flexible with my working hours so that I can fit in my coaching appointments.

I mainly coach aspiring cricketers aged 11 to 17. My private coaching includes one-to-one sessions as well as coaching a local cricket club, the Redbacks, and the Wesley school team, where I work alongside my old friend Paul Terry.

The boys I coach know I don't just care about technique and their performance in the game, but also about their well-being and their development as individuals. Grayson Heath had a huge impact on me as a human being, never mind as a batsman, and I would love them to see me as a mentor. I was really chuffed when one of the parents called to ask if I could meet him and his son for a coffee to talk about the psychology of the game.

I have to be selective about who I coach. I really don't like turning down requests but I just don't have time. It means I can pick the ones who are passionate and enthusiastic, and who want to learn a proper Test match technique rather than play T20 shots all the time. The students tell me they have watched videos of me on YouTube, particularly facing the West Indian fast bowlers. They are so enthusiastic about the game and about life. That's the most rewarding thing about it, seeing them enjoy their cricket and try to better themselves. I get immense pleasure from seeing those with less natural talent do well, and I use the shining example of Kippy to show what can be achieved through concentration and hard work. The biggest satisfaction for me is when somebody is in the C or D team at under-14 level, and a year later they're playing for the under-15 As.

I also love seeing the youngsters improve their technique, both in defence and attack. One of the guys I coach was picked to play for Australia under-16s last year. Greg Chappell, who is the chairman of selectors, asked him whether he had a coach. When he mentioned my name, Greg said, 'Now I see why you've got such a good technique.' I felt so much pride when he told me that story.

There's another, older, guy who asked if I would coach him as he was a fan of mine. He's 65, he's had two heart attacks and a stroke, he's buggered after every session – and he absolutely loves it! I always look forward to our weekly sessions.

As I write this, I've just come back from nearly seven hours of coaching in 37-degree heat. The time went like *that*. I just love it. If I won the lottery tomorrow, I might politely tell Kippy where to stick his job, but I would carry on coaching for free.

It probably seems like a contradiction – to reinvent myself after cricket I went back to cricket. But it was a very important step because it allowed me to fall back in love with the beautiful game, which in turn meant I started to make peace with my contribution in the cricket world, rather than hiding from it because I didn't want people to know what had become of the Judge.

It also gave me the confidence to take bigger steps out of my comfort zone. Even something like not drinking for 340–350 days of the year would have been unimaginable a few years ago – as would doing a psychology degree, which I'm scheduled to start later this year. I've been tutored for five hours a week for the past 18 months as preparation and can't wait to start the course itself. I know it's a big challenge. I couldn't retain information at 16, never mind at 55, and the words in my psychology textbooks are a bit different from the vocabulary that was used in the Hampshire dressing room. Alan Mullally wasn't big on discussing the Zone of Proximal Development.

I really wish I'd done something like this 30 years ago. It's a new world for me, and a huge challenge, but I'm finding it very engaging. It has really helped me to understand my own life experiences and also my cricket career, particularly with concepts like stereotype threat. If it goes well, I hope that with my mixture of theory and experience I'll be of benefit to other sportspeople, either during or after their careers.

The other thing that has involved a big step out of my comfort zone is writing this book. At first, I didn't really want to do it. Actually, scratch that – I really didn't want to do it. I'd had various offers to write my autobiography over the years, the first when I was 28 and the No. 2 batsman in the world. It seemed pointless to write about my life when I hadn't lived enough of it yet, so instead I did a book that focused on the mental side of sport.

When I read about somebody I wanted to know about their mind and the development of their character and personality in the context of their achievements. It seemed like in most autobiographies there was too much focus on what and when – their 'journey' – rather than how and why.

Maybe it's my humble nature, but I also never felt worthy of an autobiography. And if I was ever going to write one, I didn't want it to be a clinical recounting of my cricketing career, I wanted it to encompass the emotional rollercoaster of being a professional sportsman, and to be a book of learnings – for me, never mind the reader. I wanted it, at different times, to be funny, sad, moving, sentimental, uplifting, poignant, unpleasant and profound. Just like life, right?

Most of all, I wanted it to be honest. I had no interest in telling my story with the bad bits airbrushed out. It was warts and all or not at all.

When my marriage to Kath broke down, it became easier to be more open about my infidelity and how I had failed her, but by then my life was a bit of a mess. Why would I want anyone to know what had become of me? I certainly didn't want a book that would end with me in the gutter.

I began to feel a little different when I met Karin and started to get back on track, and especially when I read the autobiographies of Graeme Fowler and Marcus Trescothick. I know Tres's came out in 2008 but I only read it a couple of years ago. Both talked about mental-health issues in a brave, sincere and incredibly personal way. The raw honesty of Trescothick's and Fowler's autobiographies – and the wonderfully positive reaction to both – helped me realise that we lived in a more understanding age, where the old perception of superhero sportsmen was being left behind. We are all human, and some of us are more fragile than spectators could believe. I know my old buddy Martin Crowe would have loved to read their books. He would have admired them even more because of their willingness to tell the truth, however painful. I wish he was still around to read my book.

I still worried about telling people about my fall from grace. I have always feared letting people down and I was nervous about the reaction to my mixed bucket of anxiety, infidelity, shyness, depression and alcohol dependence, never mind all those contradictions in my character. If I didn't write a book, most people would just have positive memories of me battling away at the crease.

When I was approached again a couple of years ago, I instantly felt that old feeling of anxiety in my chest and negative thoughts in my head. 'People want to read about the Judge,' I said to Karin, 'not some loser called Robin Arnold Smith.'

My instinct was to say no. Though my life was much more well balanced, I knew I was most susceptible to needing a drink when I was in a state of anxiety, or where I thought I couldn't be the person someone expected me to be. In other words, while writing a book like this. I was still apprehensive about revisiting so many distressing memories – and, actually, also of revisiting the happy memories. What if the guilt, or the good times in the past, tipped me over the edge?

As in so many things in the last few years, Karin gently encouraged and persuaded me. She told me she would support me throughout and emphasised that it was a rare opportunity for catharsis. She also stressed that, by talking openly about my vulnerabilities and weaknesses, I might be able to help others in the way Marcus Trescothick and 'Foxy' Fowler helped me.

That really made me think, and it's one of the main reasons I decided to go ahead with the book. It's encouraging that people are able to talk about mental health more openly now, and it's so important to continue the conversation because, although every story is unique, so many themes are universal. I don't believe I've got clinical depression but I know what a black hole looks like, and I know that anyone who is in a similar position should seek help rather than try to get through it on their own. My experience is that when you're in that position you struggle to think rationally and therefore might think your life is beyond salvation. But no matter how low you go, there is always a way out once you start to seek help.

I spoke to Harrison and Margaux and told them everything I was going to put in the book if I did it, adding that I wouldn't touch it if they had even the slightest reservations. They gave me their blessing and have supported me all the way. I also worried about how Kath might feel about me being so honest about my infidelity, but she encouraged me to be completely honest.

I knew it would be painful for me sometimes, but I also knew I would come out the other side with nothing to hide. I thought of Grayson Heath's words, said in the car as we drove up to Headingley for my Test debut in 1988. 'Robin, you will say to me, "It wasn't as hard as I thought it would be."'

Well, Grayson, I can report that the book was a lot bloody harder than I thought it would be! But it really has been worth it. I lived a lie for so long that it's a relief to let it all go. There's nothing more confronting than the moment you agree to write the whole truth about your life. But there's nothing more liberating than actually completing it.

It wasn't always easy, though. I've cried many times, once in a shopping mall one day when I was proof-reading a couple of chapters before coaching. And there was one extraordinary day which is burned on my soul.

Sunday 25 February 2018 was supposed to be a day of contemplation, when I would sit with Karin and write the most painful bits of this book. The plan was to revisit my darkest moments. Instead, they revisited me.

Karin and I had booked a room at the Rendezvous Hotel in Perth, the place where I had planned to take my life seven years earlier. We spent an idyllic morning on the beach, chatting and kissing. We joked that we had run away from home, left our children and my parents to escape to this paradise by the sea. In reality, we had taken the break so that I could clear my mind and find the courage to evoke the memories and feelings I had suppressed.

When we got back to the hotel, I stood on the balcony and looked down, trying to take myself back to the black hole I had been in. I had no idea where to start, so I took a long hard drag on my cigarette. Before I had time to exhale, I saw a woman plummeting from 11 storeys above me. She landed with a sickening thud a couple of metres from me on the rooftop platform that jutted out directly below our balcony.

'Shit, Karin!' I yelled. 'KARIN! Fuck, I just saw someone trying to commit suicide but I think she's still breathing!'

I snatched my mobile and dialled emergency as we raced across a barrier to find her. She was wedged sideways in a storm drain and as I touched her, she moved her arm slightly. I stared at an elegant, suntanned middle-aged woman, her eyes open and cast downwards. We each held her hand and I stroked her arm while Karin whispered something in her ear. Blood rushed from her mouth and moments later she took her last breath.

I prayed that she had found peace because I could empathise with the pain she must have been feeling. I understood her better than she will ever know. But seeing the reality of suicide, and of what almost happened to me, helped give me the courage to share my experience. It also helped me understand the person I had become in those times. I became angry at the thought of people who say suicide is selfish, never thinking of the pain of those they leave behind. It was so wrong. I understood that the irrational reason people build the courage to kill themselves is because they believe they will stop any intense pain they cause others by stopping their own.

The opportunity to confront dark memories that I had suppressed is the main reason this book has been so cathartic and liberating, but it has helped me in other ways too. I have reflected on every aspect of my life, to try to see things from both sides, and to try to get some closure on the things that haunted me, particularly being rejected by both England and Hampshire.

I was caught up in the emotion of it all at the time. I'm much more philosophical about it and I sympathise, for example, with Hampshire's reasons for not offering me a new contract in 2003. When I look at it in the cold light of day, do you want to continue with a 40-year-old who's averaging in the thirties or a young bloke who's averaging in the twenties? Probably the younger bloke. I wish I could have felt like that back then.

I still think I was handled poorly by Keith Fletcher and Ray Illingworth, and I will always be sad about those lost years with England, but they are not bad people and I'm sure they were doing what they thought was best. And these days I think about it less and less. Or at least I will once I've finished this book!

I look back on my Test career with a lot of pride. A batting average is seen as an accurate barometer of a player's ability, and it usually is. But what we sometimes forget is how often a cricketer goes out to the middle feeling nowhere near their best. They still have to struggle on and grind out runs or grab a few wickets. The public doesn't see Mike Atherton doubled up in agony in the dressing room because his back is in spasm, or, more recently, Rashid Khan grieving the death of his father while continuing to play in the Big Bash League.

When I consider my mental fragility and all I went through, especially in the second half of my career, I'm proud of a Test average of 43.67. Of the two generations I straddled, only David Gower and Graham Thorpe finished with a higher average for England. But the statistic from my England career that makes me happiest is the one with Lamby, that our average partnership of 79 is the highest for England in Tests since the war. Not bad for two 'South African-born batsmen' who enjoyed living life to the full.

A lot of these things passed me by during my career. It's nice to reflect on them now, especially those that I achieved with Kippy. The fact we scored over 50,000 runs for one club, and that this may be a post-war record, means a lot – as does the fact we are one of only ten pairs of brothers who have both been named as Wisden Cricketers of the Year. We were just two kids from Durban who practised tirelessly in the back garden. We fed the bowling machine, sledged each other and encouraged each other. We thought that maybe – maybe – one of us might become a professional cricketer, but for both of us to do so, and to score so many runs for a club we both loved so much, is really special. It also shows what you can achieve in life through dedication and hard work.

I've also reflected on the macho, adrenalin-fuelled behaviour that defined my life for so long. I certainly don't want to reject my past – I had some amazing times and I'm proud, for example, of the way I fought at the crease against fast bowling. But I also realise that what it means to be a man is pretty complicated. There's so much macho bullshit still going around that does nobody any favours.

I don't really regret the socialising during my playing days, even though it caused problems later in life. I was young and loved nothing more than relaxing with my teammates over a few beers. That was the culture I grew up in. Whether it was good for me, who knows, but I loved the camaraderie and especially the laughter. Having said that, if I had my time again I wouldn't be quite as enthusiastic as I was. You get carried away in that bubble, that fantasy world of spending time with the blokes you admired as a kid. I had seriously loyal mates. It's easy to say they were bad influences but I don't agree with that. It was up to me to find the right balance between work and play, not them. And it was up to me to forge a second career, not them. I was naïve. Maybe I thought I'd be a cricketer forever.

I feel comfortable and happy these days. I lead a very busy life, which is so much better for me – maybe not quite the 100mph life-style of old, but I'm still going at about 70mph. I'm up at 5.30 a.m. every day – I feel guilty as Karin has usually been up for an hour working – and busy with work and coaching until around 8 p.m. I do around 70 hours a week between Kippy's place and my coaching, and I also look after Mom and Dad. I take care of Mom every day until she goes to bed around 10 p.m. I float between three apartments in the same block – theirs, Karin's and mine.

You might not recognise me these days. The Judge's wig has long gone – it's more wavy than crinkly, and it has whitened over the years. Karin tells me it's a salt-and-pepper colour and that it looks distinguished.

I do worry about Mom and Dad. They are now in their late eighties and I look after them as best I can. I don't care if it means I get two hours' sleep a night. Mom hasn't been well lately and she had to go to hospital recently because of complications with her diabetes. That was really hard, but I stayed firmly on the rails this time.

I draw so much strength from being with Karin. I adore her, and we've been together five and a half years as I write this. The Islamabad episode was tough but we got through it and our relationship is everything to me. I've never been unfaithful to Karin and never will.

I take so much pleasure from the fact Harrison and Margaux have forged happy lives in Australia. Harrison recently moved to Sydney for two years to work as a teacher and live with his outstanding girl-friend, Yen. That was a bittersweet moment because I loved having him around, but I am so happy for him. He teaches high school visual art and does some abstract painting in his spare time.

Margaux is a joy. She loves travelling and did her degree in tourism and events at Murdoch University. In the four years since she turned 21, she has visited almost 20 countries, including places as varied as Cambodia, Denmark, Borneo and Morocco. I love that she always goes in a small, unofficial group so that she can learn about the culture and have some authentic experiences rather than go in a tour party.

Margaux loves visiting Asia in particular. The trip to Bali was her gateway to that part of the world, and every time she comes back from there she is bursting with enthusiasm about the people, the food and the culture. Karin adores Asian culture, too, and I'm so happy when I hear the two of them chatting about it. I hope one day the three of us can go for a holiday to Japan or Singapore.

I'm not a great fan of tattoos but I was touched when Margaux had a discreet one of some bananas and a palm tree under her wrist. She said the reason she got it is that it reminded her of those child-hood holidays in Barbados, when I would take her to the beach and we would wait under the palm tree for the pineapple man. She said that because I love bananas so much and, apparently, I have fingers like bananas, she got those instead. I love that those holidays made such an impression on her.

I have agonised so much in the last decade about whether it was the right decision to uproot the family, and I am always seeking reassurance by asking them if they are happy. I really think they are, because they always tell me it was one of the better decisions I have made.

You go through many ups and downs during a separation, but Kath and I always maintained one core value – that we would remain as a family. It's so important to both of us. We still get on pretty well and always get the family together for the big milestones in the children's lives. When Harrison had an exhibition of his artwork in north Perth, Kath did all the catering and we had the whole family, including Karin, together.

I still get occasional anxiety attacks but, though they are still uncomfortable, I find they are easier to manage now. I came off my anti-depressant medication recently, too, and this time I managed to do it properly. It's hard to know what the future holds but at the moment I feel stable and happy. I know I need to be vigilant when it comes to my other medicine. I don't think I'll ever rely on alcohol like I once did but I'm self-aware enough to know there might be the occasional relapse. I could be relaxing on a beach in Bali without a problem in the world and there would still be a shadow I have to watch; my own shadow. I thought – I still do think, to some extent – that drink has the power to transform me into more interesting, energetic and charming company. Everyone I know tells me that's nonsense, and that I am much better company sober. I am starting to feel much more confident and comfortable in social situations while I sit with a cup of coffee or a glass of lemon, lime and bitters.

I'd like to think that at some stage in ten years' time if I've proved to myself that I'm no longer reliant on alcohol, maybe I could treat myself to the occasional glass of wine with Karin. I'd have to be very sure in my own mind that I would be able have a sensible drink. At this stage I know, if I'm completely honest, that one glass of wine is too many and a thousand isn't enough.

There's an Afrikaans word, *bietgie*, which sums up my life. It basically means a bit, as in a bit more. And whether it's alcohol, sugar in my coffee (four) or practise in the nets, I've always had to have a *bietgie* more. I barely cooked until I met Karin, who started to teach me. She says it was a nightmare – the first night I'd do something really well, but then the next time I did the same dish I'd put a *bietgie* more of something in and it was ruined. I think it's fine because it's only a bit more, but then a bit more and a bit more becomes a whole lot more; too much.

That's what I'm like with alcohol. The feeling is so good that I have another one, because it's only a little bit more. What harm can that do? First you drink for the buzz, then you drink because it's normal, and before you know it you are drinking to function.

I don't want to drink excessively, so I don't any more, even though life does get tough at times. I sometimes struggle with the poignancy of everyday life. It might be watching an elderly couple queuing up in the supermarket, economising on their pension, or walking past a homeless person. I wish I could win $100 million on the lottery so that I could drive round and give every homeless person $1,000.

I get really moved when I see animals struggling, too. Karin always reminds me of a time when I was driving her to do some tutoring at the State Library. As we went down Wellington Street, we saw a pigeon with a broken wing, so I did a U-turn and we picked up the pigeon and took it to the zoo. I'm just a big softie, really.

I know I am so blessed to be in the position I am now; I couldn't have imagined this when I was at rock bottom a few years ago. I have a different lust for life than when I was 25, with less adrenalin and less of the Judge persona. I lead a simple, structured life, and there isn't much spare time for hobbies. I barely even have a chance to look at my Facebook! I'm fortunate that my biggest hobby, coaching, also counts as work. When I do have a few spare hours, usually on a Sunday afternoon, I love going for a long stroll along the Swan River with Karin, stopping at one of our coffee shops on the way, or taking the ferry across Elizabeth Quay and sitting in the sunshine having a coffee – and, if we're feeling really indulgent, maybe a gelato as well.

I meet up with Margaux once a week, which is always a highlight, and Harrison comes back from Sydney for a long weekend every couple of months. Earlier today, he took me for a wonderful iced coffee at a Vietnamese restaurant in Northbridge. Those simple pleasures mean everything to me.

I appreciate my life more than ever. As hard as the dark times were, I think they have made me a better person – more rounded and broad-minded, with a greater understanding of life, people, emotions and mental health. I see those difficult experiences as humbling rather than humiliating.

It's never nice to recall, though. The drink-driving, and jeopardising Margaux's safety, will always haunt me. I've learned my lesson and I'll never do anything like that again.

I feel positive about the future, which for so long wasn't the case. Luck favours the bold and I'm going to continue reinventing myself. It's a strange thing to say at the age of 55, but I feel like I'm just starting to understand who I am. For so long, I didn't stop to analyse my life, I just lived it. Now I'm starting to really appreciate the two sides of my character, how they depend on each other and make up my personality.

This is the second part of my life. I have now realised that my cricket career was a stage of my life, not the whole thing. I made some mistakes, especially at the end of the first bit, and maybe I pissed some of my career and life up the wall, but I've generated great opportunities now. And I'm going to make damn sure the second part of my life has a happy ending.

Epilogue

In April 2018, I received an email from Jack Bransgrove, the son of the Hampshire chairman Rod. He was organising a Captains' Dinner at the club and told me they wanted the 12 living captains to attend. It would be at the Hilton Hotel which is on the premises of the Ageas Bowl, and would include each captain going up onstage for a Q&A session.

I didn't answer Jack's email. I was very apprehensive about going back because I felt people would only be happy if I went in the character of the Judge, the happy, lager-swigging bloke they had always known. I wasn't him any more. I was older, greyer on top, and no longer the life and soul of the party. I was worried not only about how people would react to the new me, but also what they had heard – true and false – about my life in the ten years since I left England.

My instinct told me not to go. My inspiration told me the opposite. 'Judie, you absolutely have to go back,' Karin said. 'Hampshire was your life. The only disappointment people will have in you is if you don't go back. You need to revisit your past. It's kind of like unfinished business, it's another experience that will be cathartic.'

For the next few days I was torn. Jack emailed to say Rod told him the dinner wouldn't go ahead without me, because of my place in the club history. That was lovely but if anything it made the decision harder.

A couple of days later, Rod's number flashed up on my phone.

'How are you, china? Jack's been waiting for your email. You're obviously coming to the Captains' Dinner, Judge!'

What could I say? That I'm too anxious to go?

'Of course, chairman, I wouldn't miss it for the world.'

I asked Karin to join me, but she said no because she had too many financial and family commitments. Then Karin's brother and son Alexander stepped in, so Karin had no reason not to come. The club booked two flights for us, and on 26 August Karin and I boarded the flight to London. Patrick Trant upgraded us to business class, which was a wonderful gesture, and Karin and I settled in for the long flight to London. We had separate seats at either side of the plane, with all the food trolleys in the middle, so we were having to shout across at each other. That set-up is perfect for sleeping but we just wanted to chat or watch the same film, so we hatched a plan.

Karin switched the ring on her finger and said we'd just got engaged, that we were going to London to celebrate and would love to sit together. We properly hammed it up, and luckily for me one of the flight attendants was a South African lady who knew her cricket. She said her father had been a big fan of mine and so she found two spare seats that were nearer each other.

When we arrived, Patrick's chauffeur Ian, who I had met many years ago, was waiting to drive us to Hampshire. I was so touched by all the goodwill and kind gestures. We arrived at the Hilton and Jack Bransgrove checked us into room 356, directly overlooking the ground. My good buddy Paul Hendy, 'Check Seven',[1] who owns many car dealerships in southern England, gave us a Ford car to drive while we were there and one of the first people I saw was Shaun Udal. I had missed him so much, so visiting the Cotton Graphics factory and seeing how he was getting on was a major highlight. We had lunch together with his lovely wife Emma and his amazing son Jack, who is also my godson.

---

[1] That was his nickname because whenever we played golf he was forever calling for the seven-iron: 'Check Seven!'

Epilogue

I couldn't believe I was back in Hampshire and that Karin could meet Shaggy and his family. The next day I took her on a tour of my old haunts – the New Forest, my old home, the pub that used to be Judge's Wine Bar, the cathedral in Romsey. It's very rare that Karin likes her photo taken but she was inspired by random and quaint things, like the bright red door of a white-painted house. 'Take a picture of me in front of that door, Judgie,' she said. Then we discovered the restaurant La Parisienne. It was closed at the time but I took a photo of Karin in front of the restaurant; her Mum, Brigitte, was born in Montmartre, Paris, so I took the photo for both of them. It felt so good to share my life and create memories of us in this place that I loved.

That night, as the sun was setting, I sat on the balcony of our hotel room and felt a mixture of apprehension and anticipation. I looked over this magnificent ground with immense pride and remembered everything that I had experienced here. It wasn't just the memories of playing for Hampshire County and becoming the captain of a club which continued to hold my soul, it was the realisation that through the vision of many people I loved immensely, the Bowl was born.

As I stared at the ground and thought back to all the struggles we had in the early years, I realised this site was a metaphor for my life. I remembered how the club had fallen in the gutter after great promise, *just like me,* how the club's finances were spent and it couldn't sustain its future, *just like me,* how the intervention of someone who believed so passionately that it could be better and stronger allowed it to regain its worth and give back to others, *just like me*, how with regenerated interest it grew on the power of reinvention, *just like me*!

I broke down, but they were tears of joy, not sadness. I'd never felt so confident that I would forge a successful future.

I woke the next morning with a familiar feeling in my stomach. Anxiety? *No, Judge, just a small bout of nerves, everyone gets them and it's okay.* It was the day of the Captains' Dinner and I knew that this evening I would see hundreds of familiar faces, people I knew and loved. Karin knew I was feeling so many intense and conflicting emotions, that tonight would be such a heightened experience and a test of my rehabilitation.

'Karin, it's so overwhelming. How can I tell everyone why I didn't keep in touch? How can I say, "I'm sorry but I was suffocating in a dark place and drowning in alcohol for years"?'

'Trust me, Judgie, they know that while you weren't here, your thoughts and love for them never left.'

'But I want them to know why. How will I tell them?'

'Judgie, they won't expect you to. They won't even be thinking about that. All they'll be thinking is, "Gee, it's so good to see Judgie here." Just live in the moment and I promise you everything will be fine.'

In the afternoon I had a lovely chat with Mark Nicholas, out in the middle at the Ageas Bowl. We rolled back the years by doing a bit of visualisation and playing some imaginary shots, including the old square cut.

I went back to the hotel to get changed into my lounge suit. As we approached the reception for the Captains' Dinner, I felt proud to have the woman I love by my side. She was a bit nervous about meeting all the people who meant so much to me. I copied her advice from the morning – 'Just live in the moment and I promise you everything will be fine' – and we both started laughing.

When we entered the room, Karin said with exaggerated excitement, 'Oh gee, Judgie, do you reckon Shane Warne might be here?' We both burst out laughing again, recalling the night we first met six years earlier when I asked her whether she had heard of any cricketers.

My old way of dealing with such a cocktail of social anxiety and raw emotion would be to take the edge off with alcohol, but this time I stayed completely dry, although I must confess to having probably one too many Red Bulls. I went to the doctor to get a prescription of Seropax, the anti-anxiety medication I used to take in my darker days. I wanted to have some with me as a safety blanket, but as it turned out I didn't need to take any.

At 8.30 p.m. it was time for the Q&A. I was seated on the far right, and I knew I was nervous because I was clenching my teeth a bit. Warney and Mark, naturals in front of a big crowd, answered their questions with panache. I had not anticipated that the other 11 captains would express gratitude not only for my contribution on the field but also for the way I captained the club. Even more heart-wrenching was how they said they had been affected by my human traits, thanking me for mentoring with compassion and for my sincere and honest friendship during my time as Hampshire's captain. The praise was overwhelming and I felt at times I was almost struggling to breathe. It was an unbelievably emotional experience.

Karin later told me the applause from the 400 guests, when the other captains talked about me, was 'a beautiful celebration of you, Judgie, and the love for you was deep and tangible.'

I'm still so grateful for the love that people have shown me, but I do still struggle to cope with it. I feel so unworthy. Maybe it's because I've been in the presence of others I greatly admire, or maybe it's because I'm only just learning to love myself.

When we got back to our room, I hugged Karin.

'Karin, are you okay?'

'Judgie, forget me, are *you* okay?'

'It's all too much, Karin. I've missed them all too much.'

We were both emotional at the same time. 'Judgie,' said Karin. 'Home is somewhere that leaves the light on waiting for you to come back, no matter how far or how long you're gone.'

I woke at 4.30 a.m. the next morning, the first day of the Test, and sat on the balcony so as not to disturb Karin. I watched the ground staff working from the moment the sun came up. I thought back to all the problems we had with the pitch when we first moved to the ground. I recalled the match against India in 2002, which was almost abandoned because of a dodgy wicket, and wondered whether this Test match would even be taking place had that game been called off and a black mark placed against the ground.

The lights went on in the England dressing room and preparations slowly intensified for the first day of the Test. I felt enormous gratitude to Rod for bringing me back after ten years of living away, and helping me realise I had taken part in something special at Hampshire; something that was never going to be forgotten. I was overwhelmed by the love I continued to have for this ground, this club, those I've played with and those who'll continue to play for Hampshire long after I'm gone.

I saw first-hand that the circle of life and cricket goes on. On the first morning of the Test match, Mark Nicholas introduced me at breakfast to Sam Curran and Keaton Jennings, two really nice young blokes trying to make their way in international cricket, with the same hopes and fears I had 30 years earlier. I had played against their fathers – Kevin Curran, a superb all-rounder and wonderful competitor for Northamptonshire who died tragically in 2012; and Ray Jennings, who used to give me all sorts of abuse from behind the stumps in South Africa. Keaton was such a polite, gentle man that I thought Mark was joking when he told me he was Ray's son.

All those concerns I had about coming over had been completely unnecessary. Karin and I travelled up to London for the day while we were over and saw the Bunburys playing at Lord's. I had a lovely catch-up with Medha Laud and David English, and I also bumped into Athers. We chatted like we'd never been apart.

In my darkest moments, when I wasn't thinking rationally, I'd feared my contribution to Hampshire and England cricket had been forgotten. It was clear that couldn't have been further from the truth.

When were at the airport waiting to fly back, Karin and I started chatting again about the idea of home. On the first day I met her, by the pool in Perth in 2013, she asked me, 'Where's home?' The question threw me, because I was born in South Africa, I lived in Perth and my heart and soul were still in England. But returning to Hampshire made everything clearer.

'Karin, you're right. The light was left on here, and it feels so good to be back. I'll always love coming to Hampshire because it was my home for twenty-six wonderful years. But that was a different phase of my life. Home is where the heart is, and my home now is in Perth.'

Acknowledgements

PHEW. I HAD NO idea how much work goes into a book like this, or how draining it can be. Reflecting on my life was often painfully uncomfortable, and I feel like I've had a lump in my throat for the last couple of years. At times, while scribbling notes on bits of scrap paper, I felt as if I was looking back on someone else's life. I steeled myself and took ownership of every amazing experience I'd had – those I was proud to tell and those that racked me with guilt.

It doesn't matter who we are, we all make mistakes. I was never perfect. And I was never just the Judge. I am Robin Arnold Smith: a contradiction of strength and weakness, truth and lies, physical strength and emotional fragility. I care immensely about those I love and those who experience the same feelings as I have done. I am not unique. We all lead a life, we are all interesting and we all have a story to tell. I see this as a book of learnings. No matter how low you fall, you can always find a way to reinvent yourself and stand tall.

There are so many people I would like to thank for their work on this book. I'm very grateful to Rayne Sullivan for providing highlights of many of my innings, which helped to jog some happy memories, and to Graham Morris, Mike Vimpany, Simon Walter, Dave Allen and Patrick Eagar for helping me find photographs from my playing days. Thanks also to Mike Brearley, Neil Fairbrother, Angus Fraser, Allan Lamb, Phil Tufnell, Tim de Lisle, Richard Isaacs, Charles Colville,

Nick Marsh, Peter Hayter, Alex Narey, Rod Bransgrove and Jack Bransgrove, who helped with everything from contacts and advice to sourcing archive footage and filling in gaps in my memory.

Ed Wilson, my literary agent, did a brilliant job in finding a great publisher, and Yellow Jersey have been a pleasure to work with. Graeme Hall, Rowena Skelton-Wallace, Josh Ireland, Maddy Hartley, Phil Brown, Tim Bainbridge, Aidan O'Neill, Gordon Clough and David Purvis are all unsung heroes who have done wonderful work behind the scenes. My thanks especially to Justine Taylor for her copy-editing, Matt Broughton for designing a cover that I absolutely love, and to the editorial director Tim Broughton (no relation) for his expertise, enthusiasm, understanding – and for putting on an amazing breakfast when I was in London!

I wouldn't have agreed to an autobiography unless I found the right person to tell the story of my complicated life. It was a godsend working with Rob Smyth. His prior knowledge of me as the Judge, and his empathy for me as Robin Smith, meant we got on straight away. He has become a great friend, even if he does live on the other side of the world!

My partner Karin Lwin encouraged me to write this book, bare my soul and release emotions I didn't even know I was harbouring. She was my rock in my darkest hours, and over six years she has got to know me better than I know myself. She captured my most intense emotions, wrote them down and passed them onto Rob. This book would never have been possible without her.

Shane Warne and Mark Nicholas, two of my greatest friends in the world, wrote forewords that made me proud and emotional. I just adore and respect them both.

I will be forever indebted to the people who made sure this book has an optimistic ending. My wonderful Mom and Dad; Kath, who was by my side for over 25 years, and my beautiful, inspirational children, Harrison and Margaux; my brother Kippy, who is my other rock, and his lovely wife Julie. And, most of all, the love of my life. Karin, I love you my darling.

Index

Index

Index

Index

Index

List of illustrations

Parents' wedding, personal collection; Mom ballerina, personal collection; Mom car window, personal collection; Bike rides, personal collection

School trophies, personal collection; Cover drive, personal collection; Rugby player, personal collection; Florence, personal collection

Fielding with Kippy, Tony Edenden; Sir Garry Sobers, personal collection; Malcolm Marshall, personal collection; Robin and Kath's wedding, personal collection

Batting with Kippy, *Southern Daily Echo*; Square cut, Patrick Eagar/Popperfoto/Getty Images

Allan Lamb, Patrick Eagar/Popperfoto/Getty Images; David Gower, David Munden/Popperfoto/Getty Images; Sir Ian Botham, Graham Morris/Cricketpix

NatWest celebrations, Graham Morris/Cricketpix; World Cup defeat, Graham Morris/Cricketpix; B&H trophy with Mark Nicholas, PA Images

Mother Teresa, Chris Cole/Getty; Gatting rickshaw, Graham Morris/Cricketpix; 167 not out, Ben Radford/Getty

Baby Harrison, Graham Morris/Cricketpix; Margaux, personal collection; Family photo, supplied by Robin Smith, original source unknown

Ian Bishop inspects, Graham Morris/Cricketpix; Nelson Mandela, Graham Morris/Cricketpix; Shaun Pollock bouncer, Clive Mason/Getty

Michael Atherton, Graham Morris/Cricketpix; Archbishop Desmond Tutu, David Munden/Popperfoto/Getty

Rose Bowl, supplied by the Hampshire Cricket Archive c/o Dave Allen; Sir Viv Richards, Hugo Philpott/Getty; Malcolm Marshall memorial, Graham Morris/Cricketpix

Final innings, Dave Allen; Martin Crowe and Shane Warne, personal collection; Rod Bransgrove, supplied by Jack Bransgrove

Margaux graduation, Harrison graduation, Margaux and Harrison, Margaux and Robin, Harrison painting, all personal collection

Photos with Karin, Paul Terry and Kippy fishing, all personal collection

Dennis Lillee reconstruction, personal collection; Coaching, personal collection

Smith family, personal collection; Captains' Dinner, Dave Vokes Photography